6th Feb 1873

PIONEERS

OF

C. L. Collins

MARION COUNTY,

CONSISTING OF A

General History of the County

FROM ITS EARLY SETTLEMENT TO THE PRESENT DATE. ALSO, THE GEOGRAPHY AND HISTORY OF EACH TOWNSHIP, INCLUDING BRIEF BIOGRAPHICAL SKETCHES OF SOME OF THE MORE PROMINENT EARLY SETTLERS IN EACH, TOGETHER WITH NUMEROUS INCIDENTS ILLUSTRATIVE OF PIONEER LIFE MORE THAN TWENTY-FIVE YEARS AGO.

By WM. M. DONNEL.

DES MOINES, IOWA:
REPUBLICAN STEAM PRINTING HOUSE.
1872.

DEDICATION.

To the following persons, who have kindly furnished me the means for its publication, this, his first effort as a historian, is respectfully dedicated by their humble servant, the Author.

JOHN C. DONNEL, THOS. FORSYTHE,
JAS. M. CATHCART, B. G. BOWEN,
A. G. YOUNG, D. T. DURHAM,
A. B. MILLER.

PREFACE.

In presenting this work to the public, it appears to me that an apology is indispensable, and I make it in the form of a preface.

It is now upwards of four years since I first entered upon the laborious but pleasant task of collecting the materials that compose this book. It was then my design to compile brief biographical sketches of the earliest settlers, together with complete accounts of their pioneer experience ; but as I proceeded with the work, materials of a more general historical character, fraught with interests that demanded attention, accumulated upon my hands, swelling the volume far beyond the limits I had first marked out for it. So, beyond giving a history of the pioneers of Marion county, I have given a history of the county itself, and retain the title originally intended for it.

If in some instances I have erred in date or statement, or have omitted any circumstances worthy of mention, the reader will please to bear in mind that in sifting and selecting from a large mass of matter collected from various sources, the liability to err is unquestionable. Notwithstanding the great difficulty of avoiding mistakes, I have carefully endeavored to do so, and it is to be hoped that few or none of importance have found their way into these pages.

I have also carefully endeavored to avoid making any statement prejudicial to any person, or offensive to any political partizan, deeming such matter not only undesirable, but uncalled for in an impartial history. This work has nothing to do with the partizan politics of the country, and may be safely relied upon as a source of useful information and entertainment to all parties. In short, I have tried to make a book well worth being made a keepsake in every family in Marion county.

In conclusion, I return my sincere thanks to the many good friends who so kindly welcomed me to their homes, and aided me with such historical facts as they had in their possession. I hope to merit their continued kindness and good will.

WM. M. DONNEL.

INTRODUCTION.

Marion county originally belonged to a large tract of country ceded to the United States by the Sac and Fox Indians, at a treaty held at Agency, in the autumn of 1842. At that treaty the entire tribe was assembled, and Keokuk was their spokesman. Among other stipulations it was agreed that the new purchase should be vacated by the Indians as far west as the red rocks on the Des Moines river, on the first day of May, 1843, and the remainder by the tenth of October, 1845. The line to distinguish the United States from Indian Territory, that crossed the river a short distance above the present site of Red Rock village, was run by Geo. W. Harrison, U. S. surveyor, in the autumn of '43. In running this line, the distance from the Missouri state line to the monument he erected over the red sand-stone bluffs, north of the river, was found to be just 69 miles.

Marion is in the third tier of counties from the south line of the State, the fifth from the east line, the seventh from the north line, and the sixth from the west line. Its center is about 52 miles north of the south line of the State, 108 west of the Mississippi river, 150 from the north line of the State, and about the same distance east of the Missouri river, calculating these distances in a straight direction. It is in the 41st degree of north latitude, and 16 degrees west of Washington. It is nearly on the same latitude with Sandusky City, Ohio, Hartford and New Haven, Connecticut, Providence and Newport, Rhode Island, Madrid, in Spain, Rome and Naples, in Italy, Constantinople, in Turkey, and Salt Lake City, in Utah.

Marion county is bounded on the north by Jasper county, on the east by Mahaska, on the south by Monroe and Lucas, and on the west by Warren. It is in an exact square of 24 miles, and therefore embraces an area of 576 square miles or sections, equal to 368,690 acres, at least seven eights of which is rich, tillable land. And this area is occupied by a population that averages a little more than 42 persons to the square mile.

The principle streams that run through the county are the Des Moines and Skunk rivers, much the larger of which is the Des Moines. This stream rises in the southern part of Minnesota, runs nearly south till it reaches the capital of Iowa, where it takes a direct southeast course, till it empties into the Mississippi at Keokuk. It enters Marion county at section 7, township 77, and range 21, being near the northwest corner, and leaves it in section 13, township 75, range 18. In the section of this stream that forms the boundary line between Red Rock and Union townships, it once made a large curve to the southwest, forming a long peninsula with a narrow neck. In 1847 this curve was so dammed with ice and drift-wood that the water was forced to cut a new channel across the neck, leaving the old one a mere bayou. This place is known as "The Cut-off." The Des Moines is navigable for small steamboats as far as the capital, during freshets.

Skunk river crosses the northeast corner of the county, entering it in section 5, township 77, range 18, and leaves it in section 24, same township and range. The Indian name for it was Chicauqua by which it was also known by the old settlers of the lower counties through which it runs. The term Chicauqua is said to signify anything of a strong odor, and is supposed to have been applied to this stream on account of the great quantity of wild onions that grew about its head waters. In accordance with this supposition, (which is probably true,) and also in order to give the little stream a more practical name than Skunk, a bill was introduced during the session of the State legislature of 1869 and 1870 enacting that it should be called Chicauqua, which however failed to pass. It is an exceedingly crooked stream, with a deep, narrow channel and abrupt banks, which give it a treacherous look during high water.

White Breast, the third stream of any importance, enters the county in section 18, township 79, range 21, runs in a northeasterly direction, and empties into the Des Moines in section 10, township 76, range 19. The Indian name for this stream was Waupo-ca-ca, the name of an Indian chief, some account of whom is given in the history of Polk township.

There are numerous smaller streams that I shall take occasion to notice in my township histories.

All streams of any considerable size, are widely margined by timber mostly of an excellent quality. Walnut, cottonwood, soft and hard maple, hackberry, elm and ash, are abundant on the bottom lands. Oak is the prevailing timber on the up-lands. Between these strips of timber are the high undulating prairies, on which innumerable small streams or feeders take their rise, flowing each way into the larger creeks, and they to the rivers. On the most elevated portions of these prairies, lasting water of an excellent quality may be found from fifteen to twenty-five feet below the surface. The soil is a black mould of vegetable formation, from eighteen inches to three feet deep. There are also many small prairies along the streams, the black soil of which is four or five feet deep.

The only railroad completed through the county is the Des Moines Valley. Its line is through the northeast corner, making Pella and Otley points in this county, and Monroe just within the limits of Jasper. Either of these points does a large amount of shipping.

Three other roads are in prospect, one of which, the Albia,

Knoxville and Des Moines, is partly graded east of Knoxville, and will undoubtedly be completed within a reasonable time. The Muscatine Western will make Pella a point, and is now graded to Monroe, Jasper county—will probably make the village of Red Rock a point; all of which will secure to Marion county abundant commercial intercourse with all parts of the United States, as its agriculture and resources demand.

PART I.

GENERAL HISTORY OF THE COUNTY.

CHAPTER I.

Dragoons—Trading Houses—Indian Payments, and How Made—Incidents—Character of the Traders.

Soon after the purchase of 1842, or about that time, a garrison of United States dragoons was quartered at Ft. Des Moines, between and at the junction of the Des Moines and Coon rivers, for the purpose of guarding the Sac and Fox Indians, the late proprietors of the lands, against the warlike encroachment of the Sioux, who had long been known as their most implacable foes; and also to prevent the settlement of those lands by the whites previous to the first day of May, 1843, and the eleventh day of October, 1845, agreeable to the stipulations of the treaty made at Agency, in the autumn of 1842. There was also a garrison at Agency, whose duty was to guard the agency and prevent immigrants from crossing the line before the first of May, as above stated.

But it is evident that no extraordinary vigilance was exercised by the garrison to enforce this restriction. Many crossed the line, either with or without their knowledge; but with the understanding on the part of the immigrants themselves, that they would be subject to arrest and seizure of their property by the dragoons, small squads of whom were scouting here and there over the country. Those who thus found their way into the forbidden territory, could do nothing toward making a permanent settlement, except to fix upon some locality that suited their fancy, and be ready to establish a claim upon it at the proper time. They dared not erect a house; and in some cases, it was found advisable to secrete their wagons and such other property as was likely to betray their intentions to become settlers.

Little was known of the country previous to its actual occupation in 1843. Some hunters and trappers had passed through it, from whom reports were received of its beautiful prairies, luxuriant vegetation and rich soil. A few trading houses had been established at different times and places, mostly along the Des Moines river, on a trail most frequently traversed by the Indians, between Des Moines and Hard Fish, an Indian town located where Eddyville now is, and Agency.

The remains of one of these houses is still visible, near the eastern border of the county, in what is now Lake Prairie Township. It was, perhaps, the first house occupied by white people within the bounds of the county. Another, known as the "Phelps' Trading House," stood some where near the same locality. The proprietor, William Phelps, previously kept the same kind of an establishment at Farmington, Van Buren county, and moved up when his Indian customers receded before the advance of civilization. At a somewhat later date others were established at and in the neighborhood of the present site of Red Rock. One of these, by a person named Shaw, stood on the opposite side of the river from the village, and another a short distance above it, was kept by John Jordan. At the last named place was once the scene of a dreadful Indian tragedy, the details of which will be given in another part of this work. About a mile and a half above Red Rock, was another trading house kept by Turner, and north of town about the same distance was yet another, known as the firm of Gaddis & Nye. Some others, who still live in the county, traded much with both the Indians and whites after the settlements commenced, among whom are G. D. Bedell, of the village, and G. H. Miksell, of the the town of Red Rock. Indeed, so far as we can learn, only the three first mentioned establishments existed previously to the date of settlement.

The houses were generally mere shanties designed for temporary occupation. That of Gaddis and Nye was but a shelter made of poles, and roofed with bark or brush. The chief business of the proprietors, especially of those of the earliest date, was with the Indians, exchanging whisky, tobacco, pipes, guns, powder and lead, blankets and a few cheap dry goods, for furs, deer skins and such other products of the hunting grounds as were of any commercial value. After their customers began to receive their yearly payments, old Mexican dollars came into circulation, and many of them very aptly found their way into the pockets of the traders. About eighty-four thousand dollars constituted a payment, and one custom was to distribute this sum among the numerous families of the tribes, each head receiving an amount proportioned to the number of his family. But the Indians sometimes adopted a different mode of payment, called "Chief payments," making their chief the recipient and treasurer. This made him a sort of financial agent for his tribe, and, therefore, to some extent, responsible for individual debts frequently contracted with the traders in anticipation of the payments. In most cases such debts were promptly paid, the savages manifesting an honesty in such transactions that seemed in strange contrast with their usually treacherous characters.

On occasion of one of these payments a contest arose between the Indians as to how it should be made. Keokuk, chief of the Sacs, was in favor of an individual payment, contrary to the wishes of other chiefs and their followers. As pay day approached the contest grew so hot that an appeal to arms seemed probable; and when it came, the hostile parties mustered their forces and even rode up in line of battle. But just then, through some agency or other, seen or unseen, the fight was postponed indefinitely. A compromise was effected, and a chief payment decided upon.

This event took place at Ft. Des Moines, but at precisely what date we are not advised, though it must have been in 1844 or 1845. We have the account from an individual who went there to collect money due him for produce and other articles he had sold the Indians on credit. But for some cause he failed to get any, and other traders also lost heavily.

In those days traders were required to obtain a license for their business, though the requirement was not compulsory. Those who chose to do so could sell to the Indians on credit, and when pay-day came, presented their claims to the agent and drew. But those who failed to fortify themselves with this legal authority had to run the risk of being swindled by absconding debtors, or having their claims repudiated altogether.

Not unfrequently these unsophisticated savages, not having the shrewdness to detect a cheat, or to understand the proper value of an article in trade, were made the victims of gross impositions by unscrupulous traders. A little incident that occurred near Red Rock will illustrate this: An Indian traded his blanket for a melon, promising to bring the article within a given time. It was a good one, and apparently made the most of his scanty wardrobe. But he had eaten the melon, and thought it was good enough to be worth the blanket that he did not feel so much the need of then, and true to his promise, paid it over at the time stipulated.

Another incident permit me to relate, illustrative of the reckless improvidence of a race of people that must consequently ere long, degenerate to a mere remnant, in contrast with the wicked shrewdness that seeks to victimize them for the sake of gain: On occasion of one of these chief payments —the last one perhaps—an individual living near Fort Desmoines, who had had extensive intercourse with the Indians, knew their character and spoke their language, conceived a plan to get some of their money on terms that some might call a fair exchange.

On the day following the payment, he sent a polite invitation to the chief and his five braves to come and dine with him. He had made ample preparations for the feast, and among other articles acceptable to the Indian palate, was a good supply of whisky. At the proper time his guests appeared, and were most flatteringly received and entertained. After dinner, when the hearts of his victims had become softened, to a consistency of great liberality, he invited them to an examination of his ponies. Thereupon half a dozen handsomely equipped animals were brough tfrom the stable and paraded before the admiring guests. The next act in the performance was to invite the chief to accept the finest one of the number as a present, which the grateful sovereign readily did. It is said to be a custom among Indians on receiving a present, to return something of supposed proportionate value. Agreeable to this custom, and, perhaps, actuated by an overwhelming sense of gratitude, the chief immediately placed in the hands of his host a box containing *one thousand dollars in gold*, which he had just received from the Government, in behalf of his tribe, for their lands. Then another pony was presented to one of the braves, which was in like manner acknowledged. Then another, and another, till each of the five braves were supplied with a pony, and their white brethren—the traders—had six thousand dollars of their hard cash.

We are not informed whether the matter terminated thus, or whether the embezzlement was discovered to the tribe, and the unworthy chief tried and punished, as he should have been. If not, it was no fault of the tribe, who were usually not slow to bring judgment upon offenders.

Most of the trading houses were abandoned soon after the Indians left the country, which was upwards of a year after settlement commenced. What became of all the traders can only be conjectured. Jordon went to California, but returned and is now supposed to be in Missouri. Shaw died at Red Rock, many years ago; Gaddis and Nye expressed their intention of following the Indians, and the last known of them they were descending the Des Moines in a canoe, and it is possible that their success in trade induced a majority of those who left the country about that time to follow their old customers.

In speaking of the character of these traders, perhaps all that we ought to say might be said in palliation of the truth: Isolation from the surroundings and restraints of civilization was by no means calculated to improve their morals. If, in some respects they resembled the savages, the fact must be attributed to association. Yet in one particular they were as wholly distinct from the savages as other men; they had a specific object in life, a business upon which was founded anticipations of pecuniary advancement. Not scrupulous as to the means, so the end might be attained, they adopted a calling condemned by the better sentiment of all mankind, as degrading and tending to evil results. Away from the restraints of law and the benificent effects of reformatory agitations, they were free to indulge their cupidity in debauching the simple savages with adulterated whisky, and cheating them in trade. We might here particularize, but there is no need of it. We have made these statements as matters of history that, perhaps, some to whom they apply, might be willing to forget. The traders have had their day, and their victims are no more. *

---

* NOTE.—The statements made in the above paragraph are not intended to apply to *all* persons who traded with the Indians, but to the majority of those whose only business was that of traders. There are some good citizens still living in the county, who dealt more or less with the natives, but not exclusively as traders.

CHAPTER II.

The Indians—Language of the Sacs and Foxes—Brief Sketches of their History—Black Hawk Beheaded—Installation of Keokuk as Chief—Indian Tragedy near Red Rock.

Enough has been written upon the manners and customs of that somewhat mysterious race of people, the Indians, so that we shall not introduce the subject here, except as it occurs in the reminiscences related from time to time. Indian life is so uniform that what relates to one tribe is mainly applicable to the whole nation, for the similarity of complexion, language and habits of the numerous tribes lead us to believe they belong to the same nationality as much as did the twelve tribes of Israel. It is true that there are some differences, but these are not materially distinct, and may be attributed to differences of climate and country. Various causes may have divided the nation into so many tribes, but the most probable cause was the same that operates to divide civilized nations into clans and communities—conflicting interests and quarrels—since which they have maintained the separation under separate leaders. Most of the tribes are noted for their warlike propensity, and if their history could be written, it might show a succession of wars as full of romance and adventure as those of the ancient Greeks and Romans. From this cause some tribes, once powerful and much dreaded, were reduced to mere remnants or totally extinguished. We venture to say that if it had not been for these divisions into tribes, and the failure of some of their most noted chiefs to unite many of them against a common enemy, our success in subduing them would have been far more difficult.

The Sacs and Foxes who occupied the country included in the purchase of 1842, were enough alike in all general respects to constitute but one tribe. We are told that they occupied the same districts, hunted upon the same hunting grounds, intermarried, and spoke the same language, with but slight difference, no more, probably, than what occurs between eastern and western people in their use of English.

As a matter of some curiosity, as well as useful instruction, we here give the translation of a few words of Indian, as spoken by these tribes, as nearly as English letters can be made to convey the somewhat difficult articulation:

Horse, nack-a-tock-a-shaw; hog, cocasho; ox or cow, nannoos; Desmoines river, koasauqua sepe; White Breast river, waupeka sepe; Skunk river, shecauqua sepe;* e-noch-enoqua, to-day I am going; Ku-che-pen-oach-ne-och-e-pe-i-ale, come a long distance; war, necanty; one, nacote; two, nish; three, ness; four, neaue; five, neollen; six, cautwassick; seven, nawhick; eight, swaussick; nine, sauk; ten, mataus or sweech; twenty, nishwaupetuck; thirty, nessswaupetuck; forty, neaueswaupetuck; fifty, shi-cau-e-collah; sixty, nessswassick-ete-swaup-etuck; one hundred, naquetauk; one thousand, mataus-naquetauk.

The history of these tribes may be traced back to a period as early as 1767, the year in which Black Hawk was born. They then occupied the country now known as the state of Wisconsin. At an early age this celebrated warrior, Black Hawk, by his prowess and skill in war against the Osages, between whom and the Sacs and Foxes a long standing grudge had existed, raised himself to some eminence as a leader and gave these tribes a notoriety in military history.

---

* This word, we are told by good authority, does not apply exclusively to *skunk*, but means anything that has a strong or offensive smell. The head waters of Skunk river were once noted for the vast quantities of wild onions that grew there. Hence Chicago is the same word a little differently spelled and pronounced.

From the time that the government came into possession of the north-western territory, by purchase from the Spanish government, these Indians did not seem favorable to the change, and conceived a dislike to the new proprietors. The treaty of 1804, was not calculated to remove this prejudice, inasmuch as it was made without the general authority of the Indians. Soon after this treaty, the whites began to erect forts and trading posts along the Mississippi in the disputed territory, which caused a war that continued, with occasional intermissions or truces, brought about by renewed treaties, till the capture of Black Hawk, in 1833.

This renowned warrior spent a pleasant captivity in traveling through the eastern part of the United States, at the expense of the government, during which time he visited Washington, and had an interview with President Jackson. After having seen much of the magnitude of the government against which he had been from time to time long and vigorously contending for what he conceived to be the just rights of his people, and had thereby an opportunity to judge of its power, he with his son and one or two of his braves who had accompanied him, returned to the west, and was released at Ft. Armstrong—now Rock Island—and immediately retired to private life, from which he no more emerged in hostile array against the whites. His death occurred in 1839, near Fairfield, Jefferson county. Soon after his death his head was severed from his body and coveyed to St. Louis. The object of this mutilation history does not state, but we may conjecture that it was either to preserve it in spirits or obtain from it a bust or painted likeness of the great chief. We have reason to suppose that the government had no cognizance of an act so unlike her wonted treatment of fallen foes. Our informant thinks that the head may be at St. Louis to this day. But this is not so very probable, for when the Indians discovered this mutilation of the body of their venerated chief, they threatened serious trouble, which nothing could avert but the return of the head; accordingly it, or some other head, *was* returned, but it is not likely that the Indians could have been easily deceived in the identity of a face they had so long been familiar with. At all events they became pacified.

After the capture of Black Hawk, and the treaty that followed, Keokuk was made chief of both the Sacs and Foxes. This chief, little less renowned than Black Hawk for bravery and cunning in war, was yet quite a contrast to the latter in person, and in his relations with the whites. Black Hawk was a person of small stature, while Keokuk was a portly Indian, weighing, probably, over two hundred pounds. Whilst Black Hawk was pursuing his hostile attempts to check the encroachments of the whites, Keokuk remained either neutral or friendly to the latter. In this he had many adherents, which prevented Black Hawk from bringing a much larger force into the field, as a strong partizan leader he had desired to do. For this reason, and in order to insure permanent peace with the Indians, the government, through its agents, obtained the appointment of Keokuk to the chieftainship of both tribes.

We have on file a number of sketches illustrative of the character and customs of these people, that occurred during their residence in this county, after its first settlement, but which, for want of room in this chapter, we shall reserve for the miscellaneous department of the work.

We shall, however, take occasion here to relate an event that transpired near Red Rock, early in the fall of 1844, and which, on account of its horrible details, is still fresh to the memory of those who witnessed it, or lived in the neighborhood at the time.

It is said to have been an occasional custom with the Indians (or at least with those who were thus disposed) to take criminal liberties with such squaws as should happen to be found abroad, unattended by any other person. Any squaw thus found alone was presumed to be not virtuous, and was therefore subject to the licentious attacks of any bad man who, under these circumstances, was not subject to punishment for the crime. The assault was called a *feast.*

On the occasion of which we speak, a Winnebago brave and his wife, a likely young squaw, of the Sac or Fox tribes, had come down the Des Moines river on a trading expedition, and were camped near Jordan's trading house that stood, as we stated in the preceding chapter, on the south side of the river, some distance above the ferry landing. About this time two Indians, named Wan-pep-cah-cah and Pac-a-tuke, chanced to be prowling in the neighborhood, and discovered the lady alone in the woods. They thereupon deemed her a fit subject for a "feast," but she escaped and returned to camp. Toward evening of that day, or the next, these Indians were at Red Rock, from which they could observe the movements of their intended victim at the camp. At about dark they made their appearance at the trading house and attacked the squaw again, as she was preparing to light the camp fire, when she took refuge in the house. Her husband, who was absent at the time, on his return asked her why she had not lighted the fire. She then told him how she had been followed and persecuted by the two bad Indians, who were still without, intending to camp on the ground. Hearing this, Jordan permitted the brave and his wife to remain in-doors that night.

But the Winnebago was not content to merely escape, for the time being, the unwelcome presence of those "sons of Baliel"—his honor had been compromised in that of his wife. He was deeply incensed, and nothing but a bloody revenge could heal the wound. With this feeling he rose and announced his purpose to go out and kill them. On accosting them angry words followed, and they both assaulted him, probably not knowing that he was armed. He resisted the assault with his hunting knife. Wan-pep-cah-cah received eleven mortal stabs, and Pac-a-tuke, one across the abdomen, letting out his bowels, which he caught and supported with his hands as they fell, and as he sank to the ground in an agonizing death.

This took place about nine o'clock at night. None but the actors witnessed the deed, but the strokes of the knife were distinctly heard within, and the scene next morning was such as to warrant the truth of the above narration.

Next morning several white men collected at the scene of the tragedy, and sent a report of it to a chief named Pashapaho,* who, with his party of about three hundred, had been down the day before, but returned and camped on what is now called Stortz's Island, two or three miles above Red Rock. Pashapaho, on hearing the news, immediately sent one of his braves down with peremptory orders to kill the murderer. Apparently no thought was entertained of giving him a trial for his life, nor even inquiring as to how far he might have been justified in the commission of the deed. The order was to kill him.

The Winnebago remained at the place, apparently trusting in the justification of the act to shield him from the punishment of a common murderer, or else desirous of seeing what action would be taken in his case. But when he saw Pashapaho's agent approaching, he comprehended at a glance his intended doom, and made an attempt to escape. But too late. The fleet-footed Fox was too near him when the flight began, and after a chase of only about one hundred and fifty yards, he was overtaken, and by the assistance of another Indian, who had just come into the action, apparently as a sort of reinforcement, was overpowered, led back to the house, and his legs bound together above the knees.

---

*Stabbing chief.

The inquiry now was, what they meant to do with him. The reply was that they would kill him. Against this the white men who were present did not feel called upon to interfere, either by command or persuasion, nor, so far as we have been able to learn, by representing the facts of the case to the Indians. They only protested against the execution being performed there, and insisted that the prisoner should be taken to his own country for that purpose. But this protest was not heeded; the Indian who had come to carry out the orders of his chief, walked into the house, seized a hatchet that belonged to the place, and, as he stepped out again by his victim, who was seated near the door, struck him a heavy blow across the back of the neck, burying the edge of the weapon in the bone. The stroke felled him, but did not render him insensible nor even speechless; and, as it was not followed immediately by others, as though it was the purpose of his executioner to prolong his agony, he partly rose upon his hands and pleadingly said: "Strike me again, friends." Then the other Indian who stood by, actuated either by a sense of pity or an eager desire to see the bloody work go on, said to the executioner in a tone as threatening as his words: "Kill that Indian or I'll kill you!" In another moment the head of the prostrate victim was nearly severed from the body. This done the Indians went their way, leaving the bodies where they had fallen, either not caring what disposition was made of them, or else taking it for granted that the whites would see to their burial. Messrs. Jordan, Bedell and a few others, when they saw that the savages would have nothing to do in the matter, proceeded to make some arrangements for the interment. Whilst this was going on, the poor woman who had witnessed the last act of the tragedy, the murder of her husband, with what feelings we are not sufficiently advised to describe, performed with her own hands the last sad rites it was the custom of her people to bestow upon the dead in preparation for the funeral. Having procured some red paint commonly used by Indians to decorate their faces, she painted their cheeks, eye-lids and lips very nicely and carefully, and then made an impression of her open hand on each cheek. This service she performed with equal care upon each, foe as well as friend. The three bodies were put into one grave near where the upper ford now is. Since then they have been washed away with the bank that has caved in more or less with the annual freshets, and what remains of this most tragic event may now be scattered and deeply embedded in the sands at the bottom of the Des Moines. The woman, who was the innocent cause of the affair, went to Red Rock. Hearing that the Indians intended to murder her also, she took refuge in the house of Robert D. Russell, where she remained secreted for upwards of a month. By this time the Indians had so far learned the facts of the case that she was finally deemed innocent, and was permitted to come forth and go west with her friends.*

The settlement of Marion county was begun at a period of some financial depression.† The monetary crash of 1837 was still felt, and those who came early were by no means rich. They were literally poor men, seeking homes and independence that could not be acquired in a country where real estate was beyond the reach of the day laborer. An opportunity was now granted to those who would brave the privations of frontier life to possess themselves of an estate that might, if rightly improved, insure independence and even wealth.

---

*Another version of this story is to the effect that two drunken Indians murdered the son of a prophet, and, after being arrested, were tried and sentenced to death, the oldest squaw of the tribe being selected to execute the sentence with a tomahawk. Also that the Indians were so much incensed at the traders for supplying the murderers with whisky, that they sat twenty days in council discussing the propriety of punishing them, but were finally pacified by those who could speak their language. But the foregoing details being from an eye-witness to the last act of the tragedy, may be deemed correct.

†The "tightness" of money matters at that period may be conceived by the fact that property, compared to present prices, was remarkably cheap. Twenty-five or thirty dollars would buy a good yoke of cattle, and forty-five would buy ber one horse.

CHAPTER III.

Poverty — Settlements — Marking off Claims — Primitive Houses and their Furniture—First Crop—Grating Corn for Meal—Hominy—Samp.

During the first year (1843) about seventy families from various parts of the east and south, settled in the county. These immigrants mostly came in companies,—families acquainted or connected,—and settled in neighborhoods that eventually formed the nucleus of what were called "settlements." These settlements were mostly designated by names derived from some leading member thereof, or from their locality, such as the English settlement, the Tong settlement, the Buffington settlement, the White Breast settlement, and the Red Rock settlement. The first division of the county into election precincts, to be hereafter described, seems to have been intended to accommodate these settlements, and will show their localities. These settlements were not only the result of the social tendency of mankind to drift into communities, but in a country so wild, and where mutual dependence upon each other was so much felt, wisdom demanded such combinations. In time these settlements were so expanded by additions as to unite with others, and thereby lost their distinction, but some of them are still known by their old names.

But these settlements were not always so compact as circumstances seemed to require. Settlers were disposed to suit themselves with a location, though it might be at a remote distance from neighbors, and families within two or three miles of each other were neighbors. Occasionally a lonely cabin was to be met with so far from any other as to be apparently out of range of any settlement.

The first business of a settler on reaching the place where he intended to settle, was to select his claim and mark it off as nearly as he could without a compass. This was done by stepping and staking or blazing the lines as he went. The absence of section lines rendered it necessary to take the sun at noon and at evening as a guide by which to run these claim lines. So many steps each way counted three hundred and twenty acres, more or less, the legal area of a claim It may be readily supposed that these lines were far from correct, but they answered all necessary claim purposes, for it was understood among the settlers that when the lands came to be surveyed and entered, all inequalities should be righted. Thus, if a surveyed line should happen to run between adjoining claims, cutting off more or less of the one or the other, the fraction was to be added to whichever lot required equalizing, yet without robbing the one from which it was taken, for an equal amount would be added to it in some other place.

The next important business of a settler was to build a house. Till this was done some had to camp on the ground or live in their wagons, perhaps the only shelter they had known for several weeks, so that the prospect of a house of some kind that could be called a home, produced a thrill of pleasure that could hardly be comprehended by those who have never suffered the same privation. To the home-loving unadventurous female, this thought must be specially applicable.

But such a home! The poor settler has neither the means nor the help to erect a palace. So far from it, the best he can do, in most instances, is to fix up the cheapest thing imaginable that could be called a house. Some of the most primitive constructions of the kind were half-faced, or, as they were sometimes called, "cat-faced" sheds or "wickeups," the Indian term for house or tent. But a claim cabin was a little more in the shape of a human habitation, made of round logs light enough for two or three men to lay up; about fourteen feet square, perhaps a little larger or smaller, roofed with bark or clapboards, and floored with puncheons (logs split into slabs), or earth. For a fire place, a wall of stone and earth—frequently the latter only when stone was not convenient—was made in the best practicable shape for the purpose, in an opening in one end of the building, extending outward, and planked on the outside by batts of wood notched together to stay it. Frequently a fire-place of this kind was made so capacious as to occupy nearly the whole width of the house. In cold weather, when much fuel was needed to keep the temperature of such a room above the freezing point, large logs were piled up in the yawning space. To protect the crumbling back wall against the effects of fire, two "back logs" were placed against it, one upon the other. Sometimes these back logs were so large as to require horse power to draw them into the house, the horse entering at one door and going out at the other, leaving the log where it could be rolled into the fire-place. For a chimney any contrivance that would conduct the smoke upwards, would do. Some were made of sods plastered inside with clay, others—the more common perhaps—were the kind we occasionally see in use now, clay and sticks, or "cat in clay," as they were sometimes called. For doors and windows, the most simple contrivances that would serve the purposes were brought into requisition. The door was not always immediately provided with a shutter, in which case a quilt or some other cloth might be spared to hang over it. As soon as convenient, however, some boards were split and put together for a shutter, hung upon wooden hinges, and held shut by a wooden pin inserted in an auger hole. As substitutes for window glass, greased paper pasted over sticks crossed in the shape of a sash, was sometimes used. It admitted the light and excluded the air, nearly equal to a glass window, but of course, lacked the transparency.

In regard to the furniture of such a house, our inventory must necessarily be as brief as our description of its architecture, unless in such instances where the settlers may have brought with them their old household supply, which, owing to the distance most of them had come, was very seldom. It may be readily understood by the reader that whatever articles could be made to substitute tables and chairs, were used for them. A table could be as easily made as a door shutter, and of the same kind of material. Indeed we have heard of instances of the door shutter being taken down and used for a table, and re-hanged again after meals. Benches and stools supplied the place of chairs. But perhaps the most important of the few domestic comforts that could be crowded into so small a space, was a bedstead or two. Any family who had been bred to the customs and conveniences of civilization could hardly accommodate themselves to the simple mode of repose in use among the savages, that of stretching them selves upon the earth. Something softer than the bosom of mother earth, and a little more elevating, was deemed indispensable, if it could be obtained. Therefore the nearest approach to a real bedstead, that could be extemporised in a hurry and with the fewest tools, was done in this wise: A forked stake was driven into the ground at a proper distance diagonally from a corner of the room, upon which poles, reaching from each wall, were laid. The wall ends of the poles may have rested in the openings between the logs or been driven into auger holes. Bark or boards were made to substitute cords. Upon this cheap article of furniture the pains-taking housewife could spread her bedding so as to hide every bit of its deformity; then hang up some sheets behind it, and thus give the sleeping corner of the homely habitation a tasty and wide-awake appearance. It was generally called the "prairie bedstead," and by some, the "prairie rascal," though for what reason the latter term was applied to it does not appear, for it is difficult to conceive of anything more honest in construction or use.

Few of these houses yet remain as monuments of the past. The writer has seen two or three foundation logs of one of the first, where it stood. Their appearance is quite antiquarian, rotten and sunken into the earth, but still bearing some marks of their ancient use. One or two cabins of a somewhat later date, still stand, or did a year since, on the premises of J. M. Brous, an old settler in Perry township. They are in tolerable preservation, considering their age. But a majority of those old cabins have passed away, as well as some of their builders and original occupants; not, however, without first serving the purposes of stables, sheds, cribs, &c., till at last too frail for even these uses, they have been reduced to fuel, and their ashes returned to the earth that first produced the living tree.

The next important duty of the settler was to prepare some ground and plant what he could at that advanced season for cropping. This was generally done in the edge of the timber, where most of the very earliest settlers located. Here the sod was easily broken, not requiring the heavy teams and plows needed to break the prairie sod. Perhaps we might safely add, as another reason for first settling in and about the timber, convenience to fuel and building timber. It may be supposed that the timber afforded some protection against those terrible conflagrations that occasionally swept across the prairies. Though they often passed through the groves, it was not with the same destructive force. By these fires much of the young timber was killed from time to time, and the forests kept thin and shrubless. Since these fires have been kept out, our timber lands have become thickly set with a new growth.

The first year's farming generally consisted of a "truck patch" planted in corn, potatoes, turnips, &c. But one man in the county planted any considerable crop of "sod corn," and this was Jas. Price, of Summit township. He broke nine acres of prairie the first year, where he still lives, and from it produced considerable more corn than he needed for his own consumption. But generally, the first year's crop fell far short of supplying even the most rigid economy of food. Most of the settlers had brought with them such provisions as were indispensable to frugal living for some time, such as flour or meal, bacon, and coffee or tea. But these supplies, unlike the poor widow's barrel of meal and cruise of oil, were not inexhaustible. A long winter must come and go before another crop could be raised. At times game was plentiful, and the skillful huntsman could supply his table with venison. When corn could be obtained, the absence or inconvenience of mills for grinding it, forced the necessity of grating it on an implement made by punching small holes through a piece of tin or sheet-iron and fastening it on a board in a concave shape, with the rough side out. Upon this implement the ear was rubbed to produce meal. But grating could not be done when the corn becomes so dry as to shell off when rubbed. Some even used a coffee mill for grinding corn. But a very common substitute for bread was hominy, a palatable and wholesome diet, made by boiling corn in weak lye till the hull or bran peals off, after which it was well washed to cleanse it of the lye, then boiled again to soften it, when it was ready for use as occasion required, by frying and seasoning it to suit the taste. Another mode of preparing hominy was by pestling. A mortar was made by burning a bowl-shaped cavity in the even end of an upright block of wood. After thoroughly clearing it of the charcoal, the corn could be put in, hot water teemed upon it, and subjected to a severe pesteling by a club of sufficient length and thickness, in the larger end of which was inserted an iron wedge banded to keep it there. The hot water would soften the corn and loosen the hull, and the pestle would crush it.

Another preparation of corn diet, called "samp," was made by cracking the kernels in a tan-bark mill, then boiling it like rice.

CHAPTER IV.

Going to Mill—Tally's Ford—Origin of Roads—First Roads Located—Returning from Mill.

But when breadstuffs were needed, they had to be obtained from the "Old Purchase," and hauled, mostly by ox teams, a distance of from sixty to eighty miles; some had to go even as far as Burlington to get a supply of wheat and corn and have it milled. Wheat could be had at fifty cents per bushel; cheap enough compared with present prices, but dear enough then considering the scarcity of money, the inferiority of the grain and the distance it had to be hauled. Owing to the want of proper means of threshing and cleaning it, wheat was more or less mixed with foreign substances, such as dirt, smut and oats. The price of corn was from fifty to seventy-five cents per bushel. It was mostly bought in the ear, and shelled by the purchaser before taking it to mill. Those mills usually resorted to were at Brighton, Washington county, and at Keosauqua and Bonaparte, Van Buren county.

But the difficulties to be encountered in reaching these distant places, were not the least among the tribulations endured by the pioneers during the first two years of settlement. The slow mode of travel by ox teams was made still slower by the almost total absence of roads and bridges, and such a thing as a ferry was hardly even dreamed of. In dry weather, common sloughs and creeks offered little impediment to the teamsters; but during floods and the breaking up of winter, proved exceedingly troublesome and dangerous. To get "stuck" in some mucky slough, and thus be delayed for an hour or more, was no uncommon circumstance. Often a raging stream would blockade the way, seeming to threaten swift destruction to whoever would attempt to ford it.

To those living south of the Des Moines, Tally's ford was the usual place of crossing that river. This ford was at what is now Bellfontaine, a little east of the county line. During low water, no difficulty was experienced in fording; but when it was too deep for this, the means for getting over were certainly trying to any wayfaring man. The only ferry boat was a small canoe. Wagons had to be unloaded and taken to pieces, and both they and their loads shipped in small cargoes at a voyage, till all were over; then the teams had to be unharnessed or unyoked and made to swim, the horses being led by the halter at the side of the canoe, and the oxen by the horns. Mrs. Tally has been known to lead an ox by the horns whilst her husband managed the canoe. Sometimes they were permitted to take their own course in swimming.

An "old settler," to whose "sketches" we are indebted for these statements, speaks thus eulogistically of the disinterested generosity of Mr. and Mrs. Tally, who kept the ferry:

"In this work the early settlers were much indebted to the kind assistance of Mr. and Mrs. Tally, who labored faithfully for their accommodation, usually without adequate compensation, and frequently without any whatever, very generously refusing any reward for their timely aid;" and also acknowledges, for himself and others, "a debt of gratitude for favors bestowed in times of real necessity;" for the good Samaritan offices of this worthy couple were not confined to the ferry: in cases of sickness, or want in other respects, they were neighbors to all within their reach. It is therefore due to them that their names should be preserved to memory, as among the benefactors of mankind in a sphere not less important because limited to a locality. Their present residence is in Decatur county.

With regard to roads, as we have said, there was nothing of the kind worthy the name. Indian trails were common, but they were unfit to travel on with vehicles. They are described as mere paths, about two feet wide, all that was required to accommodate the single-file manner of Indian travelling. Riding, or walking in companies, it seems to have ever been a national custom with them to follow each other singly.

An interesting theory respecting the origin of the routes now pursued by many of our public highways, is given in a speech made by Thomas Benton, many years ago. It possesses a spice of romance, which, however, does not render it a whit less probable. Indeed, the truth of it is practically demonstrated in many instances. He says the buffaloes were the first road engineers, and the paths trodden by them were, as a matter of convenience, followed by the Indians, and lastly by the whites, with such improvements and changes as were found necessary for civilized modes of travel. It is but reasonable to suppose that those monster beasts, the buffaloes, would instinctively choose the most practicable routes and fords in their migrations from one pasture to another. Then the Indians, following, possessed of about as much enterprise as their predecessors, the buffaloes, made no improvements, and were finally driven from the track by those who would.

Among the many roads in this county known to be only Indian trails at the period of which we are writing, is one from Red Rock to Knoxville, and those traversing the bottoms on either side of the river above and below Red Rock. Under the cliffs south of the river, above town, this trail was so narrow as to barely permit the passage of a horseman between the bayou and the rocky wall. Would it be a great stretch of the imagination to suppose that these paths were made and trodden by thousands of buffaloes passing and repassing between pastures, long before the Indians came to drive them from their haunts? If so, Red Rock must have been their fording place hundreds, if not more than a thousand years ago. So, perhaps, were the other fords that have since been in use. The imagination might here paint a wild scene: Standing upon the abrupt bank of the river at Red Rock, on some sultry summer day when the air is still, and the clear, shallow water moves slowly down the sand-margined channel, our ears catch a low, rumbling sound like that of distant thunder, only continuous, and each moment growing more distinct, mingled with the lowings of the herd. Suddenly a grand panorama bursts upon our astonished vision. Emerging from the thick forest, crowding each other as though driven by fright, or impelled by heat and thirst, comes the immense multitude, and without a moment's halt in their peculiar rolling gait, down they plunge over the worn sandy bank into the river, where they assuage their thirst, and lash the waters about them as a protection against annoying insects. Then the advance passes on as the rear presses it, and it soon disappears. Thus for hours they continue to move ; and if we grow weary of what may at length become a monotonous scene, we may exchange it for another equally if not more imposing, by stepping out upon the open prairie, a few miles northward, where we find it almost covered by the vast herd, who have sought it as a pasture after having exhausted some other range.

Whilst speaking of roads, it may be deemed proper, though at the risk of being considered tedious, to state that the first county road that we have any record of as being legally established, was established in 1845, and is thus described in the petition asking for it : "To commence at the house of Samuel Nicholson, thence running in a northerly direction so as to strike John Conrey's claim near the south-west corner of it, thence by the nearest and best route to Knoxville." Viewers, John T. Pierce, Reuben S. Lowry, and Garret W. Clark; surveyor, Isaac B. Power. The next one was petitioned for in January, 1846, and is described to run "from McPherson's, by way of Durham's ford, to Knoxville;" and the next related to the "re-location of a territorial road where it crosses the lake in Lake Prairie; thence to the termination of it." About the same year the road from Red Rock, via Burch's mill, to Knoxville was established. The want of technicality in the descriptions of these roads was owing to the fact that the country had not yet been sectionized,which was not done till 1846–7, and then only so far as the west line of that part of the purchase open to settlement in 1843, as described in the introductory; therefore the points named in the descriptions were the best known of any that could be named. Several more road transactions followed these, but they are not of sufficient interest to record here. It was not until a much later period than this chapter is mainly intended to treat of, that road matters began to be looked after with any considerable interest. Next in importance to the possession of a homestead was a good and convenient way to pass to and from it; and its importance became greater as the country increased in population, villages and cities sprang into being, and the lands around them began to be fenced into farms.

At the time of which we are speaking, when the early settlers were compelled to make those long and difficult trips to mill, a portion of the way to be traversed was on the prairie, between Oskaloosa and Blue Point, a stretch of about forty miles, where there was not a house. During the summer, when grass was plentiful, the passage of this comparative desert could be made without much difficulty, by traveling till night, then camping out and feeding the teams on the range; but in winter, an attempt to cross it, without sufficient time to do so by daylight, was attended with no little danger. The road was too obscure to be safely followed at night, and there was no object in the dim horizon to guide the traveler in any certain direction. Though the utmost economy of time was necessary for persons going so far to mill, and who had families at home to feed, they were compelled to time their travel so as to stay a night at either of the points above named going or coming.

When the goal was at last reached, after a week or more of

toilsome travel, attended by more or less exposure, the details of some of which we propose to give in other chapters, and the poor man was impatient to be soon on his return with the needed staff of life, he was often shocked with the information that his turn would come in a week. Then he must look about for some means to save expenses, and he was lucky who could find employment at whatever he could do by the day or by the job. Then, when his turn came, he had to be on hand to bolt his flour, as in those days the bolting machine was not an attached part of the other mill machinery. This done, the anxious soul was ready to endure the trials of a return trip, his heart more or less concerned about the affairs of home; and as this feeling increased, the miles seemed to grow longer, and the journey proportionately tedious.

These milling trips often occupied from three weeks to more than a month each, and were attended with an expense, one way or another, that rendered the cost of breadstuff extremely high. If made in the winter, when more or less grain feed was required for the team, the load would be found so considerably reduced on reaching home, that the cost of what was left, adding other expenses, could be safely estimated at from three to five dollars per bushel. And these trips could not always be made at the most favorable season for traveling. In spring and summer so much time could hardly be spared from other necessary labor; yet, for a large family, it was almost impossible to avoid making three or four trips during the year.

CHAPTER V.

An Unpropitious Season—Primitive Mode of Cleaning Wheat-Dirty Bread—Wolves and other Beasts of Prey—Failure of Crops—Better Times in Prospect—Erection of First Mill in the County.

The winter of 1843-4 was one of great severity and length, followed by a late spring. The Des Moines river remained closed till the middle of April; then, about the last of May, heavy rains began and continued till the middle of July, so that what could be planted was but indifferently cultivated. Finally came a keen September frost that cut short what was already much curtailed by late planting and poor cultivation. Some wheat had been sown, but it not only yielded poorly, but was more or less effected by rust and smut; and, owing to the rude manner of threshing and cleaning it, it became compounded with a grit not pleasant to masticate and hard to digest.

As the time may come when the simple modes of threshing and cleaning wheat in use by the pioneers, for the want of better means, may be forgotten, it may be well to preserve a description of them here. Possibly it may never be needed as a recipe, but may some day be regarded as an interesting scrap of history. The plan was, to clean off a spot of ground of a necessary circumference, and, if the earth was dry, dampen it and beat it so as to render it somewhat compact; then unbind and spread the sheaves in a circle, so that the heads would be uppermost, leaving room in the centre to be occupied by the person whose business it is to stir and turn the straw in the process of threshing. Then bring upon it as many oxen or horses as could conveniently "swing around the circle," and keep them thus moving till the wheat was well trodden out. After several "floorings," or layers, were threshed the straw was carefully raked off, and the wheat shoveled into a heap to be cleaned. This was sometimes done by waving a sheet up and down to fan out the chaff as the grain was dropped before it; but this trouble was frequently obviated by the strong winds of autumn, when all that was needed was the necessary exposure to permit the chaff to blow away.

By such imperfect modes of preparing the grain for flouring, it is not surprising that a considerable amount of black soil got mixed with it, that unavoidably went into the bread. This, with the addition of smut, often rendered it so dark as to have less the appearance of bread than of mud; yet upon such diet the people were compelled to subsist or do without; and it may be a matter of wonder that this wholesale consumption of dirt did not result in an epidemic.

It may be worthy of record here that in those days the wheat crop was much more subject to rust than it is now. The reason of this we will not venture to give, but leave it to those whose experience and observation much better qualifies them todo so.

Among other things calculated to annoy and distress the pioneers, was the prevalence of wild animals of prey, the most numerous and troublesome of which was the wolf. While it was true in a figurative sense, that it required much care and exertion to "keep the wolf from the door," it was almost as true in a literal sense. There were two species of these animals,—the large, black, timber wolf, and the smaller gray wolf that usually inhabited the prairie. At first it was next to impossible for a settler to keep small stock of any kind that would serve as prey for these ravenous beasts. Sheep were not deemed safe property till years later, when their enemies were supposed to be nearly exterminated. Large numbers of wolves were destroyed during the first two or three years of settlement,—as many as fifty in a day, in a regular wolf hunt. When they were hungry, which was not uncommon, particularly during the winter, they were too indiscreet for their own safety, and would often approach within easy shot of a dwelling. At certain seasons their wild, plaintive yelping would be heard in all directions, at all hours of the night, creating an intense excitement among the dogs, whose barking and howling added much to the dismal melody. It has been found by experiment that but one of the canine species, the hound, has both the fleetness and courage to cope with the wolf. Attempts were often made to take them with the common cur; but this animal generally proved himself totally unreliable for such service. So long as wolf would run, cur would follow; but wolf, being apparently acquainted with the character of his pursuer, would either turn and place himself in a combative attitude, or else act upon the principle that "discretion is the better part of valor," and throw himself upon his back in token of surrender, which strategical performance would so win upon the generous nature of Mr. Cur that peace was instantly made. Not unfrequently dogs and wolves have been seen playing together like pups. But the hound was never known to recognize a flag of truce; his baying, when upon the scent, that sounds like music to the sportsman's ear, seems to say "no quarter!" and the terrified wolf understands it.

Smaller animals, such as panthers, lynxes, wild-cats, catamounts and polecats, were also sufficiently numerous to be troublesome. Of these, as well as of the wolf, none remain except an occasional straggler in the wildest sections of the county, where they may still find a hiding-place. We must except the polecat, who has a strong proclivity for domesticating himself wherever there is a chicken-roost, much to the abhorrence of many farmer's wives, who claim special if not exclusive proprietorship of the feathered stock on the premises.

We think it hardly fair to conclude this list of troubles without mentioning one more that might seem too insignificant to be noticed. But small and contemptible as the mosquito is, it always succeeds in attracting attention, and often very feelingly. This was particularly the fact during the early times of which we are writing, when they came up in such pestiferous swarms, demanding blood in the most imperative tones, that at times neither man nor beast could labor or rest comfortably, except under the protection of smoke. Persons have been driven from the field by their unmerciful charges. But since the country has become thickly settled, and many of the ponds and water-courses that bred them drained, or dried up by cultivation, these little tormentors have been greatly diminished in numbers.

The partial failure of the crop of the summer of 1844, compelled many to resort to the Old Purchase for another year's supply of provisions. A few fortunate ones may have grown enough and some to spare, but the supply came far short of the demand. This discouraging circumstance, together with others already but briefly described, was calculated to drive the struggling pioneers from their purpose; but, so far as we know, but few abandoned their new homes to return to their old ones. With all their hardships and discouragements the country possessed attractions that fixed their choice, and a fortunate choice it eventually proved to be.

But as though Providence had repented of the burden He had imposed upon the people, and was now seeking to make amends, a more prosperous state of things began with the winter of 1844–5. It was one of such unusual mildness that the ground was but little frozen at any time, and plowing could have been done in January. Then came an early spring, and grass enough in April for grazing. That season an abundant crop rewarded the labors of the husbandman. There was no more dependence on the Old Purchase for grain, though it was still necessary to resort to those distant mills to get it ground.

In due time, however, this trouble was also shortened by the erection of flouring mills in Mahaska, and at length in our own county. About the year 1844, Duncan's mill, on Skunk river, north of Oskaloosa, came into operation, and was for several years the most convenient flouring mill. Afterwards Warren's, on the same stream, north of Pella, shortened the distance materially. Then in 1844 Andrew Foster built a saw mill on English creek, in what is now Clay township, to which he afterwards added an apparatus for grinding corn, and this proved to be a great convenience in that department of bread-stuff. To throw a sack of corn on a horse, take it to mill and get home again with the meal, all in one day, was the beginning of a comparatively happy period in the history of thatsettlement.

About the same time, or probably at a little earlier date, a Mr. Babcock erected a "corn-cracker," near the present site of Bussing's mill. It was afterward moved to Coalport. There was also one on Cedar creek, built and owned by H. Haymaker; and in 1844 or 1845, L. J. Burch erected one on White Breast, that still stands and is used occasionally.

Many others, both for sawing and grinding, were erected in various parts of the county, at later dates. But the most of them were rudely constructed, designed to relieve the pressing demands of their neighborhoods. Being water mills they could not be run at all seasons; so, when better accommodations could be afforded, they were abondoned, and some of them are now in ruins. Of these we shall speak more definitely hereafter.

Now, with an increased population and an adequate supply of home productions and machinery, the people of Marion county began to deem themselves sufficiently self-sustaining to support an independent municipality. To this end they applied to the territorial government for a distinct county organization and a name, which were granted in the yerr 1845. This event marks an epoch in its history, at which we must close this chapter for the purpose of noticing other important events of an earlier date, after which we shall refer to it again with as complete an account as we have been able to obtain.

CHAPTER VI.

Claim Law, and Club Law.

The manner of taking claims having been described in another place, we now proceed to a description of the government adopted by the settlers, mainly intended for the regulation of their claim interests, as soon as circumstances rendered such government necessary.

As we have stated, most of the settlers were poor men, who had sought the country for the purpose of advancing their pecuniary interests, prompted by the liberal advantage offered by the general government, which was a claim interest in a certain amount of the public lands till these lands should be subject to sale. In this they saw an opening that seemed to promise admission into comparative independence, if not actual wealth; and for the most of them, we are happy to say, this hope has been, to a greater or less extent, realized. Their sacrifices and labors have been rewarded; they are wealthy; the proprietors of the soil they acquired with so much hardship, they now rest from their labors, with all the comforts and many of the luxuries of life at their command. Though more than twenty-five years have passed away since some of them established their homes in this then trackless wilderness, and those who were in the summer of life then, are now in the autumn of decline, the scenes of their early trials are still fresh to their memories, and they love to " fight their battles over again," in the secure retreat of their own happy homes.

As above stated, an act of congress granted to each settler the privilege of locating upon and claiming three hundred and twenty acres of land until the time of the sale, when he could enter and secure a permanent title to the same. This claim right was regulated by what was called the "claim law," that had its origin in a large meeting of citizens at Locust Grove, Jefferson county, and was legalized by the territorial legislature of 1839.

The provisions of this law were briefly these: Any person twenty-one years old, or any other person at the head of a family, could possess him or herself of three hundred and twenty acres of land belonging to the government, and not legally claimed or occupied by any other person or persons. This could be claimed in one or two tracts, as suited the interest or convenience of the claimant. Said claims had to be defined by well blazed or well staked lines, as it might happen to be, in the timber or on the prairie, said lines not to cross or conflict with those of other claims. Then the claimant was required to build a house on the land, live in it, and cultivate a certain amount yearly, as evidence of his intention to become a permanent settler thereon. In case he should absent himself from it six months at any one time, it was forfeited, and subject to be "jumped," that is, any other person legally entitled to a claim, could take possession of and hold it as though it had never beeh claimed. But, unlike the present homestead right, claims were transferable at any time, and many who found themselves unable to buy of the government, sold to individuals, sometimes for enough to enter other tracts, and thus secured a permanent title to some portion of Uncle Sam's dominions.

Notwithstanding this apparently just and comprehensive mode of regulating these affairs, difficulties often occurred between settlers in relation to their claims. With no other title than that obtained by mere possession, it did not always appear so clear and unquestionable as to secure the holder in undisturbed possession thereof. In a community where all are in eager pursuit of the same object—the acquisition of property—it is not uncommon to find a few not thoroughly governed by a sense of honesty. So, in a community remote from the influence of law and order, rogues were not disposed to be less roguish. There were no convenient courts of justice, through whose influence men could be restrained from intruding upon each other's rights. The nearest one at that early day was in Washington county, about seventy-five miles distant. Thus isolated from comparative civilization, it is not strange that quarrels often occurred between the settlers that sometimes threatened serious results.

This state of things called for some kind of law, and each settlement of any considerable number found it necessary to adopt certain rules and regulations for its government in all affairs pertaining to claims. At first they were intended to regulate such differences as might arise between the claimants only, but were afterwards deemed a necessary protection against the encroachments of speculators and a monied class of settlers. These "by-laws," as they were called, embodied the purest "squatter sovereignty" principle. That of each settlement differed more or less, according to circumstances, but in all the object was the same. Under them the settlers were organized into "clubs," duly officered and obligated to serve on all necessary occasions.

As a matter of historical curiosity let us here introduce a *verbatim* copy of a set of these by-laws. It is of somewhat later date than most of them, but contains the substance of what has just been said of them generally. Having lain in obscurity for more than twenty years, they now come forth with the color of intiquity, and, as a relic of old times, deserve a place more enduring than the yellow, half-worn sheets of old-fashioned writing paper from which we copy them:

"BY-LAWS.

"At a meeting held at the house of Jesse Johnson, in Perry township, Marion county, State of Iowa, on Saturday, the 19th day of August, 1848, Peter Brans was called to the chair, and James M. Brans was appointed secretary. The object of the meeting being stated, the meeting then proceeded to adopt the following preamble and resolutions:

"WHEREAS, It has become a custom in the western states, as soon as the Indian title to the public lands has been extinguished by the general government, for the citizens of the United States to settle upon and improve said lands, and heretofore the improvement and claim of the settler, to the extent of three hundred and twenty acres, has been respected by both the citizens and laws of Iowa.

"*Resolved*. That we will protect all citizens upon the public lands, in the peaceable possession of their claims, to the extent of three hundred and twenty acres, for two years after the land sales, and longer, if necessary.

"*Resolved*, That if any person or persons shall enter the claim of any settler, that he or they shall immediately deed it back again to said settler, and wait three years without interest.

"*Resolved*, That if he refuses to comply with the above requisitions, he shall be subject to such punishment as the settlers shall choose to inflict.

"*Resolved*, That we will remove any person or persons who may enter the claim of any settler and settle upon it, peaceably if we can, forcibly if we must, even if their removal should lead to bloodshead, being compelled to do so for our own common safety, that we may not be driven by ruthless speculators from our firesides and our homes.

"*Resolved*, That a committee of five be appointed to settle all differences that may arise."

Here follow the names of this important committee, and a resolution appointing a captain. Then a concluding resolution, ordering the publication of these proceedings in certain newspapers favorable to the cause.

The next meeting (the only one we have any record of besides the above) came off at the same place, on the 9th of September of the same year, at which the following additional resolutions were adopted:

"*Resolved*, That each settler that applies first shall have his or her name registered, and if any two claims should conflict, then it shall be the duty of the second settler for the same piece of land to call the committee together and have the matter settled; and each settler that expects the benefit of these resolutions, must have his or her claim registered by the 20th of the present month.

* * * * * * *

"*Resolved*, That it shall be the duty of each settler to sign these by-laws, and he that refuses to do so, cannot, and shal not be protected by us.

"*Resolved*, That any settler who may have signed these by-laws, and refuses to render service when called upon by the proper officers, and without a reasonable excuse, shall be fined the sum of ten dollars, to be divided among those that may have rendered the service necessary."

A lieutenant and ensign were elected at the conclusion of this meeting, but their duties are not prescribed.

Appended to this venerable document are the names of thirty-five settlers. Two more who, though their hearts were in the cause, were omitted, for prudential reasons that may not appear on the face of the instrument, when it is known that they held the civil offices of justice of the peace and constable.

Such a company of strong, resolute men, united in a common cause, to which they were the more attached because it affected their home interests, might seem sufficient to strike terror to the heart of any lonely speculator who might have strayed into the settlement and made choice of some valuable tract claimed by one of the number.

Without doubt, the intent of the claim law was to secure to actual settlers the lands in small portions, so as to facilitate the rapid settlement and improvement of the country, thereby increasing its wealth and strength, a result slowly reached through the impediments of speculation. Yet there was no law forbidding speculation in these lands, nor even the entering of claims belonging to actual settlers without due compensation to the owners; and to supply this want these by-laws were instituted. Though the settlers were admitted to the first choice, some regulations were necessary to secure them in their possession after they were subject to entry. Though conducted very much upon the mob principle, their intent was legal so far as it went to enforce the intent of the law. Going beyond this, they were very mobs without any legal authority. But as an auxiliary to the enforcement of the law itself, these by-laws must be regarded as the best thing that could have been gotten up. Indeed, they were but the natural result of the then state of things. They placed the law in the hands of who were directly interested in its enforcement, without which we have reason to suppose that it might have been nearly a dead letter upon the statute book.

When the lands came into market, and speculators and other buyers made their appearance, the settlers naturally became suspicious of their motives, and these suspicions were founded on some practical reasons. Many of the settlers had made improvements on their claims, and valued them accordingly. In case they were not prepared to enter them, they did not wish to part with them for less than what they deemed them worth. Yet these claims were subject to entry, and as there was no law forcing the purchaser to pay more than the $1.25 per acre he paid to the government, it depended upon his magnanimity whether he would pay more or not. Some men cannot afford to be magnanimous without the authority of law. They cling to the letter of it so long as it suits their convenience; and it did not suit the convenience of some of these speculators to pay twice for the same property. The little cabin that constituted the poor settlers home, and the ground on which he had cultivated a few crops of corn and vegetables, and the fence that enclosed them, were of much greater value in the estimation of the occupant, than of him who might have been already the possessor of large landed estates, and who could easily secure other tracts equally as good, and unoccupied a little farther west. If he entered the land regardless of the settler's rights, and refused to pay him what was deemed a just compensation for his labor, or indeed anything, the only remedy was the club law; and, as intimated in some of the resolutions just quoted, it was somewhat dangerous to disregard its authority. An instance of this will be the subject of another chapter.

As it appears in one or two resolutions, differences between settlers relative to claims, were settled by arbitration. All decisions by such a court were considered final. There was no other, neither above nor below it, to appeal to. In case either of the contending parties should refuse to submit to the decision of the arbitrators, and continued to make himself troublesome about the matter, his case was submitted to Judge Lynch, where it was apt to end. Any claim holder not a member of a club, was not entitled to the benefits thereof; and, further—though perhaps not a universal rule,–any such person positively refusing to subscribe to, or comply with, the rules and regulations of a settlement, as set forth in its by-laws, thereby indicating an opposition to them, was subject to a species of ostracism difficult to endure in any country, much less in a new and sparsely settled district, where the conveniences of social intercourse were occasionally felt to be indispensable. Against such an offender "non-intercourse" was declared, which withheld from him all aid and comfort, either in sickness or in health. Such a punishment was apt to be severely felt, and, sooner or later, would bring the rebellious individual to terms.

But strict fidelity to the facts of history will not permit us to say that the spirit of monopoly was confined entirely to speculators. Many settlers were not content with the amount of land the law entitled them to, but made pretended claims to so large a portion of the territory that, in some instances, it was difficult for a buyer to find an unclaimed lot. Of course such claims were without improvements, but the pretended claimants, by representing themselves as the real owners thereof, would frequently impose upon some unwary buyer, or, by threats, extort from him sums, varying in proportion to the supposed value of the claim, or whatever sum could be obtained. For an instance of this, part of the land on which the author resides was once a pretended claim, for which the present owner was compelled to pay a small sum, he having entered it after learning by due inquiry that it was unoccupied. In this case, the club followed him and another individual named Brown, who was charged with a similar offense, as far as Oskaloosa. Brown stubbornly refused to comply with their demands, and went his way, whilst J. C. Donnel, who had offended to the amount of eighty acres, satisfied the claimants, for the time being, with a note of hand for thirty-five dollars, the half of which was afterwards paid upon compromise of the parties. Judgment had been rendered for the whole by J. D. Bedell, justice of the peace, at Red Rock, but rather than carry the case to the district court, each agreed to divide the difference, and pay his own cost.

We mention this case somewhat particularly, because it was about the last demonstration made by the club, which soon after mutually abandoned its organization, as a thing no longer needed in the eastern part of the county. This was in 1848.

CHAPTER VII.

The Majors' War.

But perhaps the most notable event connected with claim troubles, occurred just previous to the date mentioned at the close of the last chapter, and as such deserves a full account, under the above title, by which it has ever since been known.

Some time during the year 1844, a family by the name of Majors emigrated from the State of Illinois, and settled in the western part of what is now Mahaska county, and formed what was known as the "Majors' Settlement."

This family consisted of five brothers, two sisters, and their mother, a widow. One of the sisters was also a widow, and had two sons eligible to secure claims. In all, there were ten persons, each of whom claimed three hundred and twenty acres of land, amounting in the aggregate to five sections.

Having secured their claims, they were among the first to organize a club in that settlement, and adopt rules and regulations for the government and protection of claimants. But in 1847, when the land sales opened, one of the brothers, Jacob H. Majors, who seems to have acted as agent for the family, entered all their claims; after which, having abundance of means at his disposal, he proceeded to enter some timbered claims, belonging to John Gillaspy, Jacob Miller, and Peter Parsons. His plea was that he did not know they were claims; but, after being informed that they were, he still evaded making restitution according to the rules of the club.

When the report of these transactions spread abroad, it created no little excitement among the settlers, based upon fears for the fate of all their claims. That the Majors were a wealthy family, seemed now unquestionable; and, if not checked in their strides toward a land monopoly, they might continue them, to the ruin of many settlers; and their example might embolden others to do the same, and thus neutralize the real purpose of the claim law.

In view of this alarming state of things, the clubs convened, and passed resolutions denouncing the conduct of Jacob Majors, and decided upon a concerted movement to force him to deed back the claims above mentioned, should he refuse, after being duly admonished to do so. It was supposed he had many friends, who might back him in a refusal, and show some hostility in his defense; and this was the cause of the general uprising of the settlers in behalf of their rights. The central committee sent word to the various clubs, requesting them to meet at the residence of Jacob H. Majors, for the purpose of inducing him to make the required settlement.

At the time specified for this meeting, the exact date of which we have not been able to obtain, a large number of people collected there, and remained all day, awaiting the return of Majors, who was at Oskaloosa, attending the county commissioners' court, as a member of that body. A message had been sent him, desiring his presence for the purpose above stated; and it was supposed he would make his appearance in the evening.

During the day the crowd was increased by fresh arrivals, and no little excitement prevailed on learning that the offender was absent, and that doubts were entertained of his return that night, and of his willingness to comply with the demand for settlement. In order to induce him to come home, he was informed that if he did not appear before sunrise the next morning, his property would be destroyed. When night came without bringing the incorrigible Majors, after having sent the above threatening notification, it was evident that something more than gentle coercion would be necessary to bring him to terms

At night some of the company went home, but most of them remained, and camped on the ground, to see what would be the result; though we are informed that it was not the design of most of them to execute the threat. And it is quite probable that Majors also regarded it as a mere threat, believing that no one would dare to render himself liable to punishment, for a crime of such a grave character, and he therefore resolved to risk it.

But early in the morning the log stable was discovered to be in flames; and soon after, the corn cribs and other granaries, all of which were consumed, with their contents. There was no live stock in the stable, but a number of hogs were either burned, or killed by the more excitable members of the mob, who were not disposed to make idle threats.

Majors, now hearing that his property was being destroyed, sent a promise that he would deed the land back to the claimants; and under this promise the settlers dispersed to their homes.

But in a few days, Mr. M. having reconsidered his promise, not only failed to fulfill it but had warrants issued for the arrest of some of the more prominent leaders of the mob. Peter Parsons was arrested and taken to Oskaloosa, and the report went abroad that he was in jail there, and that the sheriff of Mahaska county was in pursuit of about fifty others, against whom indictments had been filed, among whom were Geo. Gillaspy and John B. Hamilton.

All this was calculated to arouse the indignation of the people to a degree that rendered it unsafe for Majors to remain at home, and he found it prudent to keep out of the way of the settlers as much as possible. Hereupon the settlers called another meeting, to rendezvous at Durham's Ford, and from thence to go to Oskaloosa, release the prisoners, and punish Majors. It was late on Saturday when the summons came. Next morning a large number collected at Knoxville, armed and equipped, and resolved to stand by the settlers' rights at all hazards. A flag was prepared, showing the "stars and stripes," and inscribed in large letters, "Settlers' Rights."

This company reached the neighborhood of Durham's Ford that day, and remained there until the next, some camping out, and some putting up at houses in the neighborhood. Here large accessions were expected, which came in that evening and the next morning, from both counties, some on horseback, and some in wagons, swelling the number to about five hundred. When all were together, and organized in a kind of military order, with arms, flags, fi e, and drum, they presented a somewhat formidable appearance. To render it still more so, and to make an impression that would be the more likely to secure the object of the expedition without serious difficulty, the horsemen were drilled as cavalry, by a Mr. Mulkey, who had seen some service in the Mexican war.

Thus the army marched into Oskaloosa, reaching that place at about the time the prisoner was to be tried. The arms were deposited in the wagons, under guard, and infantry and cavalry formed in the public square. When this formidable demonstration was observed, and its object made known, the trial of Parsons was indefinitely postponed, and he was released without bail, though he had not been confined in jail, as was at first reported.

I. C. Curtis, more recently a citizen of Pella, as spokesman for the settlers, stated the object of the visitation, and was answered by a Mr. Harbour, of Oskaloosa, on behalf of the authorities. Then followed other speeches and replies, that consumed the afternoon, and tended, and probably were intended, to kill time, and thus give excitement a chance to cool, rather than to effect any definite compromise.

During all this time Majors was there, but invisible to those who most desired to see him. But in the evening he again promised to comply with the demands of the settlers, and next morning redeemed his promise by furnishing deeds to those persons whose land he had entered. Whereupon the army disbanded, and returned home.

This, then, was regarded as a treaty of peace—a final conclusion of the war. It was all that had been contended for. But Majors was not satisfied with such a conclusion. He was in a rage, considering himself a persecuted man, and the fire of revenge thus kindled in his breast rendered him rash, and regardless of consequences. A mob had followed him, destroyed his property, and forced him to surrender. The law was, therefore, evidently in his favor, and to the law he would appeal. Though the offense of Majors was such as to demand redress, and his persistent refusal to grant it voluntarily, rendered compulsion the only means that could be employed for that purpose, yet, as a means unauthorized by civil law, the uprising could hardly be dignified by a better term than *mob;* but we are not prepared to say that in all cases a stigma should attach to the term; and reason will back us up in the conclusion that, in the absence of any civil law to right a flagrant wrong, *mob law is right.*

Not long after this, Majors made preparations to bring the matter into court, but such was the unpopularity of his course, that it was found almost impossible to secure the arrest of persons indicted. Just previous to this, John M. Jones, who was, politically, on the winning side, was beaten in an election for sheriff of Mahaska county, solely because he was a friend of Majors. The officer who was authorized to make the arrests was kind enough, whenever he conveniently could, to notify the intended prisoners when he should call for them, and consequently, when he did call, they were often absent, and their whereabouts unknown.

Majors was repeatedly advised not to appear against them, but he persisted in so doing, and thereby subjected himself to the accumulated wrath of his enemies. He having added insult to insult, they were now determined to punish him at all events. For this purpose a select company was sent in search of him, with orders to seize him wherever he could be found, and convey him to Knoxville. Majors, conscious of his danger, did not remain at his home, but frequently stayed at Dr. Buyer's, a few miles south-west of Oskaloosa. To this place the detachment went, but not finding him there, they continued the search till they discovered him in Hallowell's saw mill, near the mouth of Cedar creek, a little south of Bellefontaine. He was at work in the mill, sawing his own lumber, and it was observed that he kept a gun near him, and carried it with him as often as he had occasion to leave the mill, if only for a moment. Thus it was evident that great caution was requisite to effect his capture without serious consequences. To this end the men secreted themselves near by, and sent one of their number, who was an entire stranger to him, to decoy him out, if possible, or throw him off his guard, till the others could steal in and seize him. The plan proved quite successful. Majors was soon engaged in conversation with his visitor, who had come to inquire after estray horses, in the meantime getting between the former and his gun, without exciting any suspicion.

Now was the crisis! Ere the victim was aware of the presence of another person, he felt himself seized by strong hands and carried out of the mill. As speedily as possible they placed him upon a horse, tied him on, and then set out for Knoxville. On their arrival there another select committee took charge of the prisoner. They were blacked, so that their identity could not be easily ascertained; and to this day, but few of those known to the circumstance can give their names. Perhaps for prudential reasons, this is kept a profound secret, for Majors still lives in Missouri, and might yet be disposed to avenge the insult he was then made to suffer.

By this committee he was taken about a mile north of town, at, or near the present site of the county fair grounds, where a preparation of tar and feathers was in waiting. Here they stripped him of all his clothing, and applied a coating of the tar and feathers to his naked body. Over this they drew his clothing, and then completed the job by adding another coating of the same materials, giving to the wearer a very portly appearance. He was then permitted to go his way, with the admonition never to repeat the offense for which he had been thus severely punished.

Instead of taking a more private route homeward, to avoid being seen in his ridiculous plight, he passed directly through Knoxville, and took the most public road thence to his place. It was sometime during the night when he reached home, and in order to avoid frightening his family unnecessarily, he stopped at some distance from the house and called to them; and when he had thus aroused them he informed them of his condition.

Sometime afterwards Majors made another attempt at prosecution, but was unable to bring his case into court for the reason that the court house was guarded at about the time set for trial, and every one, lawyers and witnesses, known to be for the prosecution, were egged away when they attempted to enter. Thus foiled again, he abandoned the case finally.

Not long after this the family sold their possessions and moved away.

Since the above was written, the following additional account appeared in a communication to the Voter :

" After receiving the generous coat of tar and feathers, Majors was indefatigable in his efforts to prosecute and convict the leaders in the various raids against him. The state of feeling, as exhibited in the late proceedings in the vicinity of Knoxville, affording but little prospect of success in Marion county, he resorted to the courts of Mahaska, where he fancied a more favorable tone of public sentiment existed. After a number of failures, he finally succeeded in obtaining bills of indictment against a number of individuals who had been disturbers of his peace during the claim difficulties.

" A young man named Bush was among those indicted. Bush had incautiously allowed himself to be arrested, against a well understood arrangement, and entered into bonds to appear at the term of court then next ensuing at Oskaloosa. Notwithstanding this violation of the rules by Bush, his friends resolved to stand by him, as they were solemnly pledged to aid and assist their friends in every emergency growing out of their difficulties.

"Accordingly they arranged matters for the approaching trial. One of their number, who very strongly resembled Bush in personal appearance, was chosen to represent him during the trial of the case. This was a bold step, but they ventured upon it.

"At the sitting of the court, Bush and his substitute were surrounded by their friends. When the case was called, the pretended Bush responded, took his seat in the criminal box, and plead "not guilty" to the indictment; but when, in the progress of the suit, it became necessary to identify the criminal at the bar as the real offending Bush, the similarity between the two individuals became at first embarrassing, and then inexplicable, and caused no little delay in the proceedings, and the court finally lost its temper, and dismissed the case. The ruse was a success, and the case was literally laughed out of court, to the utter confusion of Majors and his attorneys, who were unprepared for this sharp practice.

"At this unlooked-for failure when everything had promised success, Majors became mortified, chagrined and discouraged, and gave up in despair. He made no further efforts to prosecute the matter, being convinced of the impossiblity of procuring a conviction in a community where the hand of every man was arrayed against him. He soon after 'left the country for his country's good.' Finding kindred spirits in Missouri, he sought a home among them, where he still resides.

"It is by no means certain that the court, bar, or spectators of the trial, ever became aware of this ruse. It was known only to the initiated. B."

CHAPTER VIII.

First Election—First Political Convention—Name Proposed for the County—Organizing Act.

At the time of its first settlement, the territory now embraced by Marion county belonged to, and was under the judicial jurisdictiou of, Washington county, together with the counties of Mahaska, Keokuk, Warren, and all other territory west of it, so far as the purchase extended. Washington was then the most western organized county in the same belt now included in the above named counties, and was, therefore, necessarily their seat of justice, and the authority from whence they derived such temporary organizations as were needed for election and judicial purposes.

In 1843, several election precincts were organized by authority of Washington county, extending through these sparsely settled districts, and one of them (perhaps the most western) included a large portion of Marion. This was called "Lake Precinct," and the election came off on Lake Prairie, on the first Monday in October, 1843. In 1844, three or four precincts were established in the county, and another election was held on the first Monday in April of that year. This was on the occasion of the organization of Mahaska county, and Stephen Druilard, who lived on White Breast Prairie, was elected as one of the county commissioners for that county, of which Marion was made an attached part, as it had been to Washington. At that election each precinct also elected two justices of the peace, and two constables, to serve until the August election of that year, the names of whom we have not been able to obtain. The last elections held in connection with Mahaska county, were in April and August, 1845.

In the spring of 1845, a movement was made to secure a separate county organization. A meeting, or convention, composed of a few of the more prominent citizens of the county, interested in the movement, was held at the house of Nathan Bass, on Lake Prairie.* The following named persons were present: Lysander W. Babbit, George Gillaspy, Reuben Matthews, Homer Matthews, David T. Durham, Nathan Bass, Joseph Druilard, John Williams, Levi Bainbridge, Isaac N. Crum, Simon Druilard, John W. Alley, and a few others. The meeting was organized by the appointment of Simon Druilard, chairman, John W. Alley, secretary.

One object of the meeting was to propose a name for the county, and another was to recommend some person to act as organizing sheriff, subject to appointment by the legislature; also to choose some of the candidates for county offices, to be voted for at the first election to be held for that purpose, the time of which was designated by the organizing act, a complete copy of which will be given in this chapter. But perhaps the most important object of the meeting was to influence a river location for a county seat. The residences of most of the above named citizens were along the river and in its neighborhood, and consequently their interests had much to do with whatever influence they could lawfully exercise to secure its location on the river. Red Rock was once an aspirant for the honor of being the seat of justice, and contended for it on the ground of its location on the river, by the navigation of which she would have the advantage of commercial communication

* The cabin at which this meeting was held, stood on the north bank of the Des Moines river, in the north-west corner of section 19, township 76, range 18, now Lake Prairie township. It has long since disappeared, and repeated freshets have washed away the bank for several rods inland from where it stood. Mr. Van Lent, a Hollander, now owns the land then claimed by Mr. Bass. We are thus particular, because it may interest the reader to be able to find upon the map, or know when he passes it, a place rendered in some degree memorable by the scene of the first political movement in the county looking to its distinct organization.

superior to any inland location. This argument might have secured her the place, but for the overwhelming fact that the town plat was occasionally found to be below high water mark. Evidences of floods that covered the place to the depth of several feet, at some remote period, are still visible upon the bark of the trees. In the spring of 1849 the town was nearly covered, and again in 1851 it was subjected to an overflow that forced the inhabitants to leave it.

This object of the meeting was opposed by the inhabitants of other parts of the county, who derisively gave it the name of "Cornstalk Convention." Perhaps this was partly suggested by the fact of immense crops of corn being produced on the rich bottom prairies along the river.

After the meeting was organized, several names were proposed for the new county. The president offered *Nebraska;* L. W. Babbit, *Pulaski;* Reuben Matthews, *Center;* after which Mr. Bainbridge spoke at some length on the fitness of names, denouncing the too common custom of honoring foreigners and noted Indian chiefs, by giving their names to our states, counties, and towns, and concluded by proposing MARION, the name of a distinguished patriot of the War of Independence, as the most suitable one that could be chosen. The proposition was seconded, and adopted by a unanimous vote.

A vote was then taken on the choice of a candidate for organizing sheriff, and the choice fell upon Joseph Druilard.

Immediately after the convention, petitions were circulated and sent to the legislature, proposing the name of the county as chosen by the convention. By private letter, also, directed to S. B. Shelledy, representative from Mahaska,* George Gillaspy was recommended for sheriff; but, for some reason, that

---

*During that session Mr. Shelledy introduced a bill for the partial organization of two tiers of counties, designating their boundaries, and applying their names. Four of these counties, Webster, Story, Madison and Warren, still retain the names then given them.

body disregarded the applications of the people for the appointment of either of the above named candidates, and appointed William Edmondson, the then sheriff of Mahaska county, to the post of organizing sheriff of Marion.

Having obtained the above facts by much labor and research, revising and correcting from time to time, as additional information rendered it necessary so to do, in order to arrive at the correct and connected datails, we here introduce—

"AN ACT.

"TO ORGANIZE THE COUNTY OF MARION.*

SECTION 1. *Be it enacted by the Council and House of Representatives of the Territory of Iowa*, That the following shall constitute and be the boundary of a new county, to be called MARION; to-wit: Beginning at the north-west corner of Mahaska county, and running west on the township line dividing townships seventy-seven and seventy-eight, north, to the north-west corner of township seventy-seven, north of range twenty-one west, thence south to the south-west corner of township seventy-four, north of range twenty-one west, thence east

---

*The following is an extract from the journal of the council of the seventh general assembly, dated May 5, 1844, giving the proceedings of that body upon this act, just previous to its passage:

" Mr. Selby, from the committee or the judiciary, to which was referred, No. 61, H. R. file, A bill to organize the county of Marion, reported the same back to the council, with amendments, to which the council agreed.

"On motion of Mr. Coop, the 13th rule was suspended, and the bill was read a third time.

" A motion was made by Mr. Hempstead, that 'Marion' be stricken out, and the word 'Polk' inserted, which passed in the negative.

" Yeas 4—nays 8.

" The yeas and nays being demanded,

" Those who voted in the affirmative were—Messrs. Abbe, Hempstead, Summers, and Mr. President.

" Those who voted in the negative were—Messrs. Bradley, Brattain, Brierly, Coop, Lefler, Selby, Stephenson and Thompson.

" The bill was then passed, and its title agreed to.

" Ordered, that the secretary acquaint the house of representatives therewith.

along the township line dividing townships seventy-three and seventy-four north, to the south-west corner of Mahaska county, thence north along the range line dividing ranges sixteen and seventeen, to the place of beginning.

"SECTION 2. That the county of Marion be, and the same is, hereby organized from and after the first Monday in August next, and the inhabitants of said county shall be entitled to the same privileges to which, by law, the inhabitants of other organized counties of this territory are entitled.

"SECTION 3. That for the purpose of organizing said county, it is hereby made the duty of the clerk of the district court of said county, and in case there should be no such clerk appointed and qualified, or for any cause said office should become vacant on or before the first Monday in August next, then it shall be the duty of the the sheriff of Mahaska county to proceed immediately after the first Monday in August, to order a special election in said county, for the purpose of electing three county commissioners, one judge of probate, one county treasurer, one clerk of the board of county commissioners, one county surveyor, one county assessor, one sheriff, one coroner, one county recorder, and such number of justices of the peace and constables as may be directed by the officer ordering the same, he having due regard for the convenience of the people, which special election shall be on the first Monday in September next; and that the officer ordering said election shall appoint as many places of election in said county as the convenience of the people may require, and shall appoint three judges of election for each place of holding in said county, and issue certificates of their appointment; and the officer ordering said election shall give at least ten days notice of the time and place of holding said election, by three advertisements, which shall be posted up at three of the most public places in the neighborhood, where each of the polls shall be opened.

" Section 4. That the officer ordering said election (aforesaid) shall receive and canvass the polls, and grant certificates to the persons elected to fill the several offices mentioned in this act; the officer ordering each of said elections shall discharge the duties of a clerk of the board of county commissioners, until there shall be one elected and qualified for said county.

" Section 5. Said election shall, in all cases not provided for in this act, be conducted according to the laws of this territory regulating general elections.

" Section 6. The officers elected under the provisions of this act shall hold their offices until the next general election, and until their successors are elected and qualified.

" Section 7. The officer ordering the election in said county shall return all the books and papers which may come into his hand by virtue of this act, to the clerk of the board of county commissioners of said county forthwith, after said clerk shall be elected and qualified.

" Section 8. That it shall be the duty of the sheriff of Mahaska county to perform the duties required by this act, until the first Monday in September next, and until a sheriff shall be elected and qualified for said county of Marion, and the said sheriff shall be allowed the same fees for services rendered by him under the provisions of this act, that are allowed for similar services performed by the sheriff in similar cases.

" Section 9. That the clerk of the district court of said county of Marion may be appointed by the judge of said district, and qualified at any time after the passage of this act, but he shall not enter upon the duties of said office prior to the first day of August next.

" Section 10. That all actions at law in the district court for the county of Mahaska, commenced prior to the organization of the said county of Marion, where the parties, or either of them, reside in the county of Marion, shall be prosecuted to judgment or decree, as fully and effectually as if this act had not passed.

"SECTION 11. That it shall be the duty of all justices of the peace residing within said county, to return all books and papers in their hands, appertaining to said office, to the next nearest justice of the peace which may be elected and qualified for said county, under the provisions of this act, and all suits at law which may be in the hands of such justice of the peace, and unfinished, shall be completed or prosecuted to final judgment, by the justice of the peace to whom such business or papers may have been returned.

"SECTION 12. That the county assessor elected under the provisions of this act for said county, shall assess the said county in the same manner, and be under the same obligations and liabilities, as now is, or may hereafter be, provided by law, in relation to the county assessor.

"SECTION 13. That Ezra M. Jones, of Van Buren county, Joseph Robinson, of Scott county, and James Montgomery, of Wapello county, be, and they are, hereby appointed commissioners to locate and establish the seat of justice of Marion county. Said commissioners, or a majority of them, shall meet at the house of Wilson Stanley,* in said county, on the second Monday in August next, or at such other time in the month of August next as may be agreed upon by them, in pursuance of their duties under this act.

SECTION 14. Said commissioners shall first take and subscribe to the following oath, or affirmation; to-wit: 'We do solemnly swear (or affirm) that we have no interest, either directly, or indirectly, in the location of the county seat of Marion county, and that we will faithfully and impartially examine the situation of said county, taking into consideration the future as well as the present population of said county, and

*The residence of Wilson Stanley was on Lake Prairie. Ezra Jones failed to meet the other commissioners.

that we will take into consideration the best interests of the whole people of the county, and that we will not be influenced by any fee or reward, or any promise thereof'; which oath shall be administered by the clerk of the district court, or by some justice of the peace of said county of Marion, and the officer administering the same shall certify and file the same in the office of the clerk of the board of county commissioners of said county, whose duty it shall be to record the same.

"SECTION 15. Said commissioners, when met and qualified under the provisions of this act, shall proceed to locate the seat of justice of said county; and, as soon as they have come to a determination, they shall commit to writing the place so selected, with a particular description thereof, signed by the commissioners, in which such seat of justice is located, whose duty it shall be to record the same, and forever keep it on file in his office, and the place thus designated shall be the seat of justice of said county.

"SECTION 16. Said commissioners shall receive the sum of two dollars per day, while necessarily employed in the duties assigned to them by this act, and two dollars for each twenty miles travel in going and returning, to be paid out of the first funds arising from the sale of lots in said seat of justice.

"SECTION 17. The county of Marion shall form a part of the second judicial district, and it shall be the duty of the judge of said district to hold one term of said court in the same, on the twelfth Monday after the first Monday in March, in each year.

SECTION 18. This act to take effect and be in force, from and after its passage.

"(Signed.) "JAMES M. MORGAN,
"*Speaker of the House of Rep's.*
"S. C. HASTINGS,
"*President of the Council.*

"Approved June 10, 1845.
"JOHN CHAMBERS, *Governor.*"

CHAPTER IX.

County Officers—First Session of Commissioners' Court —First Business Transacted—Changing the Name of the County Seat—The Rose Ann McGregor Case.

The officers chosen at the first election (the first Monday of September, 1845), were the following :

Conrad Walters, William Welch, David Durham, *County Commissioners.*

Sanford Doud, *Commissioners' Clerk.*

Francis A. Parker, *Probate Judge.*

James Walters, *Sheriff.*

David T. Durham, *Treasurer.*

Reuben Lowry, *Recorder.*

Isaac B. Power, *Surveyor.*

Green T. Clark, *Assessor.*

Wellington Nossaman, *Coroner.**

About two hundred votes were polled at this election, and

* The election at which these officers were chosen was a *special* election, and their terms of office expired at the August election in 1846. Then, by an old act of the territorial code, regulating the terms of county commissioners, the one receiving the highest number of votes served three years, the next highest two, and the lowest one. At the regular election (at the date above mentioned), Samuel Tibbett received the highest number of votes, David Durham the next, and Hugh Glenn the lowest. By authority of an act of the state legislature in 1846-7, the county was required to be divided into commissioners' districts, which was accordingly done at the April term, 1847. All that part of the county north of the river was made to constitute one district, and, in 1867, Thomas Pollock was elected therein to take the place of Hugh Glenn. All that part of the county south of the river and east of the line between ranges nineteen and twenty constituted the second district; and all south of the river and west of said line, constituted the third. Martin Neel was elected commissioner from the second, in 1848, and Miles Jordon from the third, in 1849, as will appear in a list of county officers in another place. At the same date all of Warren county, which then belonged to Marion, was declared "Warren Precinct," and all the territory west of Warren, also belonging to Marion, was called "Black Oak Precinct."

the probable population of the county was about twelve hundred.

For some reason, Sanford Doud, elected as county commissioners' clerk, failed to appear and be qualified in due time, and Lysander W. Babbitt was appointed in his stead, at the first meeting of the board, which was on the 12th of September, 1845. The records, in Mr. B.'s hand, from which we obtained the matter for a large portion of this chapter, are still to be seen in the office of the probate judge, in a good state of preservation.

At the date above mentioned, the commissioners met at Knoxville for business. That place had just been selected by the commissioners appointed in the act given in the preceding chapter, as the seat of justice for Marion county. The house in which the first session was held is described as a "claim pen," made of linn poles, about twelve by sixteen feet square, chincked and daubed in the usual manner of enclosing such buildings, covered with "clapboards," and a square hole cut in the side wall for a window, that could boast of neither sash nor glass. This cabin stood in what is now block thirty-three, in the east part of the city.

As a matter of historical record, we here introduce a *verbatim* copy of the first entry made upon the minute book of this court. The first meeting of the first commissioners' court was, certainly, a sufficiently important event in the history of the county, all circumstances considered, to be distinctly remembered, and the tone of the preamble seems to have emanated from a due appreciation of this fact:

"*Be it remembered*, That on the 12th day of September, A. D. 1845, Conrad Walters, David Durham, and William Welch, county commissioners, duly elected and qualified within and for the county of Marion, in the territory of Iowa, met at Knoxville, the seat of justice for said county, for the purpose of holding a called session of the county commissioners' court of said county."

The court was then opened by L. C. Conrey, deputy sheriff, and the only important business transacted related to the county seat. The two commissioners who had made the location presented their report, which was received and placed upon file. It was dated August 25th, and designated the north-west quarter of section seven, township seventy-five, range nineteen,* as the most suitable place for the seat of justice for Marion county. This was on a high, level prairie or plateau, about one mile south of the exact center of the county, and in the near neighborhood of excellent timber, so that no better location for the convenience of the people then, and for all time to come could have been selected. For those living north of the Des Moines river it may be deemed more or less inconvenient to reach it at certain seasons of the year, when that stream is an obstruction to travel; but this difficulty could not have been overcome by any other location; it was one that could not be removed, but might be materially modified by ferries and bridges.

Within the last few years, some of the citizens north of the river have spoken favorably of dividing the county and erecting a new one from the strip of territory lying between Des Moines and Skunk rivers, consisting of parts of Mahaska, Jasper, and Marion counties, thus obviating the necessity of crossing either of those streams to reach their county seat. But it appears evident that the expense of organizing a new county of such a narrow, irregular shape, and maintaining its government at, necessarily, the same cost of larger counties, would be much greater than that required to build a substantial bridge at each of two or three convenient places across the Des Moines and Skunk; or, if bridge building is found to be impracticable, let a portion of the business requiring the attendance of the people living there, at the county seat, be

*Though the country had not yet been sectionized, the locality above described could be easily ascertained by its nearness to the north-west corner of the township lying only one mile south of that point.

transacted at some given point north of the river. This is a digression from the true line of our history, but, in our opinion, not less important. We deprecate a division of the county as tending to no beneficial results.

The locating commissioners suggested the name of Knoxville for the county seat, in honor of the memory of General Knox, a distinguished leader in the war for independence, and the authorities of Knoxville afterwards complimented the commissioners by naming two of the principal streets crossing east and west, Montgomery and Robinson.

The name of Knoxville proved generally satisfactory to all concerned except to one individual—L. W. Babbitt—who seems to have had a preference for odd or uncommon names. Some time after, when he kept the post office there, he thought the liability of mistaking Knoxville, Iowa, for some other place of the same name—for instance, the one in Tennessee—in the posting of mail matter, would justify him in obtaining a change of the name. So, having business in Iowa City on the occasion of the first session of the state legislature, in the winter of 1846–7, he there took the opportunity, on his own responsibility, to solicit an act of that body legalizing the change. Having drafted a bill to that effect, he presented it, and had the satisfaction of seeing it adopted. On his return home, he first stated to D. T. Durham, who attended to the post office and clerkship during his absence, that such was the fact--that Knoxville was no more Knoxville, but Osceola. But so soon as this unauthorized transaction was publicly known, the people were much displeased thereat, and not in the least disposed to pocket the joke. As speedily as possible, a petition was extensively circulated and signed, asking for the repeal of this change, and sent to Iowa City by the hand of James Willes, who delivered it to Hon. Simeon Reynolds, representative from Marion. Mr. R., in response thereto, drafted and presented a bill to repeal the name of Osceola, but, by an oversight, (which was also the fault of the petition), failed to reinsert the name of Knoxville. The act passed; but now, a worse joke was apparent, from the fact that the repeal of the last name did not restore the former, and, therefore, Knoxville was neither Knoxville nor Osceola. But, after the joke had run a brief season, the matter was readjusted, and Knoxville was herself again.

At the second session of the board of county commissioners, which was on the second Monday of October, a subject of peculiar interest was brought up, by an order which is said to have been originated by the noted Bab.itt, whose exploits have some how rendered him a prominent personage in this history. Said order required that all blacks or mulattos residing in the county should appear before some justice of the peace and give bonds for their good behavior, or be expelled from the county. This order was, in accordance with an act of the territorial legislature, entitled "An Act to regulate blacks and mulattos," dated June 21, 1839. But, in order to a more comprehensive introduction to the subject, we here insert clauses of said act bearing more directly upon the case in hand:

"SECTION 1. *Be it enacted, &c.*, That from and after the first day of April next, no black or mulatto shall be permitted to settle or reside in this territory, unless he or she shall produce a fair certificate from some court within the United States of his or her actual freedom, which certificate shall be attested by the clerk of said court, and the seal thereof annexed thereto by the said court, and give bond, with good and sufficient security, to be approved of by the board of county commissioners of the proper county in which such person of color may reside, payable to the United States, in the penal sum of five hundred dollars. * * * * * *

"SECTION 2. If any negro or mulatto, coming into this territory as aforesaid, shall fail to comply with the provisions of the first section of this act, it shall be and is hereby made the duty of the county commissioners in any county where such negro or mulatto may be found, to summon him, her, or them to appear before some justice of the peace to show cause why he, she, or they shall not comply with the provisions of this act * * * * * * * And if such negro or mulatto shall still fail to give the bond and security required by the first section of this act, * * * * it shall be the duty of the county commissioners of such county to hire out such negro or mulatto for six months, for the best price in cash that can be had. The proceeds of such hiring shall be paid into the county treasury of the proper county, for the use of such negro or mulatto, in such manner as shall be directed by the board of county commissioners aforesaid."

A history of the case may now be in order, and may not prove wholly uninteresting, even to those personally acquainted with the facts. It was known that there was a negro (or, rather, a negress) in the county, else such an order would have been regarded as an idle formality.

Some time in 1844 or 1845, a man named Thomas McGregor came from Illinois to what is now the northeast corner of Indiana township, and called upon Mr. George Henry, a settler in that neighborhood, and asked his assistance in selecting a claim. Mr. Henry readily gave him the required assistance, after which McGregor asked the privilege of moving into the house with him till he could get a cabin fixed up on his claim. Mr. Henry, being desirous of accommodating those who were to become his neighbors, and, inasmuch as the family of Mr. McGregor was small, consisting of only the man and his wife, he readily assented to that arrangement also. But when the guests arrived, the astonishment of Mr. Henry may, possibly, be imagined, when he first beheld in Mrs. McGregor a full-blooded African, about as dark as the darkest of the race, possessing all the charms that could be summed up in a figure of ample proportions, and features of combined brilliancy and prominence. As a matter of course after this discovery, he lost no time in reconsidering his promise. He was not disposed to encourage further "domestic relations" with this interesting pair, and honestly signified to Mac that his mind had undergone a change on the subject. So the latter, with his lovely spouse, was compelled to seek some other shelter. Not finding a house, they camped out, as they had previously done, until their cabin was built. But the nature of their relationship was such that they were not permitted to long enjoy it in peace. It was taken for granted that they were living in violation of a statute of the territory forbidding matrimonial connection between blacks and whites, and, for this offense, were arrested and brought before Justice Levi Bainbridge, on Lake prairie, and tried. Not being very well pleased with the rulings of this court, they took a change of *venue*, and their case was turned over to Justice Mike Morris, who happened to be present. After giving it a hearing, Mike referred the matter to the Mahaska county grand jury—this being previous to the organization of Marion—where it ended, the jury not finding a true bill against the offenders.

But the end was not yet. This was only a brief truce in the tribulations of this unfortunate couple. As we have seen, the lady was deemed an offender against another statute, and that statute made it the duty of the county commissioners to take action in the premises; hence the order noticed on another page. But, for some reason, Mrs. McGregor did not heed the threatening mandate; she was either not aware of its existence, or determined to risk the consequences of disregarding it. But another soon followed, of a more specific character, to the effect that Rose Ann McGregor should appear and give the required bonds, on or before the 29th of January, or "*be sold to the highest bidder.*" But even this failed to bring the stubborn Rose Ann to terms. The fearful penalty of non-compliance therewith, though it may have caused the culprit to tremble in anticipation, moved her not otherwise. It was, therefore, found necessary to bring into action the practical force of law, and the sheriff was armed with authority to bring Rose Ann bodily to the seat of justice. Armed with this authority, and attended by his deputy, Dr L. C. Conrey, the two proceeded to the residence of the McGregors. Apparently, this visitation had been expected by the wary Rose Ann; for, when the officers reached the house they found the doors barred, and their application for admittance pointedly refused. Not wishing to perpetrate any violence in the execution of their duty (and, perhaps, actuated by a sense of caution, for Rose Ann was reported to be the possessor of a gun, a good marksman, and, to quote the words of our informant, "some in a bear fight"), they resorted to a little stragetical compromise, by which the beseiged promised to go to town the next morning. But the officers, having no faith in this promise, retired a few rods from the house and secreted themselves behind a shock of corn fodder, to watch the movements of their intended prisoner, and seize her if a favorable opportunity presented. Presently they saw her emerge from the house, with gun in hand, and survey the premises with a cautious glance. Seeing no danger, she returned within doors, where she left the gun, and immediately reappeared, going to the woodpile for fuel. Now was the best opportunity to nab her. The two men started at their utmost speed, intending, if possible, to get between her and the house; but "the race is not always to the swift." Rose Ann soon discovered them, and so far outran them that she had time to bar the door before they reached it. Here now was a crisis that required prompt decision, activity, and nerve; such a thing as being out-generaled by a nigger could not be thought of. Parley was out of the question; and what sort of a report should they make on returning to Knoxville without their prisoner? Their reputation was at stake, and rather than risk it they would risk their lives. So Walters ordered the Doctor to make a battering-ram of an old sled tongue that happened to be lying near at hand, and batter in the door. The order was immediately obeyed, and as the door swung back, Walters bounded into the room and caught the determined Rose Ann in the act of raising the hammer of her gun. The Doctor followed, and seized the weapon just in time to save his own life, for it was already aimed at him with the evident intention of firing. Having disarmed the prisoner, she had no other choice but to surrender unconditionally. The doctor then fired off the gun, the report of which indicated a heavy charge, very probably intended for the use she attempted to make of it.

The battle now over, and the victory so fortunately won, the victors immediately set out on their return to headquarters with the prisoner. It was growing late in the evening, and some haste was necessary to reach town before dark; so, in order to make better speed, and, perhaps, also prompted by a feeling of generosity, the Doctor mounted Rose Ann on his horse, he going before, leading the way in the narrow Indian trail that, as we have heretofore stated, was then about the only kind of a road in the country.

As it happened, the sheriff had business in another direction, and accompanied them only part of the way; consequently, the deputy was left in sole charge of the prisoner. Having been so completely conquered, and afterwards so kindly treated to a means of conveyance, it was not supposed that she would become treacherous or troublesome on the way. But Rose Ann was not to be won by any such evidences of kindness, so long as she was subjected to the humiliating condition of a prisoner for no fault except race and color. She was disposed to take advantage of her captors' confidence, and she did. A short time after the sheriff left them,—the Doctor walking a few steps in advance,—Rose Ann suddenly turned about and dashed homeward on a full gallop, to the astonishment and mortification of her captor, who looked after her a moment without any decisive purpose what to do about it. But he concluded to pursue her at all events, and did so as rapidly as he was able. On the way he found his pill bags which he was then in the habit of carrying with him, being in the practice of medicine; they had bounded off in the extraordinary flight of the captive. After a mile or two of pursuit, the Doctor became weary, and turned in for the night at the residence of John Welch.

Next day Rose Ann made her appearance at court with the required bond, duly signed by herself, with Thomas McGregor (her husband) and Amos Strickland as sureties.

Thus ended this troublesome case. One of the actors in the play (which we may properly style a farce), in relating the incidents of the capture, says that he felt quite conscientious in the performance of his duty, believing, as the great apostle did when persecuting the church, that he was doing God's service. But the persecuted pair did not remain long in the neighborhood. It was supposed by some that McGregor's interest in his ebony spouse was of a pecuniary character, and that his intention was to take her to Missouri for sale; yet, this was not apparent in his attempt to settle with her in a free state.

CHAPTER X.

*County Revenue — Warrants — Stationery — First County Seal—Buying the County Seat—Building Court Houses —The First Court House—Precincting the County—Road Districts—First Juries—First District Court—Boarding Houses—Sleeping in the Court Room—A Sketch of Judge Williams.**

Isaac B. Powers, county surveyor, platted part of the town of Knoxville shortly after it was located, and Claiborn Hall laid out the remainder in the winter of 1846–7. George Gillaspy was appointed auctioneer to sell lots, and the first sale came off on the 21st of October, 1845, and the second in April, 1846. In those days, as has been heretofore stated, money was far from being plentiful; besides the prospect of speculation in town property in that wild, open country, far away from any important outlet or means of communication, was not encouraging, so that few investments were made.

The proceeds of these sales were immediately absorbed by the expenses of location, survey, and sales, and also for the erection of a court house, the need of which was now being keenly felt, as we shall further notice in due time.†

Besides the sale of these lots there was no other source of revenue till about the close of 1846, or during the winter of 1846–7, when the first taxes were collected. Previous to the organization, the county had been assessed by authority of

---

* Since the above was written, we have been informed of the death of Judge Williams, near Fort Scott, Kansas, aged 69 years.

† Owing to the want of suitable offices, the county officers kept their books and performed their official work at their dwellings and boarding-houses.

Mahaska,* and the legislature had authorized the officers of that county to collect the taxes of this assessment after the separation, which the citizens of Marion persistently and successfully refused to pay. There was then but little real estate taxable, and when the taxes were collected at the date mentioned above they amounted to the small sum of three hundred dollars!

At about this time the finances of the county were found to be in a deplorably embarrassed condition. Debts had rapidly accumulated from the date of its organization. Three elections had been held during this time, the expenses of which were paid in warrants, till these promises to pay had so far outfigured the revenue that they dwindled away to the meagre sum of thirty-seven and one-half cents to the dollar. In these the county officers were paid, if paid at all, with the slight hope that they would eventually be redeemed at their full face. The salary of officers then being nearly the same as now, there could be little to prompt aspirants for places aside from the mere honor pertaining thereto. Indeed, to such a strait had money matters come, that the officers were compelled to purchase their needed stationery on credit, at exhorbitant prices, and become personally responsible for the payment of the same. The board of commissioners found it necessary to send to Oskaloosa for one quire of foolscap, a bundle of quills,—steel pens had not come in use then,—and a bottle of ink; but before they could obtain them these officers were compelled to become personally responsible or the debt, which could not have been seriously burdensome even at a period of financial depression. Many of these warrants were sold to shavers to pay these debts. Those who bought these warrants made a profitable investment of their money, paying thirty-seven and a-half to forty cents per dollar,

* This assessment was made in the spring of 1845, as the law then directed. Green T. Clark, who had been elected county assessor, not having any official work to do, went away on business, and did not return in time to serve in the next asssessment. George Gillaspy, who had previously applied for the office, was then appointed by the commissioners, and assessed the county in the spring of 1846.

receiving six per centum on their full face, till the county redeemed them at par.

An official seal was also needed by the board of commissioners, and there being no means of obtaining one specially made for the purpose, they legalized one out of the eagle side of a twenty-five cent United States silver coin. With a stick and mallet an impression could be made of the bird of liberty, which mark served as a token of the official authority of that court. The first seal of the probate court was the eagle side of a five cent coin.

The land on which the county seat was located was occupied as a claim by L. C. Conrey. There were no improvements on it, except the cabin that was required to hold it; but so soon as the location was made, Mr. C. surrendered his title gratuitously for the benefit of the county; but it necessarily yet remained the property of the government. It was supposed that enough funds could be spared from the revenue arising from the sale of lots to enter it as soon as it should be subject to entry; but such was the all-prevailing poverty of both town and county that two hundred dollars could not be raised for that purpose. At the January session in 1847, the commissioners appointed Thomas Pollock an agent to borrow the money; but owing either to its scarcity or the want of confidence in the financial stability of the county, he failed to obtain it. In this emergency a Rev. Mr. Gibson came to the rescue with a land warrant, which he offered to apply on time; but owing to some obstruction, of the nature of which the author is not informed, the warrant could not be used. At length, however, Dr. Weir, a resident of Fairfield, where the land was subject to entry, entered it on time, and thus ended the strife, securing to Marion county, in due time, a clear title to her shire town.

By the organizing act Marion county was added to the second judicial district, and the first term of the district court for the county was fixed for March, the following year. But the county was yet without any kind of a court house, except the cabin in which the commissioners met, described in another place. So at their session in January, 1846, that body inaugurated a movement toward the erection of a temple of justice. To this end they authorized their clerk to receive proposals for a building twenty four by thirty feet square, two stories high, to be completed on or before the 20th of May following. The lowest bidder was Lewis M. Pearce, who proposed to do the job for four hundred and fifty dollars. His bid was accepted on the 29th of the month, and he immediately commenced the work. The heavy frame timbers had to be culled from the forest, and the lumber to be sawed, and all the materials conveyed, much of them from a distance of several miles, to the building-ground. All this labor occupied much more time and money than was stipulated in the contract, and the building was not completed till some time in autumn, and at a cost to the county of a little more than six hundred dollars.*

This comparatively temporary structure remained in use as a court house till 1858, when it was relieved from public service by the new one. Since that time it has been variously occupied; part of the time the upper story being used as a printing office, from which the "Democratic Standard" was issued, and part of the time as a private dwelling. In June, 1864, it was sold at auction by order of the board of supervisors, and was purchased by A. B. Miller for nine hundred and twenty-eight dollars, and is still his property. It still stands

---

*Mr. Pearce's contract was only for the wood-work, and the cost of the building in excess of his bid was for plastering and finishing, which was not completed till some time in 1848. This correction was made upon information received since the above was written.

The lumber for this court house was sawed by Andrew Foster, at his mill near the mouth of English creek, nine miles from Knoxville. Mr. Pearce took the framing timber from his claim on Walnut creek, east of Athica, and about eight miles from Knoxville.

where it was first erected, opposite the north-west corner of the square, and part of the lower story is at present occupied by B. F. Williams as a marble factory, and another part by Rufus Eldredge, produce dealer. The upper story is occupied by a family.

The new court house was built by Steven Woodruff, at a cost to the county of nineteen thousand dollars. It is a substantial two-story brick building, seventy by forty-eight feet, with an entry door at each end, and a hall about ten feet wide extending between each. This hall is flanked on either side by a tier of rooms appropriated to the various county offices. Two broad stairways, and a narrow one from the clerk's office, lead to the upper story or court room, a large apartment, well lighted, and furnished with seats enough to accommodate four hundred persons. This house stands in the center of a well enclosed square, and is surrounded by a fine growth of young cottonwoods.

On the 13th of March, 1846, the first district court convened. Joseph Williams, district judge, made his appearance at the time specified for holding court, but, as we have said, there was no place worthy the name of court house in which to hold it. The commissioners, however, had made such temporary preparations for the occasion as circumstances permitted. There was a hewed log house in the neighborhood, about sixteen by eighteen feet square, owned by Dr. Conrey, that offered the best if not the only prospect for a court room. This the commissioners purchased, and employed George W. Harrison to move to the west side of the square, near where Reaver's grocery now stands, and fit up for the purpose. In further preparation for this important event, jurors had to be selected. To do this in the order prescribed by law, it was necessary to district the county into voting precincts, and select from each the number of jurors in proportion to its number of electors supposed or known to be mentally qualified to perform the service of jurors. On the second day of March these precincts were described and named as follows. For the sake of convenience we abbreviate from the original record, and also place the name before the description:—

Lake Precinct.—Town. 77, and all of 75 and 76, range 18, north of the Des Moines river; election at the house of Samuel Peters. *Judges*—Samuel Peters, Asa Koons, and Jacob C. Brown.

This, it will be observed, included what is now Lake Prairie township.

Red Rock.—Town. 77, and all of 76, range 19, north of the river, and all of 77, range 20, east of the old Indian boundary line, and north of the river; election at Robert D. Russell's. *Judges*—James Chestnut, Claiborn Hall, and Reuben Mathews.

This included all of the present township of Summit, part of Polk, and about one tier of sections off the east side of Red Rock.

Gopher Prairie.—All west of the old Indian boundary line and north of the river; election at Asa Hughs's. *Judges*—Alfred Vertrice, Asa Hughs, and Joshua Lindsey.

This included the remainder of Red Rock township, and all of Perry.

Pleasant Grove.—All of Marion county, and the attached portion thereof south of the river and north and west of White Breast creek; election at Wm. Glenn's. *Judges*—Wm. M. Young, John P. Glenn, and Wm. Glenn.

This included the present townships of Union, Swan, and Pleasant Grove, parts of Polk, Knoxville, and Franklin, the north-west corner of Dallas, and all of Warren county lying between the above named streams.

Knoxville.—Town. 75, range 19, and all of 76, range 19, south of the river, and east and south of White Breast creek, and all of 75 and 76, range 20, east of the old Indian boundary line; election at the place of holding district court. *Judges*—Lawson G. Terry, Landon Burch, and Moses Long.

This included the larger portion of Knoxville township and the south-east corner of Polk.

English—All of the county and attached portions thereof west of the old Indian boundary line, and south and east of White Breast creek; election at Wm. Tibbett's. *Judges*—Wm. Tibbet, Elisha B. Ryan and Samuel Nicholson.

This included what is now the south-west and some of the west part of Knoxville township, the larger portions of Washington and Dallas, and part of Warren county.

Round Grove—Town. 74, range 19, and all of 74, range 20, east of the old Indian boundary line; election at Alexander May's. *Judges*—Alexander May, John T. Pierce and Jeremiah Gullion.

This embraced all of what is now Indiana township, and about one and a half tiers of sections off the east side of Washington.

Cedar—Town. 74, range 18, and all of 75, range 18, south of the river; election at Jasper Koons's. *Judges*—Joseph Clark, David T. Durham and Francis A. Barker.

This embraced all of Liberty township, and all of Clay except what belongs to town. 76, range 18.*

These precincts continued in use until the population rendered smaller divisions necessary, when township organizations were substituted from time to time, with numerous changes, till they finally assumed the geographical phase shown by the large and beautiful map of the county, gotten up by Messrs. Shirwood and Pyle, in 1855. These township

---

*It is apparent that this point was entirely overlooked by the commissioners and not assigned to any precinct. It is the north-west corner of Clay.

We have been particular in these descriptions, to enable the reader, by the help of the map, to find the localities of these precincts, and get an idea of the civil geography of the county at that date. We hope the details will not be deemed too tedious to be interesting.

organizations will be detailed at some length, in the order of date, in another part of this book.

During the following month (April 14) the county was also divided into road districts, and a supervisor appointed for each Several of the precincts described above were each constituted a road district, numbered as follows:

No. 1. Town. 77, range 18, and all of 76, range 18, north of a line running west of the south-east corner of section 12. *Supervisor*, Samuel Peter.

No. 2. All of town. 76, range 18, south of a line running west from the south-east corner of section 12, and north of the river; and all of town. 75, range 18, north of the river. *Supervisor*, Wm. Welch.

No. 3. Red Rock precinct; *Supervisor*, Claiborn Hall.

No. 4. Gopher Prairie precinct; *Supervisor*, Joshua Lindsey.

No. 5. Pleasant Grove precinct; *Supervisor*, Wm. M. Young.

No. 6. Knoxville precinct; *Supervisor*, Lewis M. Pierce.

No. 7. English precinct; *Supervisor*, Wm. Tibbet.

No. 8. Round Grove precinct; *Supervisor*, David Sweem.

No. 9. All of towns. 75 and 76, range 18, south of the river; *Supervisor*, John Wise.

No. 10. Town. 74, range 18; *Supervisor*, Hugh Glenn.

As has already been noticed, few legally established roads then existed, and comparatively little work of the kind was required to be done, which may account for the size of the districts.

The following are the names of the grand and petit jurors impaneled for the first term of the district court, March 13th, 1846. We have taken pains to ascertain, so far as possible, who of the number still live, and who are dead, with dates and places, which we append to the list:

GRAND JURORS.

1. Stanford Doud, *foreman*, lives in Van Buren county.
2. John B. Hamilton; lives in Texas.
3. Asa Koons; died at his residence in Clay, in 1847.
4. Wilson Stanley; lives near Denver.
5. Samuel Buffington; moved to Mahaska county.
6. Ed. Billops; went to California in 1849.
7. Joseph S. West; lives in Summit.
8. Osee Mathews; went to Idaho in 1867, and now lives in Ohio.
9. James Chestnut; died on his return from California in 1850.
10. Andrew Storts; lives in Union township.
11. John P. Glenn; dead.
12. Conrad Walters; died in Knoxville, July 28, 1870, aged 77 years.
13. Alexander May; lives in Indiana township.
14. Thomas Gregory; died in Clay in 1849.
15. Benajah Williams; died in Mahaska county.

PETIT JURORS.

1. Jacob C. Brown; lives in Monroe, Jasper county.
2. Nathan Bass; died on his way to California in 1849.
3. Granville Hendrix; unknown.
4. George Gillaspy; lives in Ottumwa.
5. Claiborn Hall; lives near Athens, Illinois.
6. Alfred Vertrice; went to California.
7. John Whitlatch; lives in Indiana township.
8. Wm. Buffington; lives in Mahaska county.
9. Wm. Glenn; dead.
10. Elijah Wilcot; dead.
11. Reuben S. Lowry; killed in Kansas by a falling tree.
12. David Sweem; died in Indiana township in 1867.

This court convened at the time and place already mentioned, Judge Joseph Williams presiding; also attended by the following named persons as attorneys: Edward H. Thomas, prosecuting attorney; John W. Alley, —— Bissell, a young lawyer, who was afterwards engaged in mercantile business in Libertyville, Jefferson county, where he died in 1851; Thomas Baker, of Oskaloosa, —— Calkin, —— Gray, —— Peters, Henry Temple, and E. G. Stanfield. The latter was prosecuting attorney at the second term, and is still a resident of Knoxville.

This term lasted but three days, during which all the cases on the very limited docket were disposed of, the history of which would hardly prove of sufficient interest to repay a perusal. From the brief records, however, we quote—"United States *vs.* Henry Hall." This was the first case tried, being one of an assault and battery, appealed from a justice of the peace. The case was dismissed, and the defendant discharged. The second case reads—"United States *vs.* F. M. Clipton; recognized to keep the peace, and discharged on paying costs, amounting to seventeen dollars and fourteen and three quarters cents." There was also tried an appeal from the Mahaska county district court, a civil case, "Edward H. Thomas *vs.* the Board of Commissioners of Mahaska county." This was the same Thomas who attended as prosecuting attorney Having sued for attorney's fees, and, Mahaska county being a party, he could hardly expect justice from a jury of that court, and appealed his case to that of Marion, by whom he was awarded judgment for three hundred and twenty-five dollars.

As there were no jury rooms attached to the temporary building used as a court house, the jurors were cempelled to make the best shift that circumstances allowed. The grand jury retired to the residence of Dr. Conrey, a small linn log cabin, that was also open as a boarding house; whilst the petit jury held their consultations in the open air, at a convenient distance from the court house, each jury being attended by a bailiff.

As may be supposed, attendants at court were subjected to some inconveniences, consequent to the lack of boarding accommodations. Besides the boarding house kept by Dr. Conrey, there was another place of entertainment at the south east corner of the square, dignified with the name of tavern, kept by L. M. Pierce. L. W. Babbitt also owned a house in town to which, in due time, he made an addition for the accommodation of boarders. Yet, in these limited quarters, beds could not be supplied for all of even the smallest number required to compose a district court, which could not have been less than thirty persons, not counting plaintiffs and defendants, with their array of attorneys and witnesses. So many as could be fed at tables and lodged in comfortable beds were thus cared for, much to their satisfaction, though the fare was not epicurian to the last degree, nor even sumptuous. But, for the surplus number; the only shift was to take what is termed in steamboat travel, steerage, or deck passage, by bringing their own beds and victuals with them; they made the court house floor their camping ground, where they could enjoy the rough fare quite independent of the restraints of hotel life as it then existed in Knoxville.

In those days men were not disposed to complain of the privations incident to frontier life. Experience had taught them to regard such as an unavoidable state of things, and gave them no choice but to accept of them as cheerfully as though there was nothing lacking. The evenings were passed with a cheerfulness and hilarity peculiar to frontier life, where there is, usually, comparative freedom from the conventional restraints of older and more fashionable society. Pecuniarily, and consequently socially, men were nearly upon an equality. Ignorance was no bar to the social circle, though there was then, as there always has been, and always will be, a material difference in the mental attainments of the accepted members of society. Only the morally debased received no encouragement to participate in the interchange of jest and merriment that constituted much of the entertainment of the company. Men could play pranks upon each other, fire volleys of sarcastic wit at each other, and jestingly make each other the subjects of ridicule, without causing an open rupture. Then they could change the programme to stories, anecdotes, and songs, and thus restore all equinimity of feeling that might have been lost in the rough but not offensive badinage that had been exchanged. If these social entertainments were made more or less lively by the enlivening influence of a spirit called by the Indians *skooti-appo* (fire-water, *alias* whisky), it must be remembered that popular sentiment had not yet voted the custom of indulging in the ardent a crime. Whisky could be easily obtained, was comparatively cheap, and was more generally used,* notwithstanding which, beastly drunkenness was not regarded with favor.

Thus, these men could partake of a supper of cold corn-dodgers and meat with, perhaps, the addition of baked beans, or a tart made of some kind of wild fruit, and then, after a time spent in social confab, stretch themselves upon their straw cots on the ground floor of the little court room, and compose themselves to sleep with the happy contentedness unsurpassed, if even equalled, by that obtained from the sumptuous fare of a first-class hotel.

In the presence of Judge Williams at one or the other of the boarding-houses, these pastimes were, if possible, less irksome to the company. With an inexhaustible fund of wit, humor, and music, he was at no loss for means of amusement, and

* Though the above statement may be mainly true, Judge Williams was heard to remark, much to the credit of those who attended the first district court, that it was the first court he had ever held where whisky had not preceded him.

took much delight in affording it. As the Judge was a somewhat noted character, more particularly for eccentricity than for legal attainments—though, we believe, he had the reputation of being a good judge—we deem it proper to close this chapter with a brief sketch of him.

With regard to his history we know but little, either previous to the time at which we are writing, or since. At that time he was about fifty years of age, and had worn the ermine many years. In a territorial act fixing the terms of the district courts, approved January, 1839, we find his name as appointee over what was then called the second district, composed of the counties of Louisa, Muscatine, Cedar, Johnson, and Slaughter. He was a person of remarkable good conversational powers, and delighted in telling anecdotes. His musical talent was much above the average, both for vocal and instrumental. Often, after delivering a temperance lecture,* full of eloquence, and interspersed with humorous passages, he would sing a favorite song called "Little Billy Neal," with an effect seldom surpassed, calling up an applause of such hearty, boisterous delight as has seldom greeted a star actor. He was master of most musical instruments, but for drawing tunes out of that sweetest toned of all, "the fiddle and the bow," he was particularly distinguished in this attainment. In addition to his vocal talent as a singer, he possessed that wierd, mysterious power of using his voice as a ventriloquist, and could imitate the cry of various kinds of animals so correctly that the uninitiated could not fail being deceived. He would sometimes imitate the squalling of a belligerent cat to the great alarm and mystification of the ladies, who could neither discover the brawlers nor learn from whence the noise came.

At this point we beg leave to introduce a couple of anecdotes bearing upon his notoriety as a musician :

---

* Judge Williams lectured on temperance at Oskaloosa during the first session of court there, and was the first person that organized a temperance society in the frontier counties.

Many years ago, on the occasion of a convention at Iowa City, in the interests of a proposed railroad from Muscatine to that place, Judge Williams and Le Grand Byington were in violent opposition to each other upon some points of which we are not informed, nor does it matter, so far as the interest of this sketch is concerned. After the convention, a young amateur in the art of drawing produced a caricature representing Joe Williams seated astride an enormous bull playing a clarionet. The bull was on the railroad, with tail erect and head down, pawing up the dirt, and prepared to combat the further progress of a locomotive which was close upon him, upon which was Le Grand Byington as engineer, and from the whistle of which ascended the words, "Music hath charms, but cannot soothe a locomotive."

On another occasion, being that of an election of supreme judge and United States senator by the state senate, Judge Williams was before the democratic caucus for the judgeship, and George W. Jones (sometimes called Nancy Jones, and known as a dancing master), for the senate. Their competitors of the same party were S. C. Hastings, formerly president of the territorial council, for the judgeship, and Hon. T. Wilson for the senate. The last named gentlemen were at Iowa City just previous to the time of election, laboring earnestly with the members of the senate to secure their choice. But at the caucus, which came off during the night preceding the day of election, it was decided to elect Williams and Jones.

The following additional particulars of this incident are from a letter of Mr. Babbitt, published in the Annals of Iowa for Oct., 1870. "After the adjournment of the caucus, all hands were invited by Jones, Dodge, Williams, and other successful candidates, to partake of an oyster supper and free whiskey, at a saloon near by, which invitation was pretty generally accepted, and at which the defeated candidates partook pretty freely of the last refreshment named. About twelve o'clock the party broke up, and the members retired to their rooms. The defeated candidates, Wilson and Hastings, roomed in adjoining rooms to the one occupied by me, and were very much excited over their defeat ; so much so, that they walked from room to room, bewailing their fate, and declaring that they had been repudiated by the democracy. When they came into my room, I attempted to console them, telling them that they were not repudiated, but that other democrats had more friends in the caucus than they, whereupon Wilson exclaimed : 'If I had been beaten by a high-minded, honorable man, I could have stood it without a murmur; but to be defeated by a dancing-master, ruins my reputation forever.' To this speech Hastings responded as follows: 'Wilson, you have been defeated by a high-minded, honorable man—a gentleman—a dancing-master—I congratulate you; but for me there is no consolation, for, by G–d, the fiddler beat me.' "

But we hardly dare to close this chapter without relating an instance of his peculiar power as a ventriloquist. It occurred during the first term of the district court at Knoxville. Most of those attending court then boarded at Babbitt's ; and it so happened that one night the little boarding house was so full that it was barely possible for all to find sleeping room. The Judge, with lawyers Knapp, Wright, and Olney, were supplied with beds in the lower story, whilst the jurors and numerous other attendants found room to stretch themselves on the loose upper floor, using blankets, coats, and whatever else they had provided for beds. When, after much ado, they had all got settled down for a nap, they were suddenly startled by the terrific squalling of what appeard to be a couple of tom-cats in mortal combat in the room. Instantly all hands were up and in search of the supposed disturbers; but no cats could be found, and the surprised boarders returned to their beds without any very satisfactory conjectures as to the whereabouts of the nocturnal brawlers. But they had hardly composed themselves again for rest, when the loud and boisterous growling and snapping of a couple of belligerent bull-dogs, apparently in their very midst, brought them all up standing. And then followed an uproar such as language could convey but an indistinct idea of—the dogs maintaining the combat with mingled growling, barking, and whining, and the men endeavoring with all the noise they could make, to oust them from the room. How they came to be there was a wonder, indeed: but the evidence of their presence was too unmistakable to admit of a doubt, even in the total darkness. Presently the fight ceased, and with that the general uproar abated. Then came a solution of the mystery. The Judge and lawyers could no longer restrain their merriment at the expense of the frightened and mystified lodgers up stairs, but let it come in a gush of laughter that quickly reminded some of the company that the Judge was a ventriloquist, and had undoubtedly just played them one of his mysterious tricks. But so far from being offended at it, they took a sensible view of its ludicrousness, and all joined heartily in the laugh.

CHAPTER XI.

List of County Commissioners—Probate Judges—County Judges—County Supervisors and County Treasurers—The Stanfield Defalcation—Robbery of the Treasury in 1867.

Before closing the political history of our county, it would be proper to give a list of some of the officers who were elected subsequently to the first whose names have already been given.

It was stated that when the term of the first board of county commissioners had expired, the terms of the succeeding members were regulated by the comparative number of votes polled for each at the election by which they were chosen. As three were required to constitute the board, it was enacted that the one who received the highest number of votes at the regular election in August, 1846, should serve three years, the next highest two, and the lowest one, so that a new member would be elected yearly. After the county was divided into commissioners' districts, as has been described, a member was elected from one or another of these districts yearly, so that no district elected a commissioner oftener than once in three years, thus keeping a quorum of two experienced members constantly in office.

At the first regular election, Hugh Glenn and Samuel Tibbett were elected to fill the places of Conrad Walters and Wm. Welch, David Durham holding over another year.

August, 1847, Thomas Pollock in place of Mr. Durham.

August, 1848, Martin Neel, in place of Hugh Glenn.

August, 1849, Miles Jordan in place of Thomas Pollock.

August, 1850, James M. Brous, in place of Samuel Tibbett.

In 1851 the commissioner system was abolished and substituted by the office of county judge, as will be further noticed after we have given a list of probate judges, as follows :

September, 1845, (special election), Francis A. Barker.

August, 1847, Claiborn Hall.

August, 1849, Thomas Collins.

August, 1850, Warren D. Everett.

In 1851 the offices of probate judge and county commissioners were abolished by an act of the legislature, and both merged into that of county judge, and the following is a list from that to the present date:

Joseph Brobst, elected August, 1851; re-elected in 1853.

F. M. Frush, elected August, 1855; re elected in 1857, and held the office till January 1, 1861.

Wm. B. Young, elected October, 1861; re-elected October, 1863, and held the office till January, 1866.

Joseph Brobst, elected October, 1865; re elected October, 1867, and held the office till January, 1869, when the office was repealed* and substituted by that of circuit judge.

By an act of the legislature, the office of county supervisor was created to assume the duties previously performed by the county judge. One member elected from each township constituted a board of supervisors The first board was elected on the second Tuesday of October, 1860, and held their first session on the first Monday of January following.

John B. Hamilton was then clerk of the district court, and, by virtue of his office, was also clerk of the board of supervisors.

The first business of the board was to regulate the terms of its members, so that half the number should be limited to one year, and the other half to two years; but as there were fifteen members, the odd number was placed in the list of short terms.

---

*By this act Judge Brobst was appointed *ex-officio* auditor till January 1, 1870.

The clerk prepared the ballots, and the members drew as follows:

NAMES.	TOWNSHIPS.	TERM.
Joseph Brobst	Knoxville	2 years.
Wm. P. Cowman	Perry	1 year.
D. F. Smith	Franklin	1 year.
H. R. Clingman	Dallas	1 year.
Wm. Blain	Union	2 years.
Geo. W. Martin	Polk	2 years.
Daniel Sherwood	Indiana	2 years.
John F. Baldwin	Summit	1 year.
Edwin Baker	Red Rock	2 years.
Joseph Clark	Clay	1 year.
J. B. Davis	Liberty	2 years.
E. F. Grafe	Lake Prairie	2 years.
Bromfield Long	Washington	1 year.
J. A. Logan	Swan	1 year.
J. Thornburg	Pleasant Grove	1 year.

The following is a list of county treasurers from the organization of the county till the present date,—1870:

David T. Durhom, elected September, 1845; re-elected August, 1846, and served till August, 1847. Isaac Walters, from August, 1847, to 1849, and re-elected from that until 1851. Claiborn Hall, 1852 and 1853. David Stanfield, 1854, 1855, 1856, and 1857. William Ellis, 1858, 1859, 1860, and 1861. A. H. Vierson, 1862 and 1863. Emery F. Sperry, 1864 and 1865; during which term Edwin Baker served as deputy. William T. Cunningham, 1866 and 1867. Edwin Baker, 1868, 1869, 1870 and 1871.

During this period the treasury suffered twice from robbery; the first time by defalcation at the close of Stanfield's second term; and the second time by burglary, during the second year of Cunningham's term. The history of the first is briefly as follows:

At the August election, in 1847, Mr. Stanfield being a candidate for a third term, was defeated, and his successor (as the custom then was) entered upon the discharge of the duties of his office as soon as the result of the election was known; and on settling up the affairs of the office a default of $4,546.20 was discovered. So soon as the discovery was made he was arrested,* and an indictment was found against him at the September term of the district court. Upon this, judgment was rendered against him and his securities for the amount. Of this amount, his assignee, C. G. Brobst, paid into the treasury in cash, notes, and judgment $2,206.93, leaving a balance of $2,339.27 due the county.

Mr. Stanfield seemed profoundly ignorant of the manner in which the loss occurred, and persistently denied his participation in it; and as the affair was, to some extent, a mystery, many persons doubted his guilt, and some even believed him entirely innocent. It was for some time a subject of a severe partizan warfare of words, in which the *Journal* and *Standard* participated vigorously, firing weekly volleys of hot shot into each other's camp, without, however, gaining any apparent advantage for either side

In October of the same year, Mr. Stanfield moved to Kansas, where, late in the fall, or during the winter, he was followed and visited by Doctor Patterson and James Walters, who on their return reported that they had found him living in almost extreme poverty, apparently confirming the truth of his plea of innocence. In consequence of these facts, no attempt was made to prosecute the case further; and, in 1867, in response to a petition of a majority of the citizens of the county, the board of supervisors released the bondsmen of

---

*Since the publication of the above statement we have been reliably informed that Mr. Stanfield was not arrested.

David Stanfield from their liability, thus finally ending the trouble.

The second robbery was one of much greater magnitude, and proved a total loss. It occurred on Saturday night of February 9th, 1867, or very early on the following morning, but was not discovered till about 8 o'clock, when it produced a sensation quite unusual for the time and place.

It was known that the treasury contained a large sum, and it was at first supposed that it had all been taken, and exciting stories of the robbery,—the manner in which it was effected, and the magnitude of the loss,—were verbally reported through the county before the facts were fully ascertained. For a detailed account of the affair, we quote the following from the *Marion County Republican*, of February 12, 1867:

"On Saturday night last, the office of the county treasurer, at the court house, in this place, was entered and robbed of all the money in it, which amounted to over forty thousand dollars. The burglars, in the first place, broke into Mr. Reed's blacksmith shop and helped themselves to all the tools they required. They entered the treasurer's office through a window that was very insecurely fastened. By the side of the door of the vault they removed a few bricks, which enabled them, with the aid of a cold chisel, to reach the bolt and drive it back, thus opening the door. The safe in the vault was purchased, during the last year, for sixteen hundred dollars. The burglars broke the knob off the door of the safe, cut into the lock, opened the door, and took the funds. The most that was taken belonged to the school fund of the county. Mr. Dan Smick, of Knovville, loses over $1,600, which he had placed there for safety. A portion of the funds was owned by the State.

"The robbery was discovered about 8 o'clock Sunday morning, and caused a great deal of excitement among our citizens all day long, hundreds visiting the court house. Prompt action was taken to find the robbers. Different persons were sent out to spread the news and place officers of the law on the watch. As it was impossible for the scoundrels to take the benefit of the railroad until yesterday, we trust they may be speedily overhauled, and the stolen funds recovered.

"The board of supervisors was called together yesterday."

The following additional particulars we quote from the same article:

"The knob was first knocked off, then a portion of the chilled iron under it cut out. Heavy blows were next struck exactly in the right place to loosen the bolts or break the fastenings, so heavy as to break the steel facing of the sledge used. Both of these operations, which we have imperfectly described, had the effect to loosen the bolts. Chisels were then used to pry open the door, which, unfortunately, was accomplished. The burglar, or burglars, seemed to know just what was requisite to do in order to accomplish their object. The one who made the safe could not have gone to work more scientifically, or with a better understanding of what was necessary to be done.

After a more critical examination of the amount taken, the losses of the various funds were found to be as follows:

School fund	$20,000 00
State fund	3,600 83
County fund	2,100 50
Bridge fund	3,300 48
Poor house fund	2,276 74
Insane fund	1,193 26
Making a total of	$32,471 81

As some circumstances connected with the robbery seemed, in the opinion of a majority of the board, to indicate the Treasurer's connec ion with it, they ordered his arrest, employed an attorney for the county, and sent to New York for a detective to examine the safe, and make such discoveries as might lead to the arrest of the robbers.

A preliminary examination of Mr. Cunningham's case came off during this called session of the board; and, as some of the evidence seemed to lead to his conviction, his case was left for the investigation of the grand jury for the March term of the district court.

In the mean time, some parties had employed a young man who claimed to have been an army detective, to ferret the matter out. Actuated by a hope of the large reward, he secured the arrest of a man named William D'Armond, who had been a citizen of Knoxville for a short time, and had moved to —— county soon after the robbery. Mr. D'Armond was brought to Knoxville and then sent to the Oskaloosa jail for a few weeks, to await his trial. The trial was had before Justice Kenedy, in Knoxville, and occupied about two days. M. V. Bennett was for the State, and J. B. Atherton for the defense, by both of whom the case was warmly contested; but the trial resulted in the acquittal of D'Armond.

A bill was found against Mr. Cunningham at the March term, whereupon he took a change of venue to Monroe county. Here, however, the State failed to get its witnesses at the time set for trial and the case was discontinued. After this, the board employed attorneys to investigate the matter, and sue on the bonds for whatever amount they supposed they could sustain an action upon. But, after investigating, they came to the conclusion that the evidence against Mr. C. was not sufficient to justify an attempt at prosecution. So the case was finally dismissed.

The great loss sustained by the county in this affair, together with the expenses of employing detectives, attorneys, the purchase of a new safe, &c., proved quite embarrassing for a time. It was at first thought advisable to issue bonds and obtain a loan for the benefit of those funds that were in the most pressing demand, particularly the school and bridge. But this was not done. Warrants were given on claims on which the county paid interest, and many of these were bought by speculators at a profitable discount. In due time, however, by strict economy, and promptness in the payment of taxes, the finances of the county so far improved as to bring her warrants to par before three years, and the whole machinery is now in as flourishing condition as it was before the robbery.

Our limits will hardly permit a full list of all the county officers who were elected and served from 1845 to the present date; nor do we deem such a list of much historical importance in a work more especially designed to record the early history of the county. Hence, we have named the incumbents of such offices as seemed to be of leading importance in the transaction of county affairs. We therefore proceed with the more legitimate thread of our narrative.

CHAPTER XII.

A Legal Mistake—Brief Sketch of Lysander W. Babbitt—First Post Office at Knoxville—"Lake Prairie" P. O.—Inconvenience of Mail Facilities—A Historical Incident—Sectioning the Laads—First Land Entered—Des Moines River Land—Fowler Lands.

At the second term of the district court, a circumstance occurred, slightly embarrassing to the few criminal prosecutions that came before it through the findings of the grand jury, which occurred in this wise: It was the business of the commissioners to select the jurors, and, after the proper number was drawn by the sheriff, it was the duty of the clerk to certify to the list. In this instance L. W. Babbitt, who, we should have stated, was appointed clerk of the district court by the judge, at the first term, instead of designating that office in his signature to the certificate of jurors. signed himself "Ex-officio Clerk of the Board of County Commissioners." This was right so far is it went, but in consequence of not adding "Clerk of the District Court," it was decided by that court that such a signature amounted to no legal signature at all; that the jurors were not legally drawn; that they were not jurors, and that their doings were null and void. So, all the indictments made out by that jury were, to use a phrase common in legal proceedings, quashed. It is, however, due to Mr. B. to state that the error was not intentional. Owing to the fact that no attempt was made to secure new indictments, it is safe to judge that the cases were of no vital importance.

As the career of Mr. Babbitt, connected with the early history of Marion county, may appear somewhat conspicuous, and as his name may not be mentioned in any future part of this work, we here take occasion to give what little we know relative to his history.*

He was born in the State of New York about 1810, came to Iowa at an early day, and was a citizen of Burlington in 1840, where he worked at the business of gunsmith, and also held some office. In 1842, he, with two others, went to the head waters of the Des Moines river on a trapping expedition, where they remained during the winter. On their return in the spring, as they were descending the river in a canoe, they were robbed of most of their furs by the Indians. On the first of May, 1843, they landed at what is now Coalport, where Babbitt remained long enough to take a claim, embracing the present site of the village and the bluffs below it, containing inexhaustible beds of coal.

Having secured his claim, Mr. B. repaired to Burlington for his wife, and was surprised to find her in mourning for him, and preparing to sell his property, with the view of returning to her former home. The report had reached her some time previously that he had been murdered by the Indians, and his failing to return within a reasonable time seemed to confirm this report beyond a doubt. He concluded, however, not to stop the sale of the property, but took the matter into his own hands, and soon after moved to his claim. Here he fitted up a temporary shop, where he employed himself in repairing guns, sharpening plow-shears, and doing other jobs in the smith trade, till he was called to the clerkships already mentioned.

He is described as a person of small stature, active movements, prepossessing manners, quick apprehension, and retentive memory. He was, evidently, ambitious of political promotion, for which his energy and talents fitted him, and carried

---

*We wrote to Mr. B. for information on this point, but failing to obtain an answer, we are dependent on other sources for these meagre and perhaps inaccurate accounts.

him, to some extent. During his official term at Knoxville he began the study of law, and so far mastered the rudiments of that profession, that he was admitted to the bar in 1847. During his residence here he twice represented Marion, and several other counties, in the State legislature. In 1846 he was appointed the first postmaster at Knoxville, and his commission authorized him to give out a contract for carrying the mail to Oskaloosa and back once a week,* but it was not till some time in June of that year that the first mail arrived, and the office was opened at Babbitt's house. He held the office till 1849, when he was succeeded by James M. Walters. In 1853 he left the county, having received the appointment of register of land office at Council Bluffs, under President Pierce, and is at present editor of the *Council Bluffs Bugle.* Since his residence there he has several times represented Pottawattamie county in the state legislature.

Some time previous to the establishment of a post office at Knoxville, one had been established on Lake Prairie, and called by that name. Augustus Blair received a commission as postmaster here, but failing to qualify, David T. Durham circulated a petition asking for the appointment of Wilson Stanley. This was after the establishment of the post route between Oskaloosa and Knoxville, passing this office. In due time Mr. S. received his commission, and retained it till he sold to the Hollanders and moved to Red Rock, in 1847, when A. B. Miller took charge of the office till it was moved to Pella, during the winter of 1847–8.

In relation to offices established in other parts of the county, see history of the townships.

Previous to the establishment of these offices, mail facilities were so inconvenient that the people of Marion county were

---

*David Durham took this contract, extending from July 1st, 1846, to July 1st' 1850—four years. He commenced in June, and made two trips during that month gratuitously, as the department did not commence paying till July.

comparatively isolated from the rest of the world. The nearest post office was at Oskaloosa, a distance of from fifteen to thirty miles, which precluded all thought of regular or frequent correspondence by mail. Only the most urgent necessity induced a settler to suffer the delay and expense of going to and returning from the post office, though the difficulty was sometimes slightly obviated by the chance of sending by persons passing and repassing to mill, or on some other business. Otherwise, no matter how desirous the recent immigrant might be to soften the loneliness of his condition in a wilderness so remote from the friends and scenes of his nativity, to hear from them at regular intervals, even once a month, the distance to the post office was found to be nearly, if not quite, an insurmountable obstacle thereto. Therefore, the establishment of means of regular mail communication within the county was regarded as next in importance to that of convenient milling privileges. It was like opening a prison door temporarily closed against intercourse with the outside world; and, after being so deprived, no people had better cause to appreciate this one great blessing of a civil government.

At the convention which came off at Iowa City in 1846, on the occasion of the formation of the first state constitution, preparatory to our admission into the Union as a state, John Conrey, of Knoxville, was our chosen delegate, representing besides Marion, the counties of Jasper, Iowa, Poweshiek, Warren, Polk, and all the territory attached to them within the bounds of the purchase. No convention had been held for the purpose of nominating candidates to be elected to this office, but thev were chosen by the common consent of the leading members of the opposing parties. Rev. James L. Warren, also of Marion, was chosen by the whigs. During the canvass, I. C. Curtis, also a whig in that time, not seeming favorably disposed towards the choice of his party, announced himself as a candidate, and succeeded in obtaining a few votes, by which Warren was defeated, Conrey being elected by a majority of about ten. After this, Curtis became identified with the democratic party. We record this as a historical incident that it seems hardly proper to omit, and not intending it to be prejudicial to the reputation of Mr. Curtis, who is now a citizen of a distant state.

We now proceed to a brief record of the sectionizing and sale of the public lands in the county. We regret that our information on these subjects is comparatively limited, for we would take pleasure in giving the amount surveyed from time to time, and the amount entered the first year after the sales commenced. The county was sectionized by ranges. Range 18, and the north half of 19, was sectionized during the winter of 1846–7, and the remainder of the county at different dates. The south half of the county was assigned to the Fairfield land district, and the north half to that of Iowa City. The first land offered for sale was that first surveyed and the first entered in this tract, and consequently the first in the county was section 29, town 74 (Liberty township), range 18, by Josiah Brobst, in May, 1847. The claimants were not generally prepared to enter their lands as fast as they came into market, and it was not till some time in 1848 that any considerable amount was taken up; and it was at this critical period that the greatest antagonism existed between the claimants and buyers, some accounts of which have been given. But soon after these troubles subsided, and the fertility of the soil and the beauty of the country became known to some extent, and local conveniences were established, population poured in, and the lands were rapidly taken up. But the greatest increase of population by immigration was between the years 1850 and 1855, after which little choice land remained in possession of the government. In 1860 there was none.

At the present time, some small tracts contiguous to the Des

Moines river are owned by the state, being remnants of what was donated by the government to be expended in improving the navigation of that stream. A brief history of this ill-fated enterprise may not be out of place here:—

By an act of congress, dated August 8th, 1846, every alternate section of the public lands on each side of the Des Moines river, within five miles of it (except the sixteen of any township coming within the tract), was granted to the state for the purposes above stated. This grant was all made within the bounds of the new purchase, and extended west as far as Fort Des Moines, which was deemed to be at the head of navigation.

A survey of this river had been made by Samuel R. Curtis and others, and slack-water navigation by dams and locks, on the principle of those used in canals, was thought practicable to facilitate the floating of steamboats when otherwise the water would be too shallow for that purpose during the dry seasons; and the enterprise was not only regarded practicable, but profitable as a means of commerce in reaching the productions of the Des Moines valley, whose fertility betokened an abundance in due time, and also of reaching the coal that was known to exist in the banks and in the vicinity of that stream, and the beautiful red building-stone near Red Rock.

In the winter of 1846–7 the legislature took charge of the grant, and fixed the minimum price of the lands at two dollars per acre, except what was already pre-empted, and made so much of it as was included in Marion county subject to pre-emption in the spring of 1848, which was some time previous to that fixed for public sale. But this law not meeting with general approval, or failing to effect its desired purpose, was repealed at the next session (1848–9), and the price reduced to its original standard.

In 1848 the first board of public works was elected, consisting of a president, secretary and treasurer, who had the superintendence of the proposed undertaking. The members of the board were: Hugh W. Sample, president; Charles Corkery, secretary; and Paul Bratten, treasurer. They appointed Col. Samuel R. Curtis, engineer, who made a survey of the river, and located points for the several dams. During the year following a new board was elected, consisting of Col. Wm. Patterson, president, Col. Jesse Williams, secretary, and George Gillaspy, treasurer; and they appointed Guy Wells, of Keokuk, engineer, in 1850. In 1851–2 the legislature repealed the act enabling the election of a board, and authorized the governor to appoint a commissioner and register instead. In accordance with this law, Gen. V. P. Van Antwerp was appointed commissioner, and George Gillaspy, register; but Mr. Gillaspy declined serving, and Paul C. Jeffries was appointed. In 1853–4 these offices were made elective by the people, and Josiah H. Banny was elected commissioner, and George Gillaspy, register. Two years later, Edwin Manning was elected commissioner, and Wm. Drake, register; and at the close of their term, the whole thing was turned over to the care and keeping of a New York company. But, as the enterprise was finally abandoned, after much of the grant had been squandered in the pretended erection of locks and dams at various points, what remained went back to the state, and was appropriated to the building of a portion of the Des Moines Valley Railroad. Only one dam was located in Marion county, at Rousseau, where a large quantity of rock was blasted in preparation for its erection; and the excavation in the cliff, on the south side of the river, and the loose boulders thrown from it, will long remain a mark of a project wild enough in its conception, but better calculated to put money into the pockets of certain individuals.

From the first, many settlers had little confidence in the enterprise; and, as the lands appropriated were mostly timbered, and without any resident agents to look after them, the timber was, in numerous instances, freely used for fencing and building purposes, thus more directly serving the purpose that nature originally designed it for. Little, if any of these lands now remain unclaimed by individuals.

One or two instances of extensive land monopolies seem worthy of mention in this connection.

At an early day, William D. Ewing entered several thousand acres of land in the state, a portion of which was located in this county, principally on the dividing ridge between Des Moines and Skunk rivers. Some of this is now occupied by his immediate heirs.

Another was that of the Fowler heirs (some thirty-six in number). It was, for some time, a subject of litigation in court, and was finally settled in 1866 or 1867. We quote a brief history of the case from the *Iowa Voter*, of December 10, 1868:

"About the close of the war with Mexico, one Joseph Fowler, of New Orleans, bought one hunded and seventy-five land warrants, or claims for warrants, for very small sums, from our soldiers as they were on their way home. The entries under these warrants were made by Samuel Fowler, of Missouri, in trust for Joseph Fowler, about the 29th of December, 1848; and the lands lie in Marion, Monroe, and Lucas counties. It seems that Mr. Fowler was among the first to enter in this region, and had his choice. He selected mostly timbered land, and got it as nearly in a body as might be. The lands so entered in this county are in Washington and Indiana townships. These one hundred and seventy-five quarter-sections made a very considerable monopoly, and retarded the settlement of the country very much. After the entries were made, Joseph Fowler died; and Samuel Fowler deeded the land to his heirs, of whom there are many. We believe there has been some dispute connected with transfers of these lands, on account of an apparent or supposed dower interest of Mrs. Fowler in them. The timber lands have been robbed considerable by settlers around them, who found no opportunity for purchasing. The greater portion of the Fowler land in this county has now been sold to settlers."

Since the above account was published, we have been informed that the object of Joseph Fowler in entering this large tract was purely, or in part, benevolent. Having a large number of poor relations living in Maryland, he conceived and adopted this plan to secure them homes in the west, where they might have a chance to better their circumstances. At the time of his death he was on his way, by sea, to gather them up to transfer them to their new homes.

CHAPTER XIII.

History of the Press in Marion County—Pella Gazette—Knoxville Journal—Democratic Standard—Pella Weekblad—Marion County Republican—Pella Blade—Marion County Democrat—Pella Gazette—Iowa Voter—Copperhead.

Between the years 1847 and 1855, the population of the county was greatly increased by immigration from all parts of the east and south, and a large majority of those who had established permanent homes within her limits were men and women of intelligence and enterprise, if not of great wealth. Farms were made on every prairie, and almost every grove sounded with the stroke of the ax. Here and there the neat frame dwelling was beginning to take the place of the rude log cabin, and yearly expanding fields of corn and wheat, and numerous orchards of all stages of growth, from the lately planted scion, to the young fruit brearer, all betokened the husbandman's thrift, and promised him ultimate wealth. Villages were laid out in all parts of the county, and many of the most needed manufactories were established in and about them, with merchandise to exchange for the products of the soil. Saw and grist mills were sufficiently numerous to be comparatively convenient to the inhabitants of all parts of the county; and these were yearly increasing in number and enlarging in capacity, as the increasing demands of the county seemed to require. Even at that early period a railroad and river navigation (one or both) were confidently expected. The Des Moines Valley Road, though yet distant, both in time and space, was talked of as a fixed fact, the arrival of which would be the beginning of a new era in the history of the county, as an avenue of trade and means of speedy correspondence with the east. How completely this hope has been realized within the last few years, the people know better than we can express it. And we must not omit to notice that, from the earliest period of our county history, the important matter of education was not neglected. In the midst of the toils, difficulties and inconveniences of pioneer life, school districts were organized in every settlement of a sufficient number of children, a claim-pen, (if one could be had), used for a school house, or a cabin hastily erected for the purpose, and a teacher selected from the more capable members of the community. With such houses, such teachers, and such books as the country could afford, schools were maintained till greater conveniences came along with all the other advantages that are the natural result of growth in population and wealth.

But, so late as 1854 and 1855, one of the great levers of commerce and general intelligence was lacking in Marion county. In the midst of all these evidences of advancement the need of a local newspaper must have been felt. This need was, in a measure, supplied by the publication of the *Pella Gazette*, early in 1855.

Early in the autumn of 1854, Edwin H. Grant, a practical printer, came from the east to Pella, and entered into co-partnership with Henry P. Scholte, for the purpose of publishing a weekly newspaper in that town. They immediately set about making the necessary preparations. A press and type were purchased, a building suitable for a newspaper office erected, and a list of subscribers obtained. At length, after a delay of several months after the enterprise was first announced to the public, the first number of the *Pella Gazette*, the first newspaper printed in the county, appeared under date of February 1, 1855; and it was, just at that time, the most western paper published in Iowa before reaching the Missouri river.

The *Des Moines Star*, published at Fort Des Moines, had suspended operations just previously.

The *Gazette* was a large sheet, seven columns to the page, beautifully printed from new type, of a size rather smaller than is generally used for a country paper. The leading editorial was a lengthy article by Mr. Scholte, consisting mostly of a brief history of the Holland Colony. In an article headed "Defining our Position," Mr. Grant said:

"It is not our intention to remain silent upon the great political questions of the day. But we wish it to be distinctly understood that we do not intend to give a blind credence to the machinations of any of the parties now dominant. We shall boldly avow our sentiments respecting any of the great movements of the age, regardless of political bias. Whenever we can consistently approve of any acts performed by either party, which seem to us to be calculated to benefit our State, or the great national confederacy, we shall cordially lend our influence to sustain and promote such measures."

In his "Address to the Public," in the same issue, the same writer added:

"The difficulties and expense which have attended us in reaching this position can hardly be appreciated by any one unacquainted with the business, and with the difficulties incident to a new country."

Like most pioneers, the *Gazette* began with a small list of subscribers, and but few of these paid in advance. Evidently, but few persons wished to risk their money in an enterprise of this kind till they could be assured of its success. Notwithstanding this, the paper held its own for several years, gradually increasing its patronage along with its more recent competitors. Mr. Grant continued his connection with the *Gazette* till some time in 1857 or 1858, after which the paper was suspended for some length of time. In the summer or fall of 1859 it was resuscitated by S. M. Hammond, published by him in quarto form, and edited by Mr. Scholte, as a campaign paper. From November till March, 1860, it was published by Hammond & Hannold, when it was finally discontinued, and the subscription list transferred to the *Knoxville Journal.**

On the first of October, 1855, just eight months after the *Gazette* was started, the first number of the *Knoxville Journal* was issued by Wm. M. Stone (since governor of Iowa), as editor and proprietor. The press upon which it was printed was that of the old *Valley Whig*, published at Keokuk.

The *Journal* was published in the interest of the republican party, but devoted much of its space to the interests of Knoxville and the surrounding country. The first few numbers contained some valuable historical matter relating to the county, all of which was, unfortunately, lost on the night of the 4th of March, 1856, when the office was burned. It is a matter of regret to the author that he was unable, after extensive advertising and diligent inquiry, to procure one of these old papers. The office was in a frame building that stood on the west side of the public square, nearly opposite where the court house now stands. It and all its contents were entirely destroyed, together with a store adjoining it.

The *Journal* was not renewed till some time during the next fall or winter, when Geo. W. Edwards, now managing editor of the *Des Moines Republican*, came to Knoxville in quest of a location for a paper. Being in possession of a press and type, he and Stone formed a co-partnership and renewed the *Journal*. During the same year Stone sold his interest in the paper to Edwards, who conducted it alone for a short time, till he sold it to John M. Bailey, and he to E. G. Stanfield, in the winter of 1857 and 1858. During Mr. Stanfield's proprietorship of the concern, the *Journal* was, for a

*It may be worthy of note that Mr. A. F. Sperry, at present editor of the *Iowa Voter*, was an occasional compositor and contributor to the *Gazette*, and wrote its first carrier's address.

time, edited by L. D Ingersoll, since well known as an author. After Ingersoll, it was published by Bigelow & Co.; then, in 1860, by Horner & Hannold, who changed the name of the paper to *Marion County Republican*, some time during the same year.

The third paper published in the county was the *Democratic Standard*,* first issued in June, 1856, about eight months later than the *Journal*, by Claiborn Hall, editor and proprietor. Mr. Hall, not being a practical printer, and also entirely unacquainted with journalism, soon found it "up-hill" work, and, financially, a "losing game" to publish a frontier country newspaper. So, after a short experience, he disposed of the concern to a company. After this the *Standard* was edited and published by different individuals successively, among whom were S. M. Hammond and M. V. B. Bennett, the latter well known as a lawyer and political stumper. It finally suspended operations some time in 1864 or 1865.

On the 28th of September, 1861, Henry Hospers, having purchased the office of the old Pella *Gazette*, commenced the publication of a newspaper in the Holland language, called the *Pella's Weekblad* (*Weekly*). This paper was, and is, in the interest of the Democratic party, and enjoyed a good patronage, being in a community where that party was largely dominant. On the 18th of June, 1870, Mr. Hospers having been appointed by the Legislature to the office of Immigrant Agent, sold the paper to H. Neyenech, by whom it is now conducted.

The Marion county *Republican* was purchased by B. F. Williams in Oct. 1861, and edited by him until he sold it to Wm. G. Cambridge, Aug. '66. In '63–4 Mr. Williams rented the office to a printer named Griffin, who reduced it to half its original size, and issued it principally as an advertising sheet. In March, '67, Mr. Cambridge sold it to Sperry and

*Like the *Journal*, no early numbers of this paper are extant, or, at least, could not be found, and its history must, therefore, be brief.

Barker, by which transaction the *Republican* was finally discontinued.

In the winter of '64–5 Mr. C. S. Wilson, since connected with the Winterset *Madisonian*, purchased the press and type belonging to the *Democratic Standard*, moved them to Pella, and on the 3d of Feb., '65, commenced the publication of the Pella *Blade.*

Mr. Wilson was a radical Republican, and a writer of rather more than ordinary genius. In the local department he made the paper especially attractive by his peculiar style. In his salutatory he says :

"Acting, up to the time of the beginning of the rebellion with the Democratic party, I have, since that time, had a heritage in none ; but, believing that upon the success of the Republican (or Union) party, and the triumph of their principles, depend the rescue of the country from the hand of treason, and its existence among the family of nations, I have acted politically with that party. The *Blade* will continue the advocacy of these principles, at the same time its columns will not fail to condemn whatever it judges to be incompatible with the public interest or the national honor.

"In the local department particular attention will be given to the spread of such intelligence concerning our city and county as will be of benefit to them.

"It will be my aim to make this journal acceptable as a family newspaper, and, to this end, the latest news, poetry, tales, agricultural affairs, and items of all kind will find a place in its columns. Believing that nothing tends more to the development of a county than a wide-awake newspaper, I shall endeavor to avoid the Rip Van Winkle style as much as possible."

As a sample of Mr. Wilson's wide-awake style, we are overtempted to copy the following from the local department of his first number of the *Blade:*

"OUR DRAFT CORRESPONDENT.—We have secured the services of one of the ablest writers of the age, at a salary of $25,000 per annum, to go West and correspond for the *Blade* from the Draft Regions. He will report weekly everything of interest that occurs among the numerous class of pilgrims who have so nobly taken their lives in their hands and—run away. If a rattlesnake should be so uncourteous as to take a nip at the heel of one of these devoted pilgrims; if a grizzley should chance to indulge in a breakfast of pilgram ham, or a Pen Perce fancy to a collation of draft steak, he will duly report. He has also another mission. We are somewhat related to the Digger Indians, and it will be the business of our correspondent to take steps to prevent any of the valient pilgrims from marrying into the nation of Diggers, as we are careful of our blood, and do not want to have it polluted by such intermingling."

After publishing the *Blade* for about a year, Mr. Wilson sold the press and type to Melick, who took them to Waterloo, Black Hawk county, and printed the Waterloo *Courier*.

Soon after this the *Blade* was renewed by R. Crosby, who shortly afterwards associated with him Jas. H. Betzer. In December, 1867, Crosby sold his interest in the concern to H. G. Curtis, and December, 1869, Curtis sold to A. T. Betzer. At this date the paper became a semi-weekly, in the firm of Betzer Brothers, and continues so to the present.

The Marion County *Democrat* (Knoxville) was first issued September 19th, 1865, by J. L. McCormack, from a press and type he obtained in Missouri. In his salutatory he said:

"It is the intention to make this sheet a welcome visitor to the fireside of every household; to give instruction, to afford pleasure and enjoyment in the perusal of its columns, and, if possible, to bring about a little better understanding in the minds of the people as to their true duties of neighborly citizenship."

After promising a fair share of its space to agricultural and mercantile interests, and also to the entertainment of the lovers of literature, he adds:

"In politics this paper will support the principles, and stand by the organization of the Democratic party. It acknowledges allegiance to none other, and will pay fealty to the behests of its regular organization alone.

"Believing that the safety of our republican institutions requires a return to the principles of the party that established the Union, we shall labor for the overthrow of the party now in power, and insist upon a return to the condition of things that existed before traitors endeavored to destroy the Government."

The *Democrat* is a large, well-conducted journal, and commands a liberal share of public patronage.

In March, 1867, another paper was started in Pella, called the Pella *Gazette*. It was printed in the Holland language, devoted to the interests of the Republican party, and edited by G. Van Ginkle. After running about eighteen months it was discontinued, and the press was purchased by Snow & Huber, a mercantil firm in Pella, who issued a monthly journal for the purpose of advertising their business.

In March, 1869, Messrs. Sperry and Baker, formerly of the Guthrie County *Vidette*, exchanged printing offices with W. G. Cambridge, of the Marion County *Republican*; and on the 20th of June issued the first number of the *Iowa Voter*, at Knoxville. In his salutatory the editor says:

"The *Iowa Voter* will be a radically Republican newspaper, working as best it may to further the cause of Republicanism and the welfare and progress of all advocating impartial suffrage for the whole nation, and striving always to be a prompt and reliable medium of general and local news—in short, a live Republican newspaper.

The *Voter* has a large circulation, enjoys a large share of public patronage, and has rendered itself worthy the reputation of a good local journal.

On the 8th of January, 1868, a newspaper called "*Copperhead*" made its appearance in Pella, under the proprietorship of Bennett, McCully and Gamble. Owing to the novelty of its title, and the peculiar notoriety of one of its editors (Bennett) as a radical Democratic politician, its advent caused some sensation in political circles. The name was evidently chosen to offset the stigma intended to be fixed upon the Democratic party by the Republicans, when they gave it the name of a most poisonous reptile.

In his address "To the Public" the editor says in his well-known radical style:

"Our chief aim will be to make it a first-class Democratic paper, devoted to the interests of the great Democratic party and the masses of devoted, industrious, honest men who support the Government, uphold its laws, and stand by its written Constitution, as expounded by the supreme judiciary of the land."

Only eleven numbers of the paper were published in Pella. In the last week in March it was moved to Ottumwa, Wapello county, where it is still published by McCully and Evans, McCully remaining at Pella to attend to the interests of the firm in this county.

During its publication in Pella it and the *Blade* waged a violent personal warfare, in which the moral character of the combatants was subjected to a rigid scrutiny. When the *Copperhead* took its departure for Ottumwa, the *Blade* came out with a roughly executed but amusing caricature of the event, representing a huge serpent borne partly on a hearse and partly on men's shoulders, followed by several mourners.

In the spring of 1870 the proprietors of the *Blade*, *Democrat*, and *Voter* entered into a written agreement pledging themselves to the advance payment system on subscription, to begin on the first of June. At first this was thought to be a rather hazardous policy where the credit system had so long been the practice. But the new rule, though rigidly adhered to, has proved quite as successful as the publishers could have desired.

CHAPTER XIV

Iowa Central University—Marion County Agricultural Society—County Poor House.

Among the public institutions that have been established in Marion county within the past few years, as evidence of her prosperity and enterprise, the three important ones mentioned above may be deemed worthy of special notice. And we regret our inability, owing to the lack of sufficient information, to give a more detailed history of them.

In the spring or summer of 1853, a society was organized by the Baptist Church, at Pella, looking to the establishment and endowment of a school there, to be called the Iowa Central University. The following are the names of the officers:

Faculty.

Rev. Elihu Gunn, Rev. E. H. Scarff, Prof. A. N. Currier, Miss S. J. Stoddard, Miss Marse.

Directors.

President, E. Gunn; Vice President, E. M. Scarff; Treasurer, Henry P. Scholte.

Besides these there were about thirty trustees chosen. From their address, delivered at the fourth annual meeting, we quote the reasons set forth for the location of this institution at Pella:

"The denomination, wherever its will has been expressed upon the subject, has always demanded a central location. Another location, provisionally made, was almost universally rejected in the state convention, and mainly on the ground that it was sectional in its location. And with the best reason. When almost all the other denominational schools were located on or near the line of the Mississippi river, why should we not take possession of the magnificent field left open to us in the central part of the State?

"Pella is situated within thirty miles of the geographical centre of the State, in the immediate vicinity of the Des Moines river—the great channel of inland communication, and the centre of the commerce and manufactures of the State for all time; near, also, to the point where several of the great railroad lines which intersect the State are to converge, and in the very heart of the great coal field of the State, the richest, perhaps, in the world, and in one of the most beautiful and healthy portions of this or any other country.

"Combining all these advantages, it is yet far enough removed from any great centre of trade and commerce to have all the advantages of a quiet country location. Of the advantages of a country over a city location for a college, one of the most respected of the living fathers of our denomination, and one of the most experienced in such matters, in a recent production on the subject, wrote as follows:

"'Instead of farmers and other persons from the villages or country sending their sons to a great commercial city, into the vortex of commercial speculation, political excitement, fashion, frivolity and dissipation in every form, those families who desire, to preserve their sons from the contamination of city intercourse will send them to a college situated in a rural village."

"Such a village is Pella; quiet and retired, it is yet populous enough to secure all the advantages of good society, and near enough to the great thoroughfares of travel to be at all times easy of access. It is also noted for the quiet and orderly habits of its people, as well as for their moral and religious character. To such a place parents can send their children with every assurance that their habits and morals will be safe."

Large endowments were secured: and, in 1856, a beautiful and commodious brick building was erected in the south-west part of the city, on ground donated for the purpose by Rev. Henry P. Scholte. It was, however, not completed till some time in 1857, and was first opened for the reception of pupils on the 1st of September of that year.

The building stands in the center of a beautiful park. The dimensions are 50 by 70 feet, three stories high, with a basement besides; contains fourteen rooms, including a large chapel, a library and a museum, and is capable of comfortably accommodating three hundred pupils. Its entire cost was between $15,000 and $18,000.

In 1857, the report of the trustees announced the reception of an endowment of $50,000, in scholarships of $100 each, and the prospect of another large endowment soon to follow. The school has been well patronized with attendance and donations, and is in a flourishing condition.

In 1856 the agricultural interests of the county seemed to demand an organized plan for its encouragement, and to facilitate the dissemination of such intelligence as might be useful in the various departments of the business. The only one calculated to effect the end desired, was to organize a society, appoint a time and place for a general meeting of the farmers, and award premiums for the best samples of live stock, grain, fruits, &c.

So the Marion County Agricultural Society was organized during the year above mentioned, and the first fair was held on the public square in Knoxville, in October. Only a few animals were exhibited, and, consequently, but few premiums were awarded. For the want of any other room for the purpose, the old court room was used as a floral hall.

The next exhibition, in Sept. of the year following, was held on the common a little west of town, where tables were set in the open air for the display of vegetables, small mechanical and artistic products.

These means of exhibition being totally inadequate to the increasing wants of the society, a joint stock company was formed in 1858, who purchased a beautiful plat of ground one mile north of town, and put it in sufficient repair for the use of the society that autumn.

Eight acres of the ground belonged to Drury Overton, and two to Thomas Clark, and were described as the north-east quarter of the north-east quarter of the north-east quarter of section (1) one, town (75) seventy-five, range (20) twenty.

The ground is beautiful and gently inclined southward, in a natural grove well shaded, enclosed by a high board fence, provided with a commodious hall, pens and stalls for the use of stock, and a good well of water.

The first fair was held in it in 1858. In June, 1870, it was deeded to the society. The fair in September of this year was well attended, and the finance of the society reported to be in a good condition.

During the last few years, previous to the robbery, the treasury was constantly subjected to heavy drafts upon the poor fund. From some cause or other the number of paupers seemed to have increased, and the expense of their support began to be looked upon as burdensomely heavy, particularly in the case of those who were invalids under the care of physicians. Some retrenchment in this department was deemed advisable, even at a considerable cost to start with.

Though it was known that many of those who were cared for at public expense, were worthy subjects thereof, it was yet supposed that not a few would prefer to make some effort to earn their own support than submit to the humiliating condition of becoming inmates of a poor house.

So, in 1865, a movement was made by the board of supervisors, looking toward the purchase of a farm and the erection of a house to become the home of such helpless persons in the county as were otherwise homeless and friendless. A committee was appointed to select a location and contract for its purchase, and in due time reported in favor of the west half of the north-west quarter, and the north-east quarter of the north-west quarter of section 14; and the west half of the south-west quarter of the north-west quarter of section 10, 120 acres, all in town 75, range 20, belonging to Elisha Elliot, and situated about two and a half miles south-west of the city of Knoxville. Cost $1,200.

The purchase of this land was made on the 15th of Dec., 1865; and in the spring and summer following, the whole of it was fenced and forty acres broke, part of it planted in corn and wheat, all at a cost of about $800.

The contract for building the house was let to the lowest bidder, and was awarded to Jacob Richards, in July, 1866, at $4,450. It is a large three story frame building, the basement story being fitted for a kitchen. The second and third are each traversed by a hall between two rows of rooms. Stables and other out buildings were added to the place some time after.

The contracts for overseer and physician were arwarded to John Robinson and Dr. Wetherell, under whose care the county poor were comfortably provided for in their new home.

The experiment proved quite a success. The number of paupers were greatly reduced, and the support of the remainder so systematized as to make it much less expensive.

PART II.

TOWNSHIP HISTORIES.

CHAPTER I.

Preliminary Remarks—Clay—Its Geography and Early History—First Birth, David Durham—Francis A. Barker, Thomas Young, G. G. Harsin—Weak Diet—A Little Adventure.

Having concluded what may be termed a general history of the county, we shall now proceed with a history of each township separately, in which we shall feel more at liberty to insert events of a local character relating to pioneer life, together with the memoirs and adventures of a few of the most prominent settlers that first located in each township. Our object in doing this is not merely to preserve a record of the difficulties and hardships that attended the early settlement of our now wealthy and prosperous county, but also to preserve the names of those who dared and suffered, to open the way to the blessings we now enjoy, and who, therefore, as much deserve honorable mention in local history as do those whose deeds have embalmed them in the pages of national history. It is true, as we have already said, that their chief object was to secure their own pecuniary independence, and this object has, in most cases, been fully attained. Thus far they have their reward; but it must not be forgotten that, in their toilsome efforts to accomplish this, they have conferred a great benefit upon community at large; and for this we deem them entitled to the grateful memory of the people. The number of these old pioneers is now few, in comparison to what it was twenty years ago, and is so constantly diminishing that in a few years more they will have become even less than a remnant. Many have emigrated farther west; others are scattered in different parts of the State; whilst many more have gone to the repose of the grave, both in the county and abroad. Should they be forgotten when nothing more is needed to preserve their memory for the instruction of future generations than this?

No regular township organizations were effected till the November term of the Commissioners' Court, in 1846. As we have already shown, the county was divided up into precincts for election and judicial purposes. For these precincts twenty justices and constables were elected at the first regular election, September 5th, 1845. At that election the rule required that the twenty persons receiving the largest number of votes of all the numerous candidates voted for, should be declared elected. This rule was necessary because there were no conventions held previous to election, for the purpose of making an organized choice of candidates, each elector choosing his own candidate on the day of election. We regret to say that we have been able to obtain the names of only a few of these officers.

CLAY.

This is a border township, occupying the center of the east side of the county, and numbers all of town. 75, range 18, lying south of the Des Moines river, and also that portion of town. 76, same range, on the south side of the river.

The only considerable streams that course through it are

English creek on the north, and Cedar, through the south-east corner. The township is well supplied with timber and coal.*

The name of Clay was given it in honor of the celebrated statesman Henry Clay, by his political friends, there being a large majority of them in the township when it was organized.

It is bounded on the north by Lake Prairie, with the Des Moines river as its northern boundary line; on the east by Mahaska county, on the south by Liberty township, and on the west by Knoxville and Polk.

Since its organization it has undergone several changes in its northern boundary. In '48 all of town. 75 north of the river was added to it by authority of the county commissioners, and on the 2d of October of the same year, in answer to a petition of Samuel Martin and others, it was "ordered that all of town. 76, range 18, south of the Des Moines river, be added to Clay township." And again, in 1850, that part of Clay included in town. 75, north of the river, was detached from Clay and reattached to Lake Prairie. This left both these townships in their present shape.

Previous to the date of its organization, (Nov. 16, 1846,) Clay belonged to what was called Cedar precinct. (See chapter 10.) At the first election in that precinct, Benajah Williams and Sennet Ramey † were elected Justices of the Peace, and Elias Williams, Constable, within the bounds of what is now Clay. When the township was organized, the place for holding elections was appointed to be at the house of Jasper Koons. At the first township election held there, John R.

---

*As an item of interest to geologists, we call attention to the existence of a bed of joint clay, about one and a half miles above Durham's Ford, and just above a ledge of limestone, on the south bank of the Des Moines. Some years ago Dr. Williams, now of Pleasantville, dug six feet through this deposit, and found it so completely filled with sea shells as to form almost its entire substance. Some of them he was enabled to remove whole, and found them to exactly resemble marine shells he had in his possession, gathered by him near Moro Castle, Cuba.

† Mr. Ramey failed to qualify and therefore did not serve.

Whaley and Garret G. Harsin were elected Justices, and David T. Durhim, Clerk.

The first election of which there is any record preserved, came off at the house of Jasper Koons, April 2d 1848. About 20 votes were cast, and the following officers elected: John Randall, Justice; Thomas Gregory, Andrew C. Sharp and Elias Moore, Trustees; D. T. Durham, Clerk; Jasper Koons, Treasurer, and Francis A. Barker, Inspector.

Those who settled in the township in 1843, were, Andrew Foster, † Thomas Kirtan, Matthew Ruple, David Durham, John Linpod and Benajah Williams. Those who came in '44, were, G. G. Harsin, John Harsin, Thomas Gregory, David Gushwa, A. C. Sharp, F. A. Barker, Thomas Tong, Sarah Clark, S. B. Zane, John Wise and Jasper Koons. The last named person had settled in what is now Lake Prairie during the year before. Andrew Foster and Thos. Gregory both died of small-pox in the summer of 1849.

Andrew Foster was the first person that built a house in the township. This was in section 33, town. 76, range 18, being near the river on some prairie. At this "raising" no teams or wagons were at hand to haul the logs to the ground, so it became necessary to cut them small so that they could be carried a distance of a quarter of a mile by the few men who had volunteered to assist at putting up the house.

This house was some time afterward occupied as a school house, and David T. Durham taught the first school in it, being the first in the township. About a dozen pupils attended this school from about five families residing within reach.

Among other enterprises begun at an early date was the planting of an orchard on a claim owned by Benajah Williams, by Mr. W. The farm is now owned by Geo. Harrin. The trees are mostly in a thrifty condition and good bearers.

† David T. Durham, Andrew Foster and —— Clark entered the county in the summer or fall of '42, in quest of location, and extended their tour as far as the point of timber where Monroe, Jasper county, now is.

One among the few first settlors who are still residents of the township, is Matthew Ruple. He lives in section 14. In his family occurred the birth of the first white child in the county. This was Frances Ruple, born July 23, 1843; she still lives in the township, and is now Mrs. Albert Spore.

But most distinguished among those who settled in the township in '43, was David Durham, a brief sketch of whom may be in order here:

Mr. D. was born in Belfast, Maine, July 7th, 1792, and immigrated to Ohio in 1828. He started on the 3d of September, and reached Dovertown, Morgan county, Ohio, on the 10th of October, where he located, and opened a farm. But, after being engaged in this business four or five years, he went to the salt works on the Muskingum river, and engaged as a laborer to Sennet Ramey, who, a year or two later, appointed him superintendent of his salt works. After serving in this capacity for some time, he purchased an establishment and went into the salt business on his own account. But owing to the plentifulness of the commodity, together with limited means of shipping it down the Muskingum in scows and canoes, and transportation by land in wagons, the business proved unprofitable, and he failed to meet all the payments on the property. This was in 1836, when money matters became close and precarious. Abandoning the salt works he then employed himself for one season in transporting flour and salt to and from Zanesville by flat boats and scows. Early in '37 he moved to Zanesville, where he engaged in various occupations, till the autumn of that year, when he moved to McClain county, Illinois. But not being able to settle there as he desired, with a large family, he moved again in the spring following, and stopped in what is now Jefferson county, Iowa. Here his companion, Nancy Durham, who had shared his varied fortune for more than twenty years, died, April 13, 1839. After about five years' residence in Jefferson county, Mr. Durham moved to

Clay township, where he took and occupied a claim till he secured a title from the government in 1847.

During his residence here, Mr. Durham was elected a member of the Board of CountyCommissioners,as stated in another place, and carried the first mail between Oskaloosa and Knoxville. After a long and somewhat eventful life, attended with many conflicts with fickle fortune, having at last secured a competence and a resting place for himself and children, he departed this life, March 15, 1866, aged about seventy years.

Mr. Durham was much respected for his noble traits of character, being of an amiable disposition, kind and obliging to all who had occasion to apply to him for help, in time of need. His departure was, therefore, lamented by a numerous circle of friends and acquaintances, but not as those who mourn without hope.

The next person whose experience as a pioneer, deserves particular notice, was Francis A. Barker. He was born near Poughkeepsie, Dutchess county, Virginia, April 2d, 1798. In his nineteenth year he went to West Virginia, where he engaged in teaching for about two years. In 1820 he went to Morgan county, Ohio, where he married in 1827, and here, after being variously engaged in business, he failed, and surrendered all his possessions for the benefit of his creditors, and, with a large family, came to Iowa, without a dollar with which to begin the world anew.

Thus poorly armed against the privations inseparable from frontier life, he was even less prepared for the afflictions that fell upon him through sickness and death.

It was late in October, 1844, when he reached the locality that he immediately chose for a home. This was section 14, Clay township, on the south side of the Des Moines river. Having obtained a house in the neighborhood in which to shelter his family for a short time, he set about improving his claim, but, in consequence of sickness among his children, it was not till two years later that he got a house of his own ready for occupation.

During this period the sickness in his family resulted in the death of two of his children, a son and a daughter. It was at such a time as this that the troubles incident to comparative isolation from society and the conveniences of a more populous settlement were most severely felt. The only neighbors within convenient call was the family of Matthew Ruple, half a mile distant; the nearest post office and store were at Oskaloosa, fifteen miles distant. Even lumber was so scarce that it was found difficult to procure enough fit to make a coffin, and, for want of help, the burying clothes for the dead children were made up by the bereaved mother and sisters.

It was in November, 1844, that Mr. Barker went on his first milling trip to Brighton, Van Buren county. Leaving a limited supply of provisions at home, it was necessary to make the trip as speedily as possible. The Des Moines was then fordable at Tally's where he crossed it; but a cold rain came down in such quantities as to flood the creeks and sloughs to a dangerous depth. In undertaking to ford a large slough below Wah's point, the cattle were unable to ascend the abrupt bank with the wagon, and in their struggles to do so, one of them was thrown down so as to be in imminent danger of drowning. To extricate the animal as speedily as need be, Mr. B. was compelled to get into the water waist deep. After much effort he succeeded in disengaging them from the wagon, when they immediately landed. But as the wind was blowing a freezing gale and not a sign of shelter short of five miles distant, our hero felt that something must be done to save himself, and the only thing that could be done to that end was to keep moving. So he put the oxen before him, and, with whip in hand, forced them into a rapid trot, he following them closely, which abated not till a house was reached. This run of five miles kept him from freezing, for the weather was so cold that his wet clothing stiffened about his limbs.

It was now late in the day, and nothing could be done toward moving the wagon till morning. So Mr. Barker remained over night, and next morning his host accompanied him out to the scene of his adventure, and assisted him to haul the wagon out of the slough, from which the water had fallen so much as to render the undertaking less difficult than it would otherwise have been.

After much delay in obtaining his needed supply of wheat and corn, which he had to buy, and in getting it ground, Mr. Barker set out for home, which he reached after about a month's absence.

Mr. Barker relates that on making another milling pilgrimage in the autum of '45, he attempted the passage of the large prairie below Oskaloosa, during the night, but got bewildered, and next morning found himself several miles out of the way.

In '46 Mr. Barker was elected probate judge of Marion county, and re-elected to the same office in '47. In '63, owing to age and failing health, he disposed of the estate that he had accumulated by years of toil and many hardships, and passed the remainder of his days in quiet retirement in the city of Knoxville.*

The neighborhood or settlement still remembered by most of the early settlers of Clay township as "the Tong settlement," was located in the southeastern part of the township. Nothing of historical interest relating to this settlement is remembered, except what relates to the individual from whom it derived its name.

Thomas Tong was born near the Potomac river, in Virginia, in the latter part of 1780, emigrated to what is now Adams county, Ohio, (then the frontier) at an early day; from thence to Darke county, in the same state; thence to Elk county,

*He died at his residence there, Jan. 17, 1871, aged 73 years.

Indiana; thence to Van Buren county, Iowa, and from thence to Marion county, in the spring of '45, with two sons and two sons-in-law, forming the settlement as above stated. He died in the winter of '50, aged 70.

Mr. Tong was what might be justly termed a frontiersman, having spent most of his long life on the frontiers of Ohio, Indiana and Iowa. He was skilled in all the arts of frontier life, pertaining to hunting, fishing and trapping. But, notwithstanding this comparatively rough education, he was in all respects a gentleman, upright and generous in all his intercourse with his fellows, and a warm friend to all with whom he had occasion to entertain friendly relations, and a Christain.

Mr. Garret G. Harsin, who is still a resident of this township, and now quite advanced in years, was born in Kentucky, in 1790. He first moved to Illinois at an early day, from thence to Henry county, Iowa, in 1839, and to his present place of residence, in the spring of 1844. On leaving the settlement the family carefully laid in provisions enough to last them till the middle of the summer. But, on reaching their destination, they were so beset by other immigrants, who were not so provident, and who were compelled to borrow or suffer, that their supply soon ran short. Indeed it was twice exhausted, and the family lived for some time on wheat boiled in milk. At this time Mr. H. was improving his claim, and once, when making rails, his noonday lunch consisted of only one green cucumber, without salt. On such diet he toiled on day after day, with failing strength, till he was finally able to make only sixteen rails per day. This was during the absence of his team, and one or two of his sons for another supply of provisions. Of Mr. Harsin's five sons, Geo. W. lives in Clay, James and Martin V. in Union township, John the oldest, near Sioux City, and Garret in Oregon.

John Wise, a native of Virginia, still lives in the township. He moved to his present place of residence in 1843, and made rapid improvement. But some years afterwards one of those destructive calamities that often reduce the most affluent to poverty, a fire, destroyed his dwelling, and all his household property. Mr. Wise enjoys the reputation of being worthy the name he wears. On coming to the country he brought sufficient gold with him to enter his claim, and kept the money through all the hard times that prevailed, till he paid it for his land.

A little adventure may be worth relating in concluding this chapter: In March, 1845, Jasper Koons and wife, crossed to the north side of the Des Moines river on the ice, going on a visit, and left Eliza J. Durham, then quite a young woman, and now Mrs. D. D. Miller, in the care of his house and two small children, on the south side of English. Expecting to return soon, the parents did not leave Miss D. and the little ones as well provided for as would have been required in case of a long absence. But on the third day of their absence the ice began to break up on the river, rendering it impossible for the Koons to return. So early one morning Mr. K. came to the bank, opposite Durhan's and called over to inform Mr. D. of the unprovided and isolated situation of Eliza and the children, and requested that some one should look after them till he should be able to get home. Father Durhan took a pony and proceeded to the rescue immediately. He found English broken up and not very safe to ford; but the case was one of emergency, and he made no delay. He found the sufferers without provisions or fire, and during the night previous, though the weather was quite cool, they had had no fire.

But how to remedy the difficulty was the most difficult part of it. The pony would not be likely to bear two grown persons in safety over such a flood, to say nothing of the addition of the two children to the cargo, and he had not been so well trained to the business as to make one or more voyages through the ice-cold flood without a pilot, or at least without some humane incentive, though it was quite possible that he was as unselfish as any brute of his kind.

But it is said that "where ever there is a will there is a way," out of almost any strait. Though there may be many exceptions to the truth of this proverb, it is true in a majority of cases, and it was in this. Eliza thought of the bed-cord, and proceeded to change it from its appropriate use to that of a tow line for pony. Being prepared for the adventure she tied one end of the cord to the halter. Mr. D. then took the children up and made the crossing, his sister paying out as they went. She then tugged away at the tow line, and Foster urged, till the unwilling vessel was compelled to launch again, and Miss D. soon joined the others in safety.

During the memorable flood of 1851, Mr. Durham and his family took refuge in their ferry boat, as it was moored along the side of the house where they remained till a place could be provided for them on dry land.

To get out of fire was no uncommon circumstance in those early days, and persons have been known to go several miles to get a supply. Matches were not convenient, and it was not every house that could be provided with them.

CHAPTER II.

Clay Township Continued—Wild Bees—Trapping Wolves —A Wolf Story—Hunting Stray Horses—Indian Treating the Dead—Postoffice and Postmaster—Small-pox.

During the first two or three years after the township was first settled, game was quite plentiful, and the settlers had little or no difficulty in supplying themselves with an abundance of fresh meat. Bees were also so plentiful that it requierd but little search by persons ordinarily skilled in the art of bee-hunting, to find a tree filled with the delicious sweetness culled from a wilderness of wild flowers, by those proverbially industrious workers. And, as there were none to claim exclusive proprietorship of these hunting grounds, the finder of a bee-tree became the undisputed owner of it by right of discovery.*

Here, also, as in other parts of the country, wolves were a great annoyance to the settlers. Many of these animals were destroyed in various ways, but they were so numerous that no apparent diminution was observed for some time. One of the settlers had a sow that fell a prey to these ravenous beasts. Such a loss was too aggravating to go unrevenged; so he immediately set a spring trap near the carcass of the hog, so that, in coming to feed upon it, the wolves would be compelled to pass over the concealed instrument, and would be almost sure to put a foot upon it, and instantly find it securely held by a pair of iron jaws. Thus captured, the culprit would submit to his fate with a meekness that might, in the case of almost any animal except the wolf, excite a feeling of pity in the executioner. [It is a somewhat surprising fact that this usually bloodthirsty

*They were so plentilul that the women would sometimes hunt them as a sort of diversion.

and often dangerously combative animal, when caught in a trap, and finding itself completely in the power of its captor, will offer no more resistance than a cur, and will humbly submit to any treatment.] Thus quite a number of these mischievous creatures were destroyed.

An instance is related showing the strength and power of endurance of the wolf. It was in the case of a large black wolf who inadvertently put his foot between the jaws of a heavy steel trap, and found it impossible to get rid of the incumbrance. But, by a violent effort, he broke the fastening by which it was supposed the trap was secured. There was a heavy block also attached to the chain, but the resolute animal took trap and block with him, going by a route not very smooth or even. He was tracked by the trail, and found two miles from where he was caught, still persevering in his efforts to escape.

A somewhat amusing story may be in order here illustrative of the daring character of at least one wolf, if not of the tribe generally. It happened on a cold day in winter, as Messrs. Ose Mathews and Wm. Beckwith were, with wagon and team, crossing a small prairie in the vicinity of English creek. Observing a wolf seated near the middle of the prairie, apparently watching their approach with a coolness quite unnatural to this species of the canine race, they concluded to get as near to him as possible in order to discover what was meant by such unaccountable tameness.

Having cautiously driven to within a few rods of him, they halted, quite surprised at the steady, defiant look that apparently gleamed from his wolfish eyes, and showed yet more unmistakably threatening in the snarling, up-turned lip, displaying a set of dangerous looking teeth. As it happened, the adventurers had no gun, else master wolf would have been speedily punished for his audacity. Still they determined to give him a sample of their courage at close quarters, provided the reckless creature persisted in thus challenging them to the combat. For this purpose they unhitched the team and armed themselves, one with a single tree and the other with a neck yoke, and, with all the caution that the critical situation demanded, marched upon the enemy. To their increased surprise the latter still sat unmoved, and the nearer they got to him the more savage he looked. At length one of the men got within striking distance of the ferocious monster, and was just about to deal him a death blow with the neck yoke, when the glassy look of his eyes betrayed the fact that he was already as deadas he could be, and frozen as hard as a horn. The cause of his death was not apparent, but it was probable that some person had seated him in this attitude for some one else to shoot at.

At an early date the want of enclosures in which to secure their animals, compelled the settlers to turn them out upon the range for pasturage. To prevent horses thus turned loose from meandering too far away, they were sometimes hobbled with ropes. But even this precaution did not always prevent them from straying so far as to give their owners no little trouble to find them. In such a vast range full of little valleys, ravines, groves and large forests, the difficulty of such a search may be easily imagined. Mr. D. T. Durham thus relates an instance of his experience in hunting stray horses:

" Having in the fall of 1844, gone to Ft. Des Moines, at the time of the annual Indian payment, in company with Joseph Clark, we lost our horses whilst there. After hunting for them one or two days, we concluded they might have returned home. We therefore came home on foot, but our horses were not there. So I procured another horse, and returned to look after them. On the way up I called early in the morning, at Jordan's trading house on the river opposite Red Rock, to make inquiries about the trail up the south side of the river, as I had never traveled it. Here they informed me that there was an

Indian about to take the trail, and advised me to go with him so that I might have the benefit of his knowledge of it.

"Our preparations were soon made, and my Indian guide mounted his pony, ladened with two small kegs of whisky, one on each side of his saddle, and a large bladder full in his hand, led the way. As we rode along he partook of the contents of the bladder occasionally, but not enough to intoxicate.

"Whilst passing over the undulating prairies, in what was called the "Three River Country," my guide rode forward at a rapid gait, telling me as he started, that he would wait for me beyond the hill. So I rode along leisurely and, on rounding the point of a grove I came in sight of him. He had dismounted at some Indian graves, and was standing with his head bowed, talking to himself, or perhaps to the spirit of his departed friends. After remaining in that posture a short time, he raised up, took his bladder and poured some of the whisky on the head of one of the graves. Then he would converse a little and pour again. Whilst this was going on I rode up, and would have stopped, but he motioned to me to pass on. I obeyed; and when he overtook me, I asked him the meaning of his conduct at the graves, and if those buried there were his friends. He was not much disposed to be communicative on the subject, but, by pointing to the graves, then to himself, then putting two of his fingers in his mouth, he gave me to understand that they were brothers or near relations.

"My guide kept tolerably sober till towards night, when we occasionally met other Indians, whom he treated, and drank freely himself at every meeting. So, by the time we came within sight of the fort, he had became apparently quite indifferent as to whether he went any farther or not, and I left him 'alone in his glory.'"

Next day Mr. D. found his horses in the hands of a party of Indians, a few miles below the fort. The legs of some of the animals were severely gaulded by the ropes with which they were hobbled, and the Indians were endeavoring to cure them and with some success. They readily gave them up.

The first post office that was established in this township was at Durham's Ford in the latter part of the winter, or early in the spring of 1849, Chas. H. Durham, P. M. In 1850 it was moved farther south, to section 4, township 75, and the name changed to "English Settlement," John H. Whaley, P. M. In 1852 the office was again removed to section 18, with Samuel Brekenridge as P. M., where it still remains under the management of Macklan Copeland. Pola post office, section 31, town. 76, was established in 1854, with Joseph Clark as P. M. D. T. Durham, present incumbent, appointed in 1856. Daily mails east and west between Pella and Knoxville.

In the summer of 1849 the township was visited by the small pox that prevailed to such an extent as caused quite a panic among the people. This was partly owing to its unexpected appearance, many being exposed to it ere they were aware of its presence. About sixty cases of it, and of that mild type known as the varioloid occurred, and much suffering was experienced by the afflicted in consequence of lack of attention. So prevalent was the fear of contracting the disease that a number of cases proved fatal. Otherwise the township has been known to be generally healthy, more especially since it has been well settled and the most of its surface reduced to cultivation.

Population of Clay by the United States census of 1870:

Native	1342
Foreign	30
Total	1372

CHAPTER III.

Lake Prairie Township—Its Geography and Early History—Names of first Settlers—Wellington Nossaman—Stump Mill—Pottery—Col. Alley—Shooting Affray—The Mathewses—First Birth—Wm. Welch—Keokuk, Iowa—An Adventure.

Lake Prairie township consists of township 77, range 18, and all of townships 75 and 76, range 18, north of the Des Moines river. It is bounded on the north by Jasper county, on the east by Mahaska county, on the south by Clay township, with the Des Moines river as its boundary line, and on the west by Polk and Summit.

The principal streams that run through it are Skunk river and Thunder creek. Skunk river runs through the northeast corner of the township, entering at section six, and after persuing a meandering course, leaves it at about thirteen. This stream is very crooked, and the numerous ponds and bayous that have been caused by the changes of its channel, making reservoirs of stagnant water, has rendered the neighborhood somewhat noted for ague. Thunder creek rises in Summit, runs through the north half of Lake Prairie, and empties into Skunk on the east line of the couuty. There are several smaller streams not named on the map, from which we obtain much ot our information about the geography of the township.

This township is well timbered along the larger streams, and the land there is more or less hilly, but beautifully undulating on the upland prairies.

No extensive coal mines have been opened.

Lake Prairie was originally what was called Lake Precinct, but in January, '46, the north half of it (township 77, range 18) was declared a township and called Jefferson, and the place of holding election was at the house of Richard Everwine. At the same time the south half was called Lake, with the place of election at Wilson Stanley's on Lake Prairie. [For an account of such changes as took place in its southern boundary, see history of Clay.] But by a special act of the State Legislature, during the winter of '47-8, both of these townships were constituted one township and called Lake Prairie. This name was taken from the long lake extending two miles below Amsterdam, between which and the river lies an extensive and beautiful prairie.* This lake, judging from its size and appearance, was at some remote period, the channel of the river, and extended so as to intersect with it at each end; but since, by the accumulation of ice or other drift at the upper end, the water was forced to cut a new channel, a large part of the old one has been gradually filling up by the washings of freshets and the eath that has been brought down from the uplands by rains, through successive ages, and forest tree are now growing over the abandoned channel.

Most prominent among those who first settled in this township, are Wellington and Levi Nossaman, William and John Welsh, Wilson Stanley, George Gillaspy, Green T. Clark, Thomas Tuttle, John B. and Robert Hamilton, James L. Warren, Asa and Jasper Koons, John Gillaspy, John and William George, William Cayton, Ose Mathews, (who afterwards settled in Red Rock,) William Bainbridge and Jacob C. Brown. We have been able to obtain biographical sketches of a few of

*On this prairie were once a couple of beautiful springs that were resorted to by the Indians of the village near by, and attracted the attention of the settlers by their peculiar appearance and character. They were from ten to fifteen feet wide, and one of them of unknown depth, filled with a very light sediment, through which no solid bottom could be reached by sounding with the longest poles. The water would rise and fall, and from the subterranean depths would occasionally come a sound resembling thunder. The Indians called it Thunder pring.

these which will now be given, together with their experiences in pioneer life.

Wellington Nossaman was born in Monroe county, Va., in 1817. At the age of two years was taken by his parents to Pike county, Ky.; in '32 moved to Marion county, Ind.; in '42 came to Jefferson county, Iowa; was married on the 17th of March; came to this county in April, '43, and made a claim in the south part of the township.

Here Mr. N. lived in a pole shanty, roofed with bark, that had been hastily put up for a temporary shelter, till a better building could be provided on his claim and a patch of corn planted. During this time Mrs. W. and Levi Nossaman were the only women in the settlement.

In the fall of '43, John B. Hamilton built the first house proper, a round log cabin, intended for something more than temporary use; and Mr. Nossaman built the next one immediately afterwards.

At this early date the difficulty of obtaining breadstuffs induced Mr. N., in connection with Wm. Welch, to put up what they called a stump mill, to grind corn. It was constructed to run by horse power, and when in motion the entire mill turned on a pivot under the burrs. It was capable of grinding about one bushel of corn per hour, and supplied quite a demand in the settlement. During the same year ('46) and at the same place they also established a horse-power saw-mill, and manufactured the first lumber in the county north of the river. In addition to these temporary, though valuable enterprises, they erected a pottery there, and manufactured some pretty good ware. The remains of the pottery are still visible four miles south of Pella. In after years Mr. Nossaman, in connection with Joseph Porter, built the first steam saw-mill in Pella, which was also the first machinery in the county run by steam. His lime kiln, four miles south of Pella, was, perhaps, the first permanent establishment of the kind in the county.

He also kept a store there, on his farm, known in the neighborhood as "the one-horse store." During the flood of '51 he erected a temporary grist mill, that was run by a band from an armed upright shaft, and ground eight bushels of corn per day. This mill was run day and night for six weeks, to supply the demand till the flood abated. In '53 Mr. N. purchased the Franklin House, in Pella, and kept hotel and a mercantile establishment in it at the same time, for about two years.

Previous to the organization of the county, Mr. Nossaman attended court at Oskaloosa, where he assisted to build the first court house of Mahaska county, and was one of the first grand jurors of that county court. In '45 he was elected to the office of coroner of this county, and, by virtue of that office, acted as high sheriff during the absence of the sheriff elect. In '46 or '47 he was appointed deputy assessor, and was the first person that assessed the Holland colony.

The first justice elected in Lake Prairie was William Bainbridge, and Wellington Nossaman was the first constable. The first election came off on Lake Prairie, at the house of Mr. Bainbridge, about half a mile above the crossing now known as Durham's ford or ferry, near the locality of an Indian village called Keokuk's town, consisting of forty or fifty huts.

The first lawyer resident in the county was John W. Alley, more commonly known as Colonel Alley. Of his history previous to his settlement on Lake Prairie, we have been able to obtain no particulars. He immigrated from Indiana, and settled at the place above mentioned at an early date, after which he moved to Red Rock and from thence to Afton, Union county, where he died.

His reputation as an attorney was so good that he was con stantly employed, and scarcely a case came upon trial in the Des Moines valley, within the bounds of the county, that the Colonel was not employed to pettifog for one side or the other and such was his popularity that it was supposed that whoever was lucky enough to secure his services was pretty sure of success in spite of justice. But, like many engaged in the profession, he was not scrupulous as to the means of winning a case, especially if the case chanced to be a difficult one, which was very frequent. At such times he would flatter the justice by language like this: "Now, in addressing a gentleman of your discernment and intelligence, it is scarcely necessary to remind you," etc., and then proceed to quote the law of some other State provided he could find none among our own statutes that could be construed favorably to his client. It is related that one of the justices' dockets contained the record of the decision of a case in something like this style: "I have examined this case pro and con. Colonel Alley knows all about it, and says it is so and so, and I believe it is," and rendered his decision accordingly. Apparently the Colonel had been giving the justice some private counsel.

During his residence in this township the Colonel had some trouble with the Koonses in relation to a claim at the lower end of White Breast prairie, and was fired upon and slightly wounded in the arm, one night, as he was on his way home. Having ascertained the person of his intended assassin, he ambushed himself near the disputed claim, and awaited the appearance of Jasper Koons, who was hauling rails. When his intended victim hove in sight and was within easy range, the Colonel fired and the bullet knocked the ox whip off the fellow's shoulder. Soon after this a compromise was effected, and Koons surrendered the claim on the receipt of a stipulated sum.

A few more instances might be related in which the Colonel was more or less concerned, but, as they transpired in Red Rock, they will more properly appear in the history of that township.

Among those mentioned in the list of early settlers, who

took claims on the first of May, '43, was Ose Matthews and his families, consisting of Drs. Reuben and Homer Matthews, Simpson B., Warren, and Ose, Jr., together with George Reynolds and Ray Alfrey, sons-in-law.

Ose Matthews, Sr., was born in Massachusetts, March 14, 1784; moved to Troy, N. Y.,—date not remembered—where he resided several years; thence to Lake county, Ohio, in 1817; thence to White Pigeon Prairie in '37 ; thence to Iowa, and stopped below Old Agency in '42; thence to Lake Prairie in '43, and settled there at the time above stated. In '46 or '47 they sold out to the Hollanders, and Mr. Matthews settled again a short distance above Red Rock village, in what is now Union township. After living here about a year he went to Red Rock village, where he lived with his son Simpson several years, till the latter went west, when he made his home with his son-in-law, George Reynolds, in Summit township, till he died, Dec. 20, 1865.

The most important event connected with this family during their residence on Lake Prairie, was the birth of a daughter to Mr. and Mrs. Alfrey, Jan. 18, '44, being the first white child born in the county north of the Des Moines river. She was called Amanda Lenora. She is now married, and lives in Des Moines.

What further relates to the Matthews and Alfreys will be found in the history of Red Rock.

Among those whose names are more or less identified with the early history of Marion county is William Welch, at present a citizen of Pella. As such, his biography deserves a place among these pages.

Mr. Welch was born in the little villiage of Huntsville, on the Yadkin river, N. C., Jan. 1st., 1800, being a little more than seventy-two years of age at this present writing. Went to Wilkes county, same State--date not mentioned—and from thence to Richmond, Indiana, in 1827 ; thence to Macbonaugh, Illinois, in '31; from thence, in consequence of the breaking out of the Black Hawk war, he, together with many other settlers, went further south, leaving their claims and some other property for whoever might succeed them. Then, in '36, Mr. W. immigrated to Iowa, and settled at what is now Bonaparte, Van Buren county. At that time the territory was under the political jurisdiction of Wisconsin, and was known only by that name. Here Mr. W. (being a potter by trade), erected the first pottery in the territory, the slight remains of which may still be seen in that locality. At one time during his residence there he was also employed as recorder, and was compelled to find his own stationery, which, owing to its exhorbitant price and difficulty of obtaining it from a distance, together with his own extreme poverty, he finally supplied himself with it at considerable sacrifice. Then it was after much delay and difficulty that he obtained only a part of his fees for this service.

In 1844, Mr. Welch came to Lake Prairie, and settled in the timber, about four miles south of the present site of Pella. Here in connection with Mr. Nossaman, as already stated in this chapter, he erected a pottery and a mill in the locality In 1845, Mr. W. was elected to the office of County Commissioner, in which office he served one year. See chapter IX.

During the first year of settlement, parties of Indians were frequently seen passing and repassing along their long frequented route up and down the Des Moines valley, visiting the trading houses and returning to their villages. These villages were little better than mere camps, consisting of huts and tents built without any regularity for streets or alleys, each family putting up their portable dwelling on whatever locality best suited their taste or convenience. Hunting and fishing were the principal occupations of the inhabitants of these villages; and should game become scarce in the neighborhood of a village, the people could easily gather up their houses and load them, with all their baggage on ponies, and dogs and women, and move to some more plentiful locality, leaving no traces of the deserted town, except a few stakes and poles that had made the scanty frame work of their huts.

Only one village was known to be located in the county, which was the one already mentioned in this chapter, called Keokuk's town. It was on Lake Prairie, near Durham's ford. Whether it was at any time the residence of the renowned chief is not known, for the place was abandoned soon after the whites began to settle in the neighborhood. But it is quite probable that he had some thing to do with its location, and possibly made it his head-quarters. The remains of this village were noticeable some time after it was taken away.*

Notwithstanding the generally friendly disposition manifested by the Indians toward the earlier settlers, it is apparent that they harbored a feeling of jealousy toward those who had come into the territory previous to the time stipulated in the treaty. Yet, restrained perhaps by fear of punishment, they made no demonstrations calculated to lead to an open rupture. The only instance of the kind, showing a resentment that their savage natures prompted them to gratify, had they dared do so, occurred as follows:

On or about the 7th of April, 1843, Green T. Clark, Robert Hamilton and Henry McPherson, with two or three others, all of whom had come into the neighborhood of Lake Prairie in search of a location, were encamped on the river near where the Curtis farm now is. They had been prospecting through the country, and on this occasion the company was divided,

---

* During the residence of the Indians at this villiage, the chief Appanoose was there at one time; and the wife of Dr. Ober, a settler, and a lady of much refinement, desiring to have a conversation with the "big Ingin," opened it by asking him what disease Wappalo died of. Appanoose could speak some plain English, but not being acquainted with the technical teterms of polite society, he promptly answered her in language that meant "diarrhea," but that brought a blush to the fair cheek of the lady, and indisposed her to continue the conversation.

and the three above named persons went up the river whilst the others went in an opposite direction. Having wended their way some distance through the heavily timbered and comparatively trackless wilderness of the Des Moines bottom, in the direction of Red Rock, the approach of night warned them that it would be prudent to return to camp as speedily as possible.

But after they had begun to retrace their steps a party of Indians confronted them in the same narrow trail. Fearing some possible mischief from the savages, they changed front and commenced a retreat, though not by flight, keeping up Indian file order, thinking to avoid contact with them. But as they were descending a slight declivity, at the bottom of which was a pond of water, around which the path led, one of the Indians, who was about a hundred and fifty yards behind and a little above them, fired at them, and the bullet passed in such close proximity to their heads as to not only be very distinctly heard, but felt by the disturbance of the air, and struck in the water in front of them. Turning to see from whence the firing had come, they saw one of the savages running from the rank as though in pursuit of something, and then suddenly stop and search with apparent carefulness among the grass for the game he made believe he had killed. Evidently the villain had fired upon them for the purpose of killing or frightening them; and then, to avoid suspicion and escape the punishment he knew he deserved for the act, he performed the game farce with the cleverness of a professional actor. But our adventurers had neither the time nor disposition just then, to bring the culprit to account for his conduct. To avoid any further attentions from such cowardly assassins, required some haste and vigilence, and they soon succeeded, returning safely to camp that night.

CHAPTER IV.

Lake Prairie continued---George Gillaspy—James L. Warren--Indian Worship—Short of Provisions--Tribute to the memory of Dr. Warren.

Among those who came to the county before the memorable First of May, was the no less distinguished personage, than George Gillaspy, and we proceed to open this chapter with a brief sketch of his history.

Mr. Gillaspy was born in Shelby county, Kentucky, July 15, 1814. At the age of 13 years his father moved to Johnson county, Indiana, where he remained about five years, and then returned to Kentucky. From thence he came to Iowa in 1840, and settled in Louisa county, and from thence to Marion county in the spring of 1843, stopping in the timber near Lake Prairie on the evening of the 24th of April. That night he took his wagon to pieces and covered it in different places to prevent the dragoons from discovering it, in which case it would have been subject to seizure and himself to expulsion from the territory.

As midnight ushered in the long desired first of May, Mr. G. marked out his claim, as did many others who had made selections and been awaiting the time to establish them legally. After securing his claim Mr. G. boarded for some time at Wellington Nossaman's, making rails for twenty-five or thirty cents per hundred. In the spring of '46 he was appointed assessor, and in August of the same year succeeded James Walters as sheriff,* and was re-elected to the same office in '48.

*When Mr. G. was canvassing the county as candidate for sheriff, he carried his horse feed with him in a sack. We note this simple fact merely in contrast with his late tours through the state as a candidate for governor.

In '49 he was elected to the office of treasurer of the board of public works. On the 7th of October, '49, he moved to Ottumwa and took charge of the state land office. In '50 was re-elected to that post, and in '52 was appointed by Gov. Hempstead register of the state land office. In '53 (the legislature having made the incumbent of that office elective by the people) he was elected to fill it two years. At the end of this term he commenced mercantile business in Ottumwa, but two years later sold out and engaged in land speculation with considerable success. In '56 he was elected a delegate to the constitutional convention that came off during the year following. In the fall of '57 he was the nominee for lieutenant governor on the same ticket with Hon. Benj. M. Samuels; and in '69 headed the democratic ticket as candidate for governor.

Mr. Gillaspy still lives in Ottumwa, engaged in buying and selling cattle and hogs, and in packing pork in Chicago. In person he is a somewhat remarkable man, being of almost giant proportions.

Not less distinguished, nor less favorably remembered among those who settled in this township at a very early date, was Dr. James L. Warren, who died at his residence near Peoria, Mahaska county, Jan. 18, 1870, aged 69 years. He was born in Green county, Tenn., July 1st, 1801; immigrated to Iowa and settled in Lee county in 1841. He made his first claim in what is now Mahaska county, where he cut some logs and employed a man to put them up in the shape of a cabin; but he afterwards abandoned the idea of settling there, and made a claim about three miles south-east of where Pella now is, where he succeeded in planting about twenty acres of corn and wheat in the spring following.

Those who came up at the same time and helped to found a settlement were John B. Hamilton, Robert Hamilton, Henry Miller, Green T. Clark and Henry McPherson. On their way up the dragoons refused to let them pass Libertyville with their wagons, so they packed on horses what provisions they thought would last them till after the first of May, and proceeded. Approaching an Indian village near the present location of Oskaloosa, the Doctor, who had some practical knowledge of military tactics, called a halt, and suggested that they march through the town in military order. This was agreed to by all except an old man named McPherson, who thought such a maneuver would be regarded by the Indians as a challenge to fight. Being excused from service the old man made a wide circuit to the north of town, still keeping in view, in order to witness the result, whilst the remainder obeyed the command to "forward march." On entering the place they found the inhabitants engaged in worship, in consequence of which they paid little or no attention to this mock military demonstration. The men were collected in a large tent, seated in a circle, singing in a monotonous, drawling tone to the equally musical rattle of beans in gourds, that they shook up and down, as an accompaniment to their voices. The door of the tent was closed against intruders, but Robert Hamilton, having an ungovernable curiosity to witness the performance, raised the tent wall near the ground and peeped under. Not one of the solemn- faced worshipers took the least notice of this breach of good manners; nor did they for an instant seem to permit their attention to be diverted from their devotions; but an old squaw, who seemed to be standing guard without, noticed the intruder, and indignantly ordered him away. Not being instantly obeyed, she took hold of Robert, gave him a violent pull, and uttered the word "Manitou" (God), as an explanation of the sacredness and privacy of the place and performance, at which he deemed it advisable to desist. Soon after leaving town our heroes were rejoined by McPherson, who was rejoiced to find them all safe and unhurt.

On the 26th of April they reached the present location of Pella, and contemplated making claims there; but, owing to its distance from timber, they thought it very probable that it would be many years ere much improvement could be made there, and the land become valuable. So they made choice of the timber about three miles to the southeast.

But ere the time came for them to get their wagons, and the remainder of their provisions, what they had brought with them began to come short. As soon as possible Green B. Clark was sent for the wagons, and some of the others resorted to hunting as a means of economizing the scanty remainder of breadstuffs. But the bread finally quite gave out, and hunting, even in those early days, was not so reliable a means of supporting the demand for food as some might suppose. It is said that game was plentiful, which was generally true, but, like fishing, the taking of it depended upon skill and good luck. An instance is related of an old settler named Cunningham, who still lived in Mahaska county, who, by hunting, maintained a half starved existence for eight or ten days, on his claim near Oskaloosa, not daring to leave it lest it should be "jumped." Our settlers now found it necessary to use energy and skill or starve. Hunger already incited them to do their best. Robert Hamilton shouldered his rifle and went in search of a turkey, or anything else he could find that would do to eat, whilst Henry Miller went in search of a bee-tree. Both were successful; and, what added much to their good fortune, their wagons came the next day, bringing breadstuffs and other conveniences.

Dr. Warren was among the first ministers of the M. E. Church who preached in the county, and organized the first class west of Libertyville. He was licensed as a local preacher in 1828; ordained deacon at Oskaloosa in 1852, and was ordained an elder by Bishop Ames in 1863. He also commenced the practice of medicine in 1831, which he continued till a short time before his death. In this he was very successful during his residence in this county, especially in the management of the miasmatic diseases, to which the early settlers were subject, and his field of practice often extended from Oskaloosa to " Tool's Point," now Monroe, Jasper county, and over a large territory north and south of this route. Over this wide field he ministered both in spiritual and temporal things. He was a man universally loved and respected by all who knew him. Many instances illustrative of his charitable nature, and many acts of kindness performed by him, have been related to us, and are well remembered by many who have shared the privations of pioneer life with him. His departure was made joyful by the hope of eternal life.

Green T. Clark and Robert Hamilton still live in the township. The latter is at present a citizen of Pella, whilst his brother, John B., lives in Kansas, whence he emigrated in 1862.

CHAPTER V.

Lake Prairie Continued—Thomas Tuttle—The Buffingtons—A sad Accident—Jacob B. Brown—First Religious Societies—First Orchard.

The first settler in the neighborhood of Pella was Thomas Tuttle, whose present residence is in Vandalia, Jasper county. He first came to the State in 1838, and settled in Jefferson county the year following. In 1843 he came to this county, arriving there on the 13th of May. Not having any children and no other help, Mrs. T. helped him to build a cabin in the edge of the nearest timber north of the present site of Pella. Soon after this they made a claim of part of the town plat of Pella, and put up a claim pen on what is now "Garden Square." This cabin remained there, and was for a portion of the time occupied several years after the city had grown up around it.

When this lonely pair took up their residence in the county they were not aware of the existence of another family of white people within twenty miles of them. After being here a month or so it was found necessary to replenish their stock of breadstuff ere it should run too low; so it was decided to go to Fort Madison for a supply, Mrs. T. to accompany her husband or to stay at home as she chose. She chose the latter, and for nine days and nights was the sole occupant of the little cabin, except a big cat,* seeing no human beings except Indians, as they passed and re-passed, and occasionally came in without first announcing their presence or uttering any kind of salutation.

*This cat was still living within the last few years; a remarkable instance of feline longevity.

In August following, four families named Buffington settled three miles north of Tuttle's, forming what was soon after styled "The Buffington Settlement," and for a year these families were their nearest neighbors. The names of those who headed these families were William, James, Samuel and Abram.

A painful accident occurred in the family of James Buffington just previous to reaching their new home. Their youngest were a pair of twin boys, about six months old. On the way it was discovered that one of them was missing from the wagon. Search being made, it could nowhere be found, and the anxious parent prosecuted the search along the trail they had come for two or three miles, and at last found the infant barely alive, with one of its thighs crushed and flattened by the passage of a wagon wheel. It had, probably, been so stunned by falling from the wagon that it was unable to utter any cry. So far as they were aware, there was no surgeon within a hundred miles; so they bound up the limb and dressed it to the best of their ability. It was, however, too badly mangled to be saved, and eventually came off at the hip joint; but, strangely enough, the child recovered.

The next family that settled in the neighborhood of Pella was that of Jacob C. Brown. He was a native of North Carolina, and became a pioneer at an early period in life. First moved to Tennessee, and from thence to Illinois, in 1830, where, with his family, and but a half dollar in money, he began the battle of life in the wilderness, and became inured to the privations of frontier life before he came to Iowa. In May, 1844, he settled near where Pella now is, where he remained till '47, when he sold his claim to the Hollanders, and moved to Summit. He now lives in Monroe, Jasper Co.

James Duese also settled near Pella, in 1845. He afterwards moved to Summit, but is now living in Minnesota.

The Methodists and Baptists were the first religious denominations that organized societies in Lake Prairie township. The first Methodist class was formed at John B. Hamilton's, and the first Baptist church was organized at Aaron Foulk's by Rev. Moses J. Post, and the place of holding service was at Nossaman's school house, four miles south of Pella. The first persons that received the ordinance of baptism, by immersion, in this township, and in the county, were Sarah Nossaman and Emily Barker, administered by the Rev. M. J. Post. The first Baptist preacher that was licensed to preach the gospel in this township, and also the first in the county, was Rev. G. C. Curtis.

The first apple orchards planted in this township were by Green T. Clark and John B. Hamilton, in the spring of '47, in sections 36 and 25, town. 76. The trees, (about fifty in all), were brought from Illinois. Most of them are still alive, and bearers, and some of the more thrifty ones measure a foot in diameter.

CHAPTER VI.

Lake Prairie continued—The Holland Colony—Organization in Holland—Voyage—Sojourn at St. Louis—Selecting the Location—Early Life in Pella—First Township Officers—Church Organization—First Hotel, Post Office, School, etc.--Amsterdam—Leersdam—Death of Henrg P. Scholte.

A large majority of the inhabitants of Lake Prairie are Hollanders, and we now proceed to give what little we have been able to obtain relating to their history as a colony. We had hoped to make this narrative something better than a mere sketch, but, owing to the difficulty of enlisting the aid of those who had it in their power to furnish us with details, we have been compelled to content ourself with what we have, and request the reader to do the same.*

It has been claimed by some that the religious intolerance exercised by the Established Church of the Netherlands, towards the Reformed Church, was the principal cause that led to the emigration of so large a body of people at one time, but though this may have been one among the reasons originally assigned, it was not the principal reason. The crowded state of the population in the old country, demanded a wider field in which the middle and lower classes might better their worldly circumstances, and this may be relied upon as the main reason.

Prominent among those who took an active and leading part in the organization of this enterprise, was Henry P. Scholte.

*It is to the kindness of Mr. A. G. Betten, who furnished me with some verbal statements, and to some manuscript from the pen of the late Henry P. Scholte, loaned me by his son, that I am indebted for the leading facts contained in this chapter.

As a leader of the colony, his life was so identified with it, that we may very conveniently blend a sketch of it in connection with this narrative.

Mr. Scholte was born in Amsterdam, Holland, in 1805, and early in life conceived the idea of entering the naval academy and becoming an officer in the navy. But, his mother being much opposed to this plan, he abandoned it. But, being of an active temperament, and averse to idleness, he learned the carpenter's trade, and made some advancement in drawing. When about 17 years of age his father died, which circumstance called his attention to the subject of religion, and his interest in this subject eventually ripened into a desire to preach the gospel. With a view to prepare himself for this occupation, he began the study of the languages, and made so much progress in this department that he was prepared to enter the seminary at Amsterdam in 1821. In 1824 he passed through the literary examination at the University of Leyden, and began the study of theology at that institution. During a powerful religious revival in Holland, in 1826, in which two converted Israelites took an active part, he became acquainted with numerous leading Christians of various denominations from England, France, Germany and the Netherlands, who were on a visit to Holland, and became so powerfully convinced of the narrowness of sectarianism that he abandoned it, regarding even church organizations of secondary importance. He was, therefore, quoting his own words, "prevented from clothing his faith in the straight-jacket of ecclesiastical formalism."

In 1830 a rebellion broke out in Belgium ; Mr. S. enlisted as a soldier to help put it down. In 1832 he returned to Leyden, passed through the theological examination at the University, and was licensed to preach. In the same year he was examined in the synod of Holland, and in the beginning of 1833 was installed as minister of the Gospel in the National Reform Church establishment.

Here, however, he began to experience trouble resulting from his refusal to submit to the established forms and doctrines that he found had produced a spiritual degeneracy in the church. His decided opposition to a sectarianism that amounted almost to bigotry, brought down upon him the enmity of the national clergy; and this, in 1835, resulted in a separation. Mr. S. and a few other ministers, followed by a large number of lay members, withdrew from the National Church, and became a separate and independent organization.

But they were not permitted to remain so undisturbed. Instigated by the Synod of Holland, the government commenced and for some time carried on a series of persecutions against the rebels, consisting of fines and imprisonments, basing the legality of these acts upon a law of Napoleon forbidding the assembling together of more than twenty persons for religious services.

But these persecutions, instead of putting down the rebellion, only increased the number of its adherents, till finally the government became weary of so unprofitable an undertaking, and soon after the accession of William II. to the throne persecution ceased entirely.

In his ministerial labors Mr. Scholte became acquainted with the middle and poorer classes of the country, and had ample opportunities to observe the disparity in the social conditions of the various classes, the result of pecuniary circumstances—how difficult it was for the poor, and even those of small means, to support themselves and their families, to say nothing of attaining to that social position that merit should entitle them. In the kindness of heart he began to think about contriving some plan by which relief could be rendered. But he could think of none that could be successfully carried out within the narrow and crowded limits of the Netherlands; so it occurred to him that immigration to some new country would be the only practicable means of attaining the end desired. In this view he associated himself with another minister of some eminence and ability, and together they made diligent efforts to inform themselves in relation to the natural, social and political conditions of various countries that might become an asylum for the poor and oppressed.

But previous to directing public attention to the subject, they wrote a letter to their Minister of Colonies, asking for vessels and a free passage to the island of Java; and for permission to make free settlement there; but as the government did not seem disposed to permit such a settlement to be made in her East Indian possessions, they turned their attention to America. Among other portions of this continent at first favorably thought of, was Texas. But after obtaining all the information that could be gathered, relating to its geography and climate, it was decided to be too warm. Missouri was also had in view, but the existence of slavery there forbade its choice as a location. Finally Iowa, then the youngest sister in the family of states, was chosen as the land of refuge.

Nothing more now remained but to enlist the interests of a sufficient number of others to form a colony self-sustaining in its corporation. The first meeting for this purpose was held in Leersdam, July, 1846; the second at Utrecht in December of the same year. At the latter meeting an organization was effected, Henry P. Scholte being elected President, A. J. Betten, Vice President, and Isaac Overcamp, Secretary. A board or committee was also appointed, whose duties were to receive members on certain conditions; regulate the supplies of provisions; and arrange for means of transportation. This board consisted of G. H. Overcamp, G. F. Cecaque, John Reedfelt, and A. Wigny. One among the conditions on which an individual could become a member of the association, was that he must be a sober, industrious, moral person. It was not strictly required that he should be religious, but that he should not be an atheist or an infidel, and should entertain a proper respect for the religious opinions of the majority. Roman Catholics were also entirely excluded from becoming members of the association. Another important condition was that all members who could command the means should take charge of one or more worthy persons or families who desired to go, but were too poor to pay their own way.

By the spring following (1847) the members of the association numbered about 1300, and between 700 and 800 were prepared to go. Four sail vessels were chartered to carry them to Baltimore, and in the early part of April three of them sailed from Rotterdam, and one from Amsterdam. It took about fifty days, more or less, to make the passage, arriving at Baltimore in the early part of June, where they were soon joined by Mr. Scholte, who, with his family, had came by steamer. During the voyage nine deaths and three births occurred.

Their conveyances from thence as far as Pittsburgh, were canal boats and rail cars, and from Pittsburgh to St. Louis they came by steamers, where they arrived in July. Here they were received by E. F. Grafe, a German, who had been for some time a resident of St. Louis, and had been apprised of their coming out here. It was necessary that they should sojourn for a few weeks to make certain preparations for the remaining portion of the journey, and for final settlement. A temporary shelter was prepared for their accommodation a little without the city limits, where they remained till the latter part of August.

Now, like the children of Israel, on their approach to the promised land, they found it advisable to send forward spies to spy out the land. To this duty were appointed Henry P. Scholte, Isaac Overcamp and John Reedfeldt. They were not in any sense of the term spies, their object being to seek out a suitable location for the colony somewhere within the limits of Iowa, the State they had chosen as the land of their adoption, and that with not only the full consent, but with the best wishes of the natives.

On reaching Fairfield the committee met with Rev. M. J. Post, whose duties as a minister of the Gospel, and also as a mail carrier, had taken him through the frontier as far as Fort Des Moines, and made him acquainted with many of the settlers along the Des Moines River. Mr. Post recommended the beautiful prairie lying between the Des Moines and Skunk rivers in Marion county as a suitable location for a colony, and piloted the commissioners to the place. They were very much pleased with it, and immediately set about making such preliminary arrangements as they could make, necessary to a permanent settlement. Mr. Scholte, as treasurer and agent of the colonists, purchased the claims of such of the settlers as resided within the limits of the two townships designed to be appropriated to the use of the colony, together with such live stock and farming utensils as were deemed indispensable to farming.

On their return to St. Louis a company of mechanics were sent forward with tools and means for procuring materials to put up temporary shelters for the accommodation of the main body of the immigrants, on their arrival. One large shed was erected near what is now the western limit of the city of Pella, in which a large number of families took shelter till they could improvise such other accommodations as they could for their better comfort, individually. Many of the famillies took up their abode in the cabins recently occupied by those who had sold their claims and moved away; while others built themselves houses of the tough sod of the prairie, roofed with the long grass that grew abundantly in the sloughs. In order to afford as much room as possible within these necessarily small structures, a cellar-like excavation was first made in the earth, around which was built a sod wall of two or three feet in height, over which was spread the grass roof on a light frame of sticks.

In some instances the walls were even less than two feet high and the roof reached nearly to the ground.

These curious looking huts were scattered promiscuously over and around where Pella now stands, the owners having temporarily settled down at such places as suited their own convenience, giving the town an irregularity and crudeness singular to behold in a civilized and Christian land. Mr. Scholte occupied the cabin built by Thomas Tuttle as a claim pen, that stood for several years in what is now Garden Square, (see Chapter V), till his more substantial and comparatively princely residence was completed.

In such houses as we have described, some of the Hollanders passed two winters. Though sufficiently close and deep to keep out the cold, it may be supposed that they were not entirely proof against the damp of a wet season. The grass roofs would leak, the walls would crumble, and the water would rise up through the floors and make it necessary to bail out or move. I am told that one family, on getting up in the morning, found their room half full of water.

And another annoyance connected with these earthy habitations was the prevalence of snakes. Attracted by the heat, or by the smell of food, they would creep into the walls and roofs, and sometimes fall inside. Not unfrequently one of these sneaking, hateful representatives of Satan, regardless of consequences, would drop himself down the sod chimney into the fireplace, and (as happened in a few instances) into the soup that was being cooked to make the most, if not the only article of food for the meal. Snakes are not numerous in Holland, and were, of course, not much admired, even as an article of food, by the newly imported natives of that country; and it is, therefore, not surprising if such an addition to the ingredients of the soup aroused a feeling of disgust not calculated to sharpen the appetite.

We may here relate an anecdote connected with sod house

life in the colony, which, though not a snake story, will be found of equally startling interest. One night some cattle happened to be grazing in the neighborhood of one of these houses, and it also happened that, as the grazing was not abundant, one of the oxen went prospecting about for something better. Seeing the house he evidently mistook it for a small haystack, and "went for it." Finding the coarse, dry grass not so very good, he got upon it with his fore feet in search of better feed, when the weak structure gave way beneath his weight, and let him plunge headlong into the regions below. The family were asleep till the crash came and awakened them to a bewildered consciousness of some awful calamity befalling them, and their exclamations of fright added terror to the already terrified beast, and he made his exit by the door with all practicable speed, probably resolving, ox fashion, for ever more to keep clear of such haystacks. Fortunately no one was hurt, and no serious damage was done, except to the house.

Soon after the settlement of the colony it was found necessary to organize some kind of government for judicial purposes, in accordance with the State and general government. But few of the Hollanders could speak or understand English, and it was therefore indispensable that at least a majority of the township officers should be chosen from among them. So to enable them to do so, the General Assembly was appealed to, who passed a special act organizing the township of Lake Prairie, and enabling the colonists to elect their own officers, so soon as they should take the oath of allegiance, indicating their intention of becoming citizens of the United States. Immediately following this, L. W. Babbitt, clerk of the District Court, administered the required oath, and on the day specified for an election, the following officers were chosen: Robert Hamilton, A. J. Betton, and P. Weller, Trustees; G. T. Clark and H. P. Scholte, Justices; James Muntingh,

Clerk; and Levi Nossaman, one of the Constables, the other not being remembered. The assessing was done by W. Nossaman, then acting as deputy Sheriff.

Pella was originally surveyed by Stanford Doud, in 1848, from the 8th to the 15th of May inclusive, on the north half of section 10, and on the south half of the south half of section 3, township 76, range 19. It was re-surveyed in 1849, by ——— Clemons, when the plat was greatly enlarged to accommodate an addition of several hundred that arrived that summer and autumn. The name of Pella was suggested by Mr. Scholte, from the signification of the term in the Hebrew, *a city of refuge*, and was the name of a small town in Palestine.

The Church, though retaining the confession of faith of the Reformed Church of Holland, was organized as the Christian Church of Pella, and admitted persons of all other orthodox denominations to communion with them. It is still, however, known as the Reformed Church, and has a numerous membership.

The first house of entertainment in Pella was kept by Mrs. Post, widow of M. J. Post, who had died April 2d, 1848. The first postoffice was the one that was originally established on Lake Prairie, and moved to Pella in 1848, and Henry P. Scholte installed as P. M. The first persons who sold goods in Pella were Walters & Smink, in a small building about a mile west of where the center of the town now is. As long as this was the only mercantile house there was no competition in trade, and the proprietors were often complained of—perhaps justly,—for selling goods at too high figures. When spoken to on the subject, Mr. Walters would reply, "Go to my neighbor." Soon after this E. F. Grafe opened an establishment near where Keahle's drug store now is; and then Mr. Walters was not so ready to recommend his "neighbor" to aggrieved customers.

Amsterdam, situated on the Des Moines river, on and near the upper end of Lake Prairie, was laid out by Stanford Doud, by order of H. P. Scholte, from May 15th to the 30th, on section 20, township 76, range 18. The place improved but little, and has no postoffice. Brick and lime are manufactured in its vicinity.

Leersdam was laid out by Kline, Vandemyer & Co., in 1860, on section 23. It exists only in name. H. W. Dyer, surveyor.

After having witnessed the growth and prosperity of the colony, the successful termination of an enterprise that had been dear to the leader from the time it was conceived, the great object of his life seemed to have been fulfilled. After a short illness that seemed to be the culmination of a chronic indisposition, Mr. Scholte departed this life on the 25th of August, 1868.

Population by the U. S. Census of 1870:

Native	3066
Foreign	1892
Total	4958

CHAPTER VII.

Red Rock Township—Its Geography and Early History—John D. Bedell—Red Rock Village—The Flood of '51.

Red Rock township consists of all of town. 77, range 20, north of the Des Moines river. It is bounded on the north by Jasper county; on the east by Summit; on the south by Union, with the Des Moines river as its boundary line; and on the west by Perry. Most of the township is well timbered, though in the northern part, approaching the upland prairie, the timber scatters into separate groves, that margin the small streams. The principal streams that course through it, running southward, are Calhoun and Miksell's* creeks, each large enough to afford saw mill water power three or four months of the year. Coal exists in many places, but has not been so extensively mined as in some other parts of the county, fuel being abundant and coal market rather distant.

Red Rock township, as first organized, January 6th, '47, included, besides its present territory, all of town. 77, range 19 (Summit); all of of town. 76, range 19, north of the river (now a part of Polk) and all of town. 77, range 20, south of the river (now belonging to Union). The place of holding elections was at the house of Benjamin Bowman. Only a part of the territory that is now known as Summit; all of Polk north of the river; and so much of the present township of Red Rock as lies east of what was known as the "old Indian boundary line," a short distance west of the present site of Red Rock village, first belonged to what was called "Red Rock precinct;" and the remainder of the township, lying on the west side of said

*Miksell's creek is called "Spor's timber" on the map.

line, including all of the present township of Perry, belonged to "Gopher Prairie" precinct.

On the 8th of Jannary, 1850, the township was extended so as to include sections 1, 2, 3, 4, 9, 10, 11, 12, 13, 14, 15, 16, 21, 22, 23, 24 of town. 76, range 20. This took the remainder of the present township of Union, and one tier of sections now belonging to Knoxville; but by the organization of Union and Summit in '50 and '52 the township was reduced to its present size and shape.

We have been unable to obtain a full list of the officers elected in this township, both before and after its township organization; but we have the name of Robert D. Russell as justice of the peace, and John Tollman as constable, as early as '45. John D. Bedell was first justice after its organization.

With Mr. Bedell's settlement in Red Rock begins the history of the township and village; and we shall therefore introduce the history by a brief sketch of his life up to the time of its location:

Mr. B. was born in Bath county, Kentucky, September 25th, 1817; from whence he emigrated to Montgomery county, Missouri, in the fall of '28; from thence to Clark county, same State, in the fall of '30, and from thence to Van Buren county, Iowa, in the fall of '42, and made a claim near the present site of Farmington, and erected a cabin. Two weeks after making this claim he sold it and returned to Missouri. But early in the spring of '43 he returned to Iowa, and at Iowaville met and formed the acquaintance of a Frenchman named Lewis Leplant, who could converse in the Indian language, with whom he formed a sort of co-partnership in an expedition into the new purchase in quest of a location for a settlement.

He then went to Agency, and applied to Captain Allen, who had command of the post there, for permission to pass the line. But the captain refused, adding that he had no authority to grant such a privilege, but that he could take it at his own risk, only being careful to avoid discovery by the dragoons who sometimes amused themselves by persecuting whites who could show no legal authority for their presence in the territory.

Mr. B. and his companion thereupon concluded to risk the dangers of the adventure, and, being lightly equipped, they set out on foot. This was in March, and during the journey up the Des Moines valley, following an Indian trail, a heavy snow fell, covering the earth to the depth of nearly three feet, and rendering their progress slow and toilsome. After several days travel, attended with no little hardship, the last one of their journey up closed as they reached Miksell's creek, near where the bridge crosses it about half a mile east of the village of Red Rock.

It was already dark when they reached this place, and here they concluded to make the best preparations they could for spending the night. Having cleared away the brush and snow, they were in the act of kindling a fire, when Leplant discovered a light about in the direction of the bluff that encloses the village. Though greatly fatigued and chilled, they deemed it best to reach this light, hoping to find more companionship and a better shelter.

On reaching it they found a party of Indians on their way to Hardfish, (so named from the well known chief) where was a trading post, but who had been compelled by the deep snow to stop there. But the suffering condition of the two travelers rendered them less choice of companions and accommodations than they might have been under other circumstances, and eagerly asked for shelter, and their request was readily granted. After partaking of the no way sumptuous fare of their dusky entertainers, they retired to the wickeup, rolled themselves in their own blankets, and enjoyed a comparatively refreshing sleep.

Next morning, before the Indians resumed their journey, the chief of the party piloted their guests to the river, for then the town plat of Red Rock was covered by a heavy growth of timber, so that the stream was not visible from the camp.

On taking what may be deemed an off-hand survey of the locality, Mr. Bedell thought the beautiful flat, partly walled up as it was by hills, would make a good sight for a trading house and a town. So he immediately decided to locate there so soon as it should be practicable to do so, and in order to effect a sort of preliminary establishment of his claim, he " blazed " a tree that stood on the bank of the river a short distance below where his store now is, and from thence blazed a line northward, taking in not only the whole town plat, but a considerable tract of land besides.

This done, he and Leplant returned to Missouri for provisions. These they brought on horseback, arriving about the last of April, 1843. On the first of May a house was built. It was a light pole cabin, fourteen feet square, covered with bark, and stood about twenty steps from the river bank, near where stands the old frame building built and formerly owned by James Harp. Their only assistant at the raising was John Jordan, who, as we have heretofore stated, kept a trading house on the other side of the river, and they finished the building ready for occupation by three o'clock in the afternoon.

About two weeks after this Mr. Bedel, in company with John Jordan, went to Keokuk and purchased a keel boat and loaded it at Alexander with about ten tuns of such merchandise as was needed to stock a frontier trading house, and hired it pushed up the Des Moines to their settlement.

The first person that succeeded Mr. Bedel as a settler there, was Amos Shaw. He built a cabin in which he also traded till he died, some time in 1845 or '46. In the spring of 1844, Ray Alfrey and wife moved in and occupied the cabin of Mr. Bedel, he boarding with them. During their residence here of two or three years, a feeling of jealousy on the part of Mrs. Alfrey, in consequence of the inconstancy of her husband, resulted in the first divorce case in the county. The case was successfully conducted by J. W. Alley. Mr. Alfrey had left the country at about the time the Indians did, and returned to find himself a "grass widower," when he soon disappeared the second time, and his whereabouts is not known.

Mr. Bedel kept trading house for two years, and also cultivated about ten acres of corn on the present site of the village, having previously deadened the timber. In August, 1845, he got it surveyed into town lots, and called it Red Rock, from the near locality of the lofty cliffs of red sand stone.* The Indian name for the place was sic-ella-musk-a chees, (red stone.) But as *stone* was not deemed a proper term by those who were accustomed to apply *rock* to every thing of the kind from the size of a pebble to a boulder, the new town was called Red Rock.

Those who became citizens of the place immediately after it had thus assumed its existence as a village, were James Harp and E. H. Baker. Mr Harp built the first cabin after the town was laid out. It stood a few rods from the river bank, and contained two rooms, one of which was occupied by E. H. Baker as a store room, and the other by Mr. H. himself, as a sort of "bachelor's hall." Baker remained here till he went to Burlington; from thence he moved to Prairie City; and is at present at Colfax station, in Jasper county. A more extended

*These stones are of the consistency capable of being dressed into any shape, and will harden after being exposed to the air, This proves it to be valuable as ornamental building stone; and, but for the lack of means of transportation, it would undoubtedly become an article of considerable trade.

Many years ago the writer saw the fleshless head and large horns of a deer suspended between some stunted cedars nearly half way down the perpendicular wall. The animal had evidently plunged over the height to escape the pursuing hunter, or may have been pushed over the precipice by another animal. There, beyond the reach of man or beast, the unfortunate animal had died, rotted and fallen into the river, leaving the head to tell, without a date the story of the fearful plunge.

notice of this eccentric character will be given in another place.

Robert D. Russell, who was the first justice in the township, lived a short distance above the town plat, both before and after it was surveyed. He was also postmaster for a short time previous to that event, after which James Harp was appointed, with Dr. Reuben Matthews and G. N. Crum as his bondsmen. Rev. M. J. Post, an early citizen of Pella, now deceased, carried the first mail to this office, from Fairfield, by way of Agency, Ottumwa, Eddyville; and from here to Fort Des Moines, making the trip once a week.

The first physician resident of Red Rock was Reuben Matthews, and C. M. Gilky and J. W. McCully were the next.

In '47 and '48 many additions were made to the population of the village, and several frame and respectable log houses were built, giving it a thriving appearance. Indeed, the prospect seemed favorable for its ultimate expansion into the proportions of a city. Situated on a stream already navigable for steamboats during high water, with the promise of being rendered constantly so by the addition of dams and locks, and surrounded by a rich farming country, rapidly increasing in population, the citizens of Red Rock could justly anticipate a prosperous future for their young city. In view of these natural advantages over any more inland locality, some effort was made to get the county seat there; but all hope of success vanished with the sweeping flood of '51. This memorable event occurred in June, a season unusual for such freshets, and the people were not prepared for it. It had been raining for some time and the water was high, but few expected the overflow that took place during the night, when the people were unconscious of it till the alarm was given. Finding the lower rooms of their houses deluged, and the water perceptibly growing deeper and deeper, the excitement grew almost to a panic.

There was a general moving up stairs by all who had such apartments to escape to, and confused cries for help came from all quarters; and all the canoes and skiffs that could be brought into service were manned for the rescue.

At this time Simpson B. Matthews lived in a hewed log house, on the south side of the river, about half a mile above town. During the night he was awakened by the sound of rushing water in the vicinity, and hearing what appeared to be cries of alarm, he quickly bounded out of bed, and to his increased surprise and alarm found the water several inches deep on the floor. Informing his wife what was taking place he left the house and waded some distance down the river, to where he hoped to make himself heard by the town people. Here he mounted a pile of drift wood and called loudly for help; but such was the alarm and confusion in town that for a long time his efforts to attract attention were unavailing. Having at length succeeded, and obtained promise of help, he returned to the house; and, by the way, found the water so increased in depth that he reached it with some risk of his life. After some delay, that in consequence of the perilous situation of the family seemed an age to them, they were released.

Just opposite the town, and close upon the bank of the river stood a house occupied by a family named Hall. One of the children belonging to this family was seriously ill, and on the day preceding the night of the flood Mrs. Chestnut, who still lives in Red Rock, went over to pass the night with the afflicted. This was a doleful night in their experience. The family were compelled to take an upper room, whilst the water rose rapidly in the lower, nearly filling it. The child lay panting in the agony of a near approaching death, and was hourly, if not momentarily, expected to expire. The heart-aching sadness produced by this solemn scene was rendered more intense by the surrounding desolation without, the roar of the flood and cries for help, distinctly heard from across the river. In addition to these causes of distress, another incident within doors was calculated to excite apprehensions for the safety of the house. The water had risen to such a depth in the lower story as to float up the bedstead lately occupied by the dying child, which, being tossed up and down by the undulations of the swelling flood, struck against the upper floor with a heavy thumping noise, peculiarly startling; and no one could restrain a fear that the flood might reach a depth sufficient to float the building, or throw it down. Of course a sleepless night was passed, and when the more than welcome day at last dawned help came, and they were all taken over the river. The sick one was taken to a house near the sugar grove, north-east of town, where it died soon after. Next day the abandoned house fell.

During that night and the day following, most of the people got out of town and prepared themselves for a temporary stay on the bluffs. With as much of their clothing as they could secure undamaged by muddy water, and as was indispensible to camp life, they spread their tents and proceeded to make themselves as comfortable as circumstances would permit, thinking that in a few days at most the water would abate enough to permit them to return to their houses. But a few days passed, and a few more, and yet the dry land did not appear.

In the meantime many persons suffered considerable loss in the destruction of property. Hogs and cattle were drowned, fences swept away, cornfields, lately planted, were ruined by the washing current, or covered by the debris of the flood. At length, at the end of about two weeks, the water went down, and there was apparent safety in returning to the town, and soon the camp was gladly deserted. But the deposit of mud in the houses rendered them unfit for occupation till they were cleaned out, which occupied considerable time and labor, and when this was done, and the citizens had fairly got settled indoors again, the relentless flood made a second raid upon the devoted city, forcing them to take refuge on the bluff for nearly another fortnight.

This second exile proved to be more distressing than the first. The weather was inclement, damp and chilly, and provisions scarce. Grist mills were inconvenient at best, and now beyond reach on account of the flooded condition of the streams. There was corn in the country, but how could it be rendered fit for use? Some relief, however, was found in a temporary mill owned by David B. Worth, who then lived about two miles north of town on Miksell's creek. This mill consisted of a pair of small burrs, turned by hand. To this mill, unable as it was to supply the demand, came people from all the surrounding country, with grists of corn varying in size from bushels to a peck, some begging the privilege of grinding a peck, or even a smaller amount, to supply the urgent demands of hunger. Coffee mills were also used to convert corn into meal, and when the grain could not be ground it was made into hominy.

But an end to these trials came at last. The water subsided and returned to its proper channel, and people returned to their homes and occupations, to recover, so far as possible, the damages they had sustained by loss of property and time. As has been stated, the corn that had been planted on the bottom lands was washed out or covered by mud. It was now apparently too late in the season to replant; yet there was need to do something in that direction, or suffer the total loss of a crop more indispensable than any other in the country. It was even so late as the fourth of July when some of this replanting was done; yet the remainder of the season was favorable to its growth in a soil already unsurpassed in fertility, and now possibly rendered more so by the sedimentary deposits of the flood, that the corn grew and matured with surprising rapidity, and well rewarded the faith and labor of the planter.

But there was a damage wrought by this flood that was irreparable to the village of Red Rock, to-wit: its reputation as a safe and therefore suitable place of business. All hope of obtaining the seat of justice was swept away. And who cared to purchase property subject, even at remote periods, to such destructive inundations?

Yet for a time one hope sustained the place, which was the promised slack-water navigation. But this soon vanished, and gave place to that of railroad connection, that was entertained for several years with some apparent certainty, and finally expired with the location of the Des Moines Valley Road up the prairie. This was the last hope.

CHAPTER VIII.

Red Rock Township and Village, continued—Drunken Squaws—Pray or Treat—Schoolmaster in a Fix—A Justice's Bet—An Indian Voter—A Female Justice—"Old Blank," and how he Lost his Nose—Stealing Honey—Nearly a Fight—Shooting—A Narrow Escape from Hanging—A Black Joke.

It is due to ourself to say that what has just been said, as well as what shall be said hereafter, relating to the history of Red Rock village, is not intended to be prejudicial to the interests of that place. For our own part we entertain the kindest feelings and best wishes for the people. We simply intend to be true to history, so far as we have been able to obtain it; and if the "o'er true tale" reflects no glory upon its subject, the fault is no more ours than was the calamity we endeavored to give an account of in the preceding chapter. To quote a phrase frequently used, we cannot afford to "spoil a good story for relation's sake."

From first to last Red Rock possessed a notoriety not enjoyed by any other village in the county. Situated on a much frequented Indian trail, and at the border of the United States territory, it early became a place of resort for the savages for the purpose of trading and obtaining whisky at the trading houses. It is said that even the squaws would some times come, obtain a supply of the bainful beverage, and then lay about in a state of beastly intoxication, their infants (those that had them) crying with starvation. In pity for these suffering innocents, the sober squaws would feed them with the soft pulp scraped from the inside of elm or linwood bark, which they would devour with evident relish Some of these squaws appeared to be desperate under the influence of liquor, and were tied to the fences to prevent them from running over the river bank.

The place also became the frequent rendezvous of the rougher portion of the settlers, and others whose character classed them with adventurers and desperadoes; and as a natural result of such a fusion of spirits, inspired more or less by the ardent, fights were of frequent occurrence. It is a fact worthy of note that Red Rock, though a comparative small place, has been the scene of several assassinations, shooting and stabbing affrays, and lawless carousals, the details of which are not pertinent to this history. But for the sake of more fully illustrating the moral status of her society at an early date, we may relate a few anecdotes.

It is not to be supposed that the place was wholly destitute of moral influences. A few professors of religion lived there and in the neighborhood, but their examples in righteous living were either in a measure wanting on their part or wholly disregarded by others.

On the occasion of religious services held in the village, by an itinerant Methodist preacher, on his first round, it was a question among the few brethren of the place who of them he would be likely to call upon to pray in closing the meeting. As the preacher was not personally acquainted with any of them, there was no certainty to whom the request might be directed; and, as praying was an exercise so little practised by them, no one really desired a call to such a performance publicly. Here, then, was a hazzard—something to bet on. So, just before meeting, some of the brethren and others took counsel together, and agreed that whoever should be called upon to pray, in case of failure to do so, should *pay a gallon of whisky.* But fortunately for all, the preacher did his own praying, thereby relieving some trembling brother from the conflicting emotions resulting from the danger of being compelled to make an awkward, spiritless prayer, or pay the liquor.

Daniel Hiskey, now a citizen of Monroe, Jasper county, taught the first school in Red Rock village, being in the winter of 1845–6. The school house was a small log cabin near the river, and the number of scholars that attended was about twenty from the village and surrounding country.

As it happened, Mr. D. was a temperance man—a teetoteler—and about the only one in the community; and in such a community it was not likely that he could enjoy his peculiar notions undisturbed. It was determined, on the first favorable occasion, to punish him for the heresy, or force him to recant. So on the day before New Year he was invited to furnish two gallons of whisky, and sugar to sweaten it, as a New Year's treat to the school. This he pointedly refused to do. But early next day he saw that it was the purpose of others than his "big scholars" to force him to a compliance, should he still refuse. Two or three young men came in in the morning who had not been there before, and took their places as scholars. But no demonstrations were made till noon, when they repeated the demand already made, which he as pointedly refused to obey. Whereupon they attempted to seize him, intending as they said, to "duck" him if he did not give up. But Mr. Hiskey defiantly told them he would die first, and fled. But there were others waiting to assist in the performance, and some of these joined in the chase. There was a solid bridge of ice on the river, and to this the pursued made his way with all his speed, followed, at various distances, by quite a number of noisy young men and boys. After an amusing chase up the river, the game was overtaken and conveyed to a hole that had been cut in the ice for that or some other purpose, and again informed with apparent sincerity that if he did not treat he should go under. But, though the prospect of a dip in the cold current at that particular season, attended with some risk of being swept beneath the ice and eaten up by mud-turtles and fish, was calculated to shake the resolution of any than a truly brave heart, the heart of Mr. Hiskey failed not. Finding it impossible to frighten him into a compliance by threats alone, they concluded to reduce the quantity of whisky and sugar one-half, and try again. But in vain. The obstinate teetoteler said "not a drop." At last, after some time spent in fruitless efforts to bring him to something like a compromise, if not a full concession, his persecutors became fully convinced that his obstinacy was sustained by an unconquerable principle. He was released and continued his school unmolested thereafter.

As may be readily supposed, whether party spirit ran high or low in local politics, an election could hardly be conducted without more or less flowing of that other spirit called ardent. It was calculated to create an interest among those who were not much otherwise concerned about the civil government of the township, and induce them to attend the election and perform their duty as citizens endowed with the privilege of voting.

An amusing instance of this came off at the first election held at Red Rock in the spring of '44. The polls was at Robert D. Russell's, and he was the candidate for justice. Many people were present from all parts of the precinct, and the voting was pretty lively, not a few of the voters receiving a drink of whiskey apparently in exchange for their tickets, which they handed through the open window of the cabin. An Indian that happened to be present noticed this proceeding, and thought it would be a nice plan for him to get a drink. So he presented himself before one of the persons who distributed the tickets, with the request delivered in his best English: "Me paper, me vote, get drink whis." His request was readily granted, and forthwith he proceeded to vote. Amused at his boldness in attempting to do so, and aware of his motive, those who had charge of the ballots took his ticket and handed him a small drink. Pleased with his success thus far, he thought the plan worth repeating, and applied for another paper. It was given him, either a ticket or some other paper that answered the same purpose with him, and again he voted with like success. Thus encouraged he continued to vote at intervals all day, till he got as much of the election as he could carry. Of course the tickets he handed in counted nothing for anybody but himself.

In those days petty lawsuits were of common occurrence, mostly connected with disputes about claims. Arbitration was the only means of settling these disputes previous to the election of any justice, and was sometimes resorted to afterwards; but eventually judgment was put in the hands of men duly authorized by law to render it. We have upon record no instances of claim suits worth mentioning, in addition to what has already been related. 'Squire Russell's court was frequently resorted to for a just settlement of these disputes,—though his administrations were not always the result of a clear head and an intelligent, unbiased mind. It is said that he was sometimes quite at a loss how to decide some cases of a complicated character, and admitted the better judgment of his wife by applying to her for an opinion, which frequently settled the case. On one occasion Mrs. Russell displayed her ability to administer justice in a summary manner. A claim case was on hand, and one of the parties entered the court room drunk, and manifested some disposition to quarrel with the mistress of the house, when she settled his case by knocking him down with a chair. The justice now looked up from his docket, and seeing the prostrate disturber of the peace, uttered, in his peculiar, low, growling tone, this sage advice, "By ——, Dick, let the old woman alone."

Among the rougher class of settlers who frequented Red Rock during its early history, the most notorious were William

Blankenship, (more familiarly called "Old Blank,") and the Williamses. Old Blank was a brother-in-law to the Williamses. Of his history, previous to coming to Marion county, we know but little, except that he emigrated from Illinois to the present site of Burlington, at a very early day, and made a claim there. After getting into some difficulty with the settlers there, and fighting his way through, as was his custom, he came as far west as Fairfield and settled again. Here, in a claim quarrel, he met with rather more than his match. Having offered to fight his opponent a regular fisticuff pitched battle for the claim, stipulating that whichever should be the victor in the fight, should be the winner of the property, the challenge was accepted. Old Blank had been successful in so many contests that he scarcely expected to fail in this one. But there are few men of such superior calibre, mentally or physically, that do not, at one time or another, meet with some one a little better than themselves. In this case our bully got to be the under dog in the fight, but would not surrender till he had reason to consider himself thoroughly whipped, when he cried enough. And enough it was, for when Blank got up, bleeding profusely, it was discovered that a considerable slice had been taken from the side of his sharp, thin nose. Instead of resenting the indignity he thus suffered in the disfiguration of his face, he merely said to his opponent, "the claim is yours, sir," and went his way.

Mr. B. then came to Marion county and settled a short distance below Red Rock, where he lived till about '49 or '50, when he went to California.

As he was a somewhat noted person in his semi-desperado character, a few sketches of his transactions in the neighborhood of Red Rock, may be proper here.

Shortly after his settlement on the Des Moines, and during the period of hard times experienced by most of the early settlers, Old Blank's family were reduced to the extreme pinchings of poverty, being for some time without anything in the character of breadstuffs, or, indeed, of any other kind of food except slippery elm bark cut fine and fried with a little grease of some kind.

After he had secured his claim, and had acquired some property in the way of live stock, his hogs would stray away and get across the river during a low stage of water. When winter approached, and the owner needed to look after the wandering swine and get them home, if the river happened to be swollen he did not trouble himself to wait till it went down to a fordable depth, or even to get a boat to cross in, but deliberately stripped himself, tied his clothes on his head to keep them dry, and swam over. When over and dressed he would run barefooted through the woods till he had found and collected all the hogs he claimed ownership of, and then, with much effort, would force them to swim.

Between Blank and a family named Johnson a feud existed, originating from the latter suing the former on an account of about sixteen dollars. Blank refused to pay this sum, and his horse was levied upon, after which he "ponied" up and threatened revenge. So one morning Johnson found his bee hives robbed, his grindstone spoiled, and other property damaged. Naturally suspecting Blank to be the perpetrator of this mischief, he decided to have him arrested on suspicion. Accordingly John W. Mikesell, who was then a constable, was sent for him. Mr. M., in order to make sure of his intended prisoner, made his visitation before daylight next morning, and found, besides Blank himself, his brother-in-law, James M. Williams, (more frequently known as "Mat") in bed. The constable took an offered seat and entered into conversation upon topics foreign to that of his visit, in order to elude suspicion of its object. At length he asked Blank what made the chair bottom so sticky, and remarked that it felt and tasted like honey. Blank, evidently thinking that the chair might have got smeared with some of the stolen sweetness, answered that he and Mat had cut a splendid bee tree only night before last. This was bringing matters to a crisis, and Mr. Miksell replied that it tasted very much like Johnson's honey; and also, inasmuch as he (Blank) was accused of having stolen it, he had come, duly armed by authority of law, to conduct him before a justice, to answer to the charge. The culprit agreed to this, and promised to appear, as specified; but gave due notice that should Johnson appear against him he would kill him; and such was the fear inspired by his threats that Johnson let the matter go by default, and Blank was acquitted.

On the occasion of a claim quarrel between Blank and this same Mat they mutually agreed to fight it out in the same manner in which our hero had lost a part of his nose, Mat first giving the challenge. Like professed duelists, they appointed the time and place for the combat, and invited two disinterested persons to be present and see fair play. We have not the date at which this interesting event was to transpire, but the place designated was across the river, opposite Red Rock, and the persons invited to witness it were Tom and Sol Morgan, a couple of gentlemen belonging to the same class of roughs.

The day on which the fight was to come off happened to be very cold, and a fire was made in a log heap on the intended battle ground. The river was frozen over hard enough for the parties to cross on the ice. At the appointed time they met equipped for the fight, that is, stripped nearly naked, their hair shaved, their sides greased, and their long finger nails peppered. In this ridiculous plight they stood around the burning log heap that was scarcely sufficient to shield their bare bodies from the frosty breeze. Apparently one was afraid to begin, and the other dare not, and no amount of "sicking" on the part of their friends could elicit more than sundry growls from the naked bull dogs. At length the temperature of their blood went so far blow fighting heat that the whole affair was merged into a compromise in which Blank promised to pay a stipulated sum for the disputed property. Then, like the fools they were they put on their clothes and went home, having played a most amusing farce at their own expense for the entertainment of their friends.

By some who had the best of reasons for it, Blank was believed to be a dangerous man. One or two performances of his were sufficient to prove such an opinion well founded, and we will relate them : A claim dispute arose between him and Elihu Alley, when the latter owned the saw mill on the river above Red Rock. One day Alley was alone at the mill making some repairs on the dam, when some noise on the bank attracted his attention, at which he looked up and saw Blank taking deliberate aim at him with his rifle. At that moment a third person came in sight when the assassin postponed the shooting and walked away without speaking. On being spoken to about this affair soon afterwards he boldly stated that if Mr. Alley had not looked up when he did, an instant later would have been his last.

At another time, when Mr. Alley with his son Cyrus, and a man named Evelyne, with whom he was in partnership, were at work in the mill at night, they were several times fired upon from the opposite side of the river, some of the bullets striking so near them as to render it unsafe to remain.

It was well known that Blank was the perpetrator of this deed, yet such was the fear of him by those most interested in securing his arrest that he was not molested. And when he took his departure for California the county deemed itself happily rid of a troublesome fellow.

But whilst on the way across the plains Blank's propensity for shooting was exercised to an extent that came very near ridding the world of him altogether. Getting into a quarrel with a man about some cattle, Blank used his revolver with deadly effect, killing the man instantly. He was immediately arrested, tried, and sentenced to be hung, and even a wagon tongue was elevated on which to execute the sentence. Here, however, it was unfortunately thought proper to put him into the hands of the Utah authorities for trial. This was accordingly done, and he escaped justice altogether, aided, it is supposed, by the power of money. He is now reported to be the wealthy owner of real estate in California.

An amusing anecdote is still occasionally related of an individual named Charley Hamlin, who, though not a settler, was a frequent lounger about Red Rock, drawn there as many others were, by the social intercourse inspired by the love of liquor. Charley had formerly been a candidate for the territorial legislature, and had come very nearly being elected. This to him was a matter worth boasting of, and when under the influence of whisky he was disposed to make a show of his vanity by bragging over his narrow defeat. But one day he was made the subject of a joke, by which his vanity was considerably mortified for the time being. Having imbibed pretty freely, he laid down to sleep, when some one smeared the palms of his hands and his fingers with blacking—then tickled his face with a straw. This would bring the blackened palms in contact with the face with a slap and a rub that imparted to it a portion of the coloring. The operation was continued till the whole physiognomy of the sleeper was changed from the ruddiness imparted by strong drink to a beautiful glossy black. On waking his attention was called to the change, and he repaired to a looking-glass to see for himself. Here, utterly ignorant of the cause, the surprised old toper thus addressed himself: "Why, Charley Hamlin, you came within two votes of going to the legislature, and now here you are in Red Rock, a nigger."

CHAPTER IX.

Red Rock Township continued—Names of some of the Early Settlers—John H. Mikesell's Indian Dress, Decorations, &c—Kish-ke-kosh—His partiality for Clean Victuals—His Politeness—Feeding the Indians—Scooti!

Besides those already mentioned in connection with the history of Red Rock village, we note the names of John H. Mikesell, Joel and David B. Worth, James Scott, Israel Nichols, William Williams with his sons, John, George, Joshua and James M.; John W. and Elihu Alley, Claiborn Hall, S. B. Matthews, Nathan Tallman and Druillard Shoemaker, as a few of the early settlers in the township. Only a few of them are still residents of the county, and we shall give such notice of them, individually, as we have been able to obtain.

John H. Mikesell was born in Franklin county, Va., June 27th, 1802. In 1804 his parents moved to Montgomery county, Ohio, and in '25 to Franklin county, Ind., where they resided three years, and then returned to Montgomery county, Ohio. From thence Mr. M. moved to St. Joe county, Ind., in '35, and from thence to Iowa in '42, landing in the territory on the 18th of October, and took a winter lease at the forks of Skunk river, about ten miles from Brighton, Van Buren county, paying for it by building a cabin on the land.

That winter was one of considerable severity, on account of the great depth of snow, and the family lived mostly on "hog and hominy," together with the milk of one cow that, with her calf, shared the little cabin with them during the coldest weather.

On the 28th of April, '43, Mr. Mikesell and two of his old est boys, set out for the "New Purchase," intending to make a claim and prepare a place for the family, previous to moving. But their progress was interrupted by high waters, so that they did not reach their destination till about the 7th or 8th of May. This was in section 25, about a mile north-east of the present site of Red Rock village. Here he selected a claim, and then returned for the remainder of the family, leaving the boys and a man named Thomas Martin, who had come with them, to hold the claim and build a house.

No great amount of labor was required to build such a house. It consisted of light logs or poles put up in the shape of a shed, with an open front and a bark roof sloped but one way. By some this temporary sort of structure was called a cat-faced or half-faced camp, or by the Indian term, *wickeup*. This house stood at the foot of the hill on which stands the more commodious brick dwelling erected by Mr. M. many years after.

On the 29th of the month he arrived with the family and took possession of their new home, and occupied the shanty most of the summer, or till another log cabin containing two rooms, was built on the site of the present house.

During the first two years of Mr. Mikesell's pioneer life he was engaged principally in trading with the Indians. Since then he has resided constantly on his farm, or till soon after the death of his wife, which occured very suddenly on the night of the 22d of March, 1869, after which he went to the village.

Through the intercourse of trade Mr. Mikesell became quite intimate with the Indians, and from him we have a number of incidents illustrating the character of this peculiar people, their manners, customs, etc.

The rude life led by these savages is, perhaps, already so well known that any additional description of it might be considered superfluous in a local history; yet we venture to insert a few items that seem sufficiently interesting for preservation even here.

The dress of these people—particularly of the men—was about as scant during summer as decency would admit of, consisting of a breech cloth about the middle and a pair of moccasins on their feet. In cold weather they added leggings, a shirt and a blanket. Ornaments, consisting of beads and rings, were quite popular with the men, and especially with the chiefs and others who could afford them. Some of the chiefs had their ears quite covered with rings, and sometimes are suspended to the nose. Profuse quantities of various colored beads were strung about their necks, some strans descending quite low on the breast. Their moccasins were also frequently decorated with these gewgaws. They were supposed to denote the rank of the wearer—the more rings and beads the bigger Indian. They had also a feminine fancy for feathers and paint, and would—though only on special occasions—decorate their top-knots with long feathers plucked from the tail or wing of fowls, and smear their faces with lines of red and black paint, giving them at once a most hideous and comical aspect. From this brief description the reader may draw, in his imagination, a full fledged warrior chief.

Unlike their white sisters, the squaws were not so much given to those decorations; but their bodies were at all times better covered than those of their masters. But even this was scant enough for female apparel, consisting mostly of a piece of blue cloth bound about the waist, descending to a little below the knees, and something like a sacque or shirt to cover the chest. They seldom had any covering for their heads. And even of this cheap and simple wardrobe they did not often have a change, unless they happened to be the wives or daughters of a chief or other wealthy brave.

As for their children, both sexes were permitted to go totally naked, with the exception of moccasins and leggins to protect them from snakes, till they were old enough for decency to demand some kind of covering for them.

The boys were each supplied with a bow and arrow so soon as they were old enough to learn the use of it, and that became the principal part of his education. They were apt scholars, and young as they were, their expertness in marksmanship was a matter of wonder to those unskilled in the art. On one occasion a party of Indians were camped near Red Rock, and it was amusing to witness those naked young ones, bow and arrow in hand, wading about in the river, searching for fish and turtles. On discovering the game they were almost sure to put an arrow into it, notwithstanding the well known difficulty of hitting a mark under water.

In diet the Indians were about as crude as they were in dress, and by no means fastidious as to cleanliness, except in rare cases where intercourse with the whites had begotten in them some regard in this respect. An anecdote of the noted chief George Washington Kish-ke-kosh, will illustrate this statement :

Kish was a sub chief, and had accompanied Black Hawk as one of his suit of braves during the tour of that renowned chief through the east as prisoner of war. With his leader he had been hospitably entertained at hotels and other places, and had conceived a high appreciation for the sumptuous and cleanly looking fare that was set before them. How he was enabled, after such an experience, to return with a good stomache to the frugal diet and indifferent cooking of his own people, we are left to conjecture. At all events he retained his partiality for clean victuals, and was even over fastidious in this respect, as the following instance will show:

One night he, with his company of three or four braves, slept at the house of a white man with whom he was on very friendly terms, and were to remain for breakfast. Kish had an eye on the preparations for this meal, and observed one neglect that his tender stomach rebelled against. The lady of the house—perhaps she did it intentionally, for she was not a willing entertainer of her savage guests—neglected to wash her hands before making up the bread. Kish thought he would rather do without his breakfast than eat after such cooking, and privately signified as much to his followers, whereupon they mounted their ponies and left, much to the relief of their hostess. Arriving at Joel Worth's, almost a mile and a half from where they had lodged, they got breakfast and related the circumstance.

Yet these people, though generally accustomed to the poorest fare, were not averse to the best that could be provided, and made themselves gluttons whenever they could get enough of it. Like the wolf, they seemed capable of enduring a long fast, and then of gorging themselves to very stupidity at a sumptuous feast.

On one occasion this same George Washington Kish-ke-kosh and his suit, consisting of several prominent personages of the tribe, being then encamped on Skunk river, came over to Mr. Mikesell on a friendly visit, and he treated them to a feast.

Besides Kish and his wife, this party consisted of his mother; Wykoma, son of Wappelo, and his two wives;* Masha Wapetine and his wife, and all their children. The old woman, on being asked by Mrs. M., how old she was, replied: "Mack-ware-renaak-we-kauk," (maybe a hundred); and indeed, her bowed form and hidiously shriveled features would justify the belief that she was even that old. Kish's wife was a person of ladylike appearance, and so were the two pretty young wives of Wykoma, though they were somewhat under medium size, and were also sisters. They were all dressed in a rather more than usually becoming style, perhaps out of respect for their host and his family.

---

*Poligamy was not an uncommon practice among these people. It is related that the chief, Pasishamone, during the encampment of his tribe near Red Rock, married a second wife to supply the place of the other, who was disabled by a snake bite.

Mr. Mikesell, knowing something of the voracious appetite of his visitors, had made ample preparations for them.

When the table was surrounded, Kish, who had learned some good manners as well as acquired a taste for cleanliness, essayed to perform the etiquette of the occasion before eating anything himself. With an amusingly awkward imitation of what he had seen done among the whites, he passed the various dishes to the others, showing the ladies special attention, and helped them to a part of everything on the table with much apparent disinterested consideration.

But when Kish came to help himself his politeness assumed the Indian phase altogether. He ate like a hungry person with a bottomless stomach, taking in everything in his reach, without regard to what should come first or last in the course of dessert, so he liked the taste of it. At length, after having drank five or six cups of coffee, and eaten a proportionate amount of solid foods, his energy in the gastilary exercise began to slacken. Seeing this, Mr. Mikesell approached him and, with apparent concern for his want of appetite, said, ‘ Why, Kish, do eat your dinner! Have another cup of coffee and eat something." In his reply to this urgent appeal, Kish's Indian politeness was again dominant. Leaning back on his seat, he lazily shook his head, drew his finger across his throat under his chin, to indicate how full he was; and then, in further explanation of his satisfied condition, he opened his capacious mouth and thrust his finger down his throat as far as he dared, as much as to say he could almost touch the victuals. Of course the others had each eaten a like proportion, making the most of what they did not get every day.

Another story of Indian gluttony deserves relating, though it occurred several years later than the period this history is intended to treat of.

A party of them numbering about fifteen or twenty men made their appearance in Red Rock, stating that they had been for some time camped on Skunk river, were out of provisions, in a state of starvation, and signified their intention of remaining a while in town to be gratuitously fed by the people. This was a contingency unlooked for, and by no means pleasant to contemplate, as nobody liked to take the dirty, unmannerly creatures into their houses. However, as they were not to be put off without more trouble than the people cared to risk, something had to be done for their accommodation. So they concluded to engage some one to supply them with one meal per day each, at fifteen cents per meal, and put the money into the hands of the Indians to pay their own fare. Mr. David B. Worth, who then kept a hotel in town, took upon himself the task of supplying the required food. And a task it was soon found to be. Mrs. W., not being acquainted with the surfeiting propensity of these human-shaped animals, furnished the table with the usual quantity and variety for common boarders, at the first meal. At the proper signal the long table was closely surrounded by the swarthy crowd, who fell to like famishing wild beasts and in an astonishingly short time, to the consternation and amazement of the hostess, swept the board of everything but the dishes. It was replenished again, and then again for the third time, before full satisfaction was attained; and this was when they were so full that they appeared in danger of choking, and would stroke their hands over their necks and breasts as if to press down the rising gorge. Then they would all move lazily away and stretch themselves in some sunny place, where they would remain almost motionless till the shades of evening would admonish them to seek shelter for the night.

This was repeated three or four days, every morning the Indians being on hand with appetites as keen as ever for the stipulated breakfast. Among other things they had a good relish for coffee, and of this they drank, at each meal, the three fillings of the largest kind of a boiler used for the purpose of making coffee at a hotel.

They used very little ceremony at the table, every fellow helping himself to what he liked best. One of them observing a glass dish containing some kind of fruit sauce, took a taste of it on the point of his knife. Finding it quite to his liking, he reached over, grasped the dish, emptied the whole of its contents upon his own plate, and then gobbled it up as any one might have done a dish of soup.

But to their credit we must say there was one redeeming circumstance connected with the affair: they all paid up promptly at the conclusion of each meal, the leader not permitting one of them to leave the table till each had paid his fifteen cents, not a cent more nor less.

In spite of this, however, the expense of feeding such a pack of wolves was deemed too unprofitable to be made a business of, and after two or three days' trial was abandoned. The Indians were very much displeased at their dismissal, but went their way without giving any trouble.

We can scarcely afford to close this chapter without giving one more anecdote, which, though rather foreign to the main subject, shows the simplicity of the Indians, and the disposition of some of the whites to annoy them:

As we have seen, companies of them were in the habit of stopping at Mikesell's, where they would sometimes remain for a day or two, trading, drinking, feasting, or whatever else their lazy habits prompted them to do. At one time one of these wandering parties, composed of two or three families, were camped near the house and cooking a large kettle of soup for supper. One of the Mikesell boys, who entertained no special friendship for these visitors, conceived the idea of perpetrating a joke on them by seasoning their soup. So, unobserved by them, he deposited in the kettle a large handful of pulverized red pepper, and stirred it well in. When the time came to eat the soup was ladled out into wooden bowls and distributed around. The first fellow that swallowed a mouthful of it rolled up his eyes, opened his mouth, and began to pant with evident agony; but not experiencing any relief from this, he suddenly jumped up, ran some distance, threw himself on the ground, crying "scooti! scooti! scooti!" that is "fire! fire! fire!" at the highest key. The same symptoms were soon experienced by several more, who performed the same kind of antics, rolling and tumbling about in the most frantic manner; and the camp was filled with the alarm of fire. So soon as they had sufficiently recovered from the paroxysm to give an intelligible reason for it, they said the soup was poisoned, and their children would starve; but they were soon assured that the soup was only peppered, and materials were supplied them for another mess, that proved all right, after being cautiously tasted of previously to being eaten.

CHAPTER X.

Red Rock Township continued — Conflict About a Stolen Saddle—Combative Squaws—A Skirmish.

It is well known by those acquainted with the Indians that they were not generally noted for honesty, and that one of their prevailing vices was theft. This vice, however, was principally confined to the poorer classes, and was not only refrained from, but strongly condemned by the chiefs. These big Indians were mostly too wealthy to render it necessary for them to steal; besides, they had too high a regard for their dignified position in life to stoop to an act so unworthy.

On one occasion Mr. Mikesell traded with an Indian for a saddle.* He had been engaged with them most of the night, and towards morning put the saddle under his bed and laid down to get some sleep, telling his wife to take notice whether the Indians, who were still prowling about, would take any thing from the house. Just about daylight he heard the saddle dragged from under the bed, and immediately got up to follow it. On going to the door he saw three Indians, each of them with a pony, one of whom had the saddle which he was just in the act of putting on the animal. Now, if he meant to recover it, there was no time to spare for deciding what might be the best plan

* An Indian saddle was a very simple contrivance. The front was a wooden fork so carved out as to fit well astride the horse's back, and from each prong of this fork was fixed a flat strip of wood of sufficient length, extending backwards along the side of the ridge. Then to the back ends of these strips was attached another of sufficient breadth, extending over and across the ridge edgewise, or with a sufficient slant to form the back part of the saddle. Over this frame was drawn a covering of raw hide, stretched and sewed so tightly with deer sinews that it kept its shape firmly. Then other skins could be added to render them soft and easy both for horse and rider. It was the business of the squaws to make these saddles.

to take for that purpose; but Mr. M. ran hastily down to where they were, and peremptorily demanded the property. But the thief had seen his approach, and had mounted his pony before his pursuer reached him, and had already started away when Mr. M. had just time to catch a firm hold upon the pony's tail. Seeing this apparently futile attempt to detain him, the rider yelled a laugh of ridicule and defiance, and lashed the animal into a plunging gallop. The scene was both exciting and amusing. Up, up the hill they went, where the road now ascends it in front of the house, with a plunge that showed that the little animal felt the weight of his appendage in the rear, but lashed to a speed that rendered it difficult for the latter to keep step, even with the long quick strides he made, his feet flying up and down with a most comical nimbleness. It was his intention to pull the pony against a tree close by, which they had to pass, and thus unhorse both rider and saddle; but the speed was too great to give him any time for his strategem, and his hold broke.

Provoked at this failure, he returned to where the other Indians were, who seemed much amused at the scene. Taking hold of the best one of their ponies, he put it in a rail pen, and forbade them to touch it till he got his saddle.

Though much angered at this summary proceeding, they made no resistance, but went away threatening vengeance. Fully expecting their return soon, Mr. M. remained near. He was not disappointed, for not an hour had elapsed ere he saw five mounted Indians coming at a galloping speed; and as they approached they raised the war song, singing in a not unmusical intonation, "te-o-ho, te-o-ho, ne-ne-y-tosse-ah, te-o-ho," (I'm a big brave, with te-o-ho for a chorus), and rode up to where the pony was and dismounted without apparently noticing the presence of their enemy.

But Mr. M. was on the ground as soon as they were, and aware of their intention, was the first to get hold of the pony's halter. One of the Indians, however, got hold of it nearly at the same time, and a "tussle" ensued. He was a big, stout fellow, and had thrown off his blanket in preparation for the contest; but it happened that Mr. M. had a slight advantage of ground, being on the slope a little above his antagonist. In the struggle to wrest the halter from the grip of the Indian he gave him a push that sent him down hill, turning a complete somersault backwards. Mr. M. then took up an ox whip that happened to be lying near him, and threatened to thrash the first one who would attempt to lay hold of the animal again. Singular as it may seem, these people were more afraid of a whip than of a deadly weapon, and would receive a sound thrashing without making any more resistance than a school boy, whilst the flourishing of a knife, gun or tomahawk would bring out their combatativeness at once. In this case the threat of a whipping had the desired effect, and the "ne-ne-y-tasse-ah" all "pococheed" and left "shnok-a-man" in possession of the "nack-a-tock-a-shaw."

But they had not quite given up the hope of recovering the pony. They next went and laid the matter before their chief, Masha Wapatine, who immediately became personally responsible for the payment of five dollars for the saddle. The pony was then given up, and Mr. M. got his money at the next payment.

On another occasion a slight unpleasantness arose between Mr. Mikesell and the Indians in relation to the unwarrantable purloining of some potatoes. The story as related by Mr. M. is in substance as follows:

Pasishamone and his band of about 300 men, women and children encamped on the creek near the ford, and entered into a contract with Mr. M. for provisions to the amount of about $500, consisting of potatoes, turnips, corn and five head of fat hogs, dressed. On applying for this contract Pasishamone brought a written recommendation from Mr. Beach, the Indian agent at Fort Des Moines, to the effect that the Indians were in needy circumstances, that Pasishamone was an honorable chief, and would be likely to pay for what he got. This recommendation was good enough, but in the opinion of Mr. M. it did not altogether answer the purpose; he wanted an order from the agent the better to secure his pay. Pasishamone thereupon went to the agent, but whether he had understood Mikesell or not is not known, for instead of the required order he brought back the same kind of a recommendation. Though not satisfied with this, Mikesell concluded to close the contract, which was set forth in writing and signed by the chief and thirty of his braves, each making "his x mark" near the written name.

This done the squaws immediately commenced carrying away the stuff, in which were engaged twenty-five or thirty ponies, going and coming, early and late. Mr. M. had dug his potatoes and pulled his turnips, and had pitted up what he had not disposed of in the contract. But the squaws, after having carried away their stipulated amount of potatoes, (three hundred bushels,) and most of the turnips, commenced taking from the pits, unknown to the owner, pretending to be engaged with the turnips.

But so soon as he discovered the theft he determined to punish them for it. Watching his opportunity, he saw several squaws fill their blankets with potatoes and tie them up ready to carry away. Calling the boys to his assistance, they seized upon the potatoes, carried them to the house, emptied them into the cellar, and threw the blankets into a loft overhead. The squaws followed with angry protestations against such an unlooked-for proceeding, and, when they reached the house, demanded their blankets. M. told them they could not have them till they paid for the potatoes they had stolen. This increased their wrath to a fighting degree, and two of the squaws, large, stout, looking ones, a contact with whom might have resulted in the discomfiture of any single-handed combatant, bared their large, brawny arms and told him they meant to whip him. Indeed, so earnest were their demonstrations, that our hero fully expected an encounter, but knew it would not be advisable to retreat, no matter how it might terminate, so he stood his ground and exchanged threats with them, telling them what a dreadful beating they might expect if they made the attempt. Finally some of the weaker squaws who seemed to be backing their champions, withdrew, seeing which the viragoes also gave up the contest, and all went away.

In a short time, however, they returned with the chief, who instituted an inquiry into the affair. Having learned the facts of the case, Pasishamone made them a speech in which he eulogized the kindness of Mr. M. in trusting them for food when they had not the ready means to pay for it; reminded them of having trusted their plunder in his hands on a former occasion, and received it again without the loss of even a stran of beads; and concluded by shaming them for being so ungrateful as to steal from a man who had treated them with so much kindness. The speech must have been one of considerable pathetic eloquence, for the culprits, notwithstanding the reputed stolidity of these people, actually wept tears of sorrow.

A compromise was then made, and they received their blankets; but Mr. Mikesell never received any pay for his produce. When pay-day came he went to Fort Des Moines and presented the copy of the written contract; but this proved to be worthless, and he lost the entire amount.

Another instance of petty thieving by the Indians may be worth relating:

A couple of settlers named James Scott and Israel Nichols took a claim where the farm now is that was recently owned by Thomas Simpson, but perhaps better known as the present location of the brick school house in sub-district No. 3, Summit township. These men had entered into a co-partnership in in the ownership and improvement of the claim, and had erected a sort of temporary house to live in, much after the fashion of all "claim pens:" and as they were bachelors they had also provided a limited supply of furniture and cooking utensils—no more than was regarded as indispensable to that prosaic kind of living, known as "keeping bach." At the risk of transcending the limits of a plain history, we may imagine that these young men were enjoying themselves to the utmost that their isolated condition and comparative freedom from domestic care entitled them to, working, hunting, cooking and eating by turns, as taste or inclination dictated. But one day their happiness was disturbed by an unexpected visitation. On coming to the cabin for their noon-day meal they were surprised to find neither pot, kettle nor skillet, in which to cook it. But it was easy to conjecture who had perpetrated the robbery; and unmistakable evidence in the case appeared in the discovery of a naked young Indian, apparently about six or seven years old, who had been left at the house either intentionally or by mistake. Here was a state of things not pleasant to contemplate. To get another pot and skillet was possible, though attended with some trouble and expense; but what to do with the wild young Fox, for whom they had no conceivable use, was a question hard to answer. The little fellow seemed greatly excited, and was disposed to run away, but they managed to soothe his fears enough to keep him with them. Though they questioned him as to whom he belonged, for want of sufficient knowledge of English he could give them no definite account of the party.

They, however, decided to follow the robbers and, if possible, recover their property. But is was first necessary to dispose of their captive, whom they did not wish to carry with them in a hasty pursuit. For this purpose they took him to Mr. Mikesell's and tied him to a tree, thinking his detention might bring some of his friends to his relief, and thereby secure a restoration of the stolen articles, provided they failed to get them otherwise. Having secured him thus, they left him under the care of Mrs. M., and proceeded to follow the trail of the Indians. But toward night the little fellow became so restless, and called so loudly for his parents, and wept so bitterly, that Mrs. M., contrary to the injunctions of his captors, released him. No persuasion of hers could induce him to remain. He made her understand, through what acquaintance she had with the language, that he had never slept a night away from his mother and grand-mother. He knew where his home was, and wanted to go. The plea was too much for the heart of a woman, and she let him go. We are not informed whether he reached the camp that night or not, though it is quite probable that his Indian instinct helped him through the difficulty.

Messrs. Scott and Nichols found the Indians camped on Calhoun creek. They had fires built and were cooking their suppers, when the young men unceremoniously entered the camp and attempted to take the stolen vessels that happened to be in use just then. Of course the act was resisted by the savages, who snatched blazing sticks from the fires and assailed the intruders, punching them with the torch-like weapons till they were glad to get away without having accomplished the object of the expedition. In the malee Scott received a severe blow on the side of the head that stunned him for a short time.

Early next day the attack was renewed with re-enforcements, but with no better success. This time the Indians had recourse to tomahawks instead of fire-brands, seeing which the boys fled with such speed that their pursuers were unable to overtake them. Whereupon the latter returned to camp for their ponies, on which they renewed the chase, though after a delay sufficient to give the fugitives time to get over the line. No one was hurt, and the only loss was a good overcoat by Hiram

Mikesell, of which some warrior was very probably the gainer.

Enraged at this unfortunate result, Scott and Nichols determined to get up an expedition to punish the obstinate rascals. Several men volunteered, and all went armed for any emergency. But the enemy had wit enough to anticipate some such a denouement, and considering "discretion the better part of valor," had evacuated the camp in time to make good their escape.

Scott and Nichols afterwards moved to Jasper county, where they opened a trading house. On the occasion of the death of Poweshiek, some of the friends of that chief applied to the traders for whisky to be used in the funeral ceremony, and obtained a few gallons of the cheap stuff in exchange for a pony.

CHAPTER XI.

Red Rock Township Continued—Moving the Indians—Bewildered—Kisk-ke-kosh Institutes a Reform--Moving Pasishamone--Fast Traveling—A Religious Feast—Religious Services at a Death Bed—Funeral—A Burnt Offering of Whisky.

In '45, as was stated in the introductory to this work, the Indian title to the western part of the "New Purchase" became extinct, and this was the year in which most of them moved away, seeking new homes and hunting grounds beyond the limits of civilization. But we have only two instances connected with this event worth relating, for which we are indebted to Mr. Mikesell, who assisted in the removal.

The first relates to the moving of Kish-ke-kosh and his band, consisting of about twenty mounted braves, and a wagon load of goods, such as blankets, saddles, beads, and the limited variety of household furniture in use among the Indians. These had been left in the care of Mr. M. during the summer, not being specially needed then, and somewhat inconvenient to carry about on the frequent removals that these unsettled people were in the habit of making.

At that time the main body of the tribe uuder the command of Kish was located on Skunk river, in Jasper county, and to this place the property was to be taken. With a yoke of oxen they succeeded in getting as far as the point of timber where Monroe now is, on the first day.

It being late in autumn, a heavy snow fell that night, and the Indians not being very well clad for the season disposed themselves upon the ground as close together as they could get, under blankets and skins, to keep warm. In this way they slept soundly, and did not appear to suffer any inconvenience from cold. On opening out next morning a perfect cloud of steam rose from the nest, suggesting the almost certainty of colds, resulting from the sudden transition from perspiring heat to frosty air; but these hardy creatures, accustomed to the exposures of their wild life, did not appear to be affected by it in the least.

Two unfortunate circumstances threatened to interrupt their further progress that day. Early in the morning it was discovered that the cattle had got loosed from the wagon to which they had been fastened, and had disappeared. Mr. M. immediately set out upon their trail, which the still falling snow had not entirely covered, but did not find them till he reached home. On returning he found the Indians at a loss as to what direction to go in resuming the journey. The bewilderment of an Indian is truly said to be an uncommon circumstance; but in this instance the cloudy weather and newly fallen snow, obscuring all trails, rendered the right direction quite uncertain. They were all more or less in a state of anxiety about the matter, and Kish, who, perhaps, felt the principal burden of responsibility resting upon himself, went out alone in search of the hidden pathway. After being some time absent he returned with a favorable report, and the journey was resumed in time to reach the town that night.

It is well known that among these people, as well as among all uncivilized races, the women are in a manner the slaves of the other sex. They are made to do all the drudgery of the camp; cultivate the corn; bring in the game after the hunter has had the sport of slaughtering it, no matter how far away it may be, (he being either too lazy, or deeming it beneath his dignity to bear the burden); procure the fuel to cook it with; catch the ponies for their masters to ride; pack up their tents and household goods when preparing to move, and set them up again when they relocate, &c., &c.

On the way and at the camp Mr. Mikesell had an opportunity to witness some of this kind of tyranny, and took occasion to lecture the chief on the injustice of it. Kish, with the good sense that he manifested in relation to such things, admitted the force of the argument. He had seen it practically demonstrated among the whites, and had reason to think it would do as well among the Indians. He regarded it as a false pride that kept the men from doing a fair share of the work that fell to the squaws, and they ought not to be ashamed of it. He would institute a reform in this matter among his own people; and he did set about it at once, ordering the men to work, and set the example by taking hold himself.

But it is not likely that this reformation was ever carried out to any great extent. The naturally lazy habits of the men, together with their long standing belief that hunting and war were the chief duties that nature had assigned to them, would tend to make such a change in their domestic life very difficult.

Poor Kish! Had he been treated as kindly as he deserved to be, and encouraged to a greater intimacy with the whites, his great, honest heart might have made him the example and leader of other reforms that would have resulted in the civilization and happiness of at least a portion of his race. But, coming in contact with white men whose intercourse with him was principally mercenary, he was shown but few examples in christian civilization worth imitating.

At the time referred to by Pasishamone in his speeh to the squaws, mentioned in the preceding chapter, he had together with the party over whom he held immediate command, also left the most of their goods in the care of Mr. Mikesell for the summer, whilst they occupied a temporary camp on Skunk river, in what is now Jasper county. In the meantime Pasishamone, with his suite of braves, had gone to Old Agency on a visit.

After spending the summer on Skunk, hunting, fishing and raising a little corn, the band moved to Four Mile creek, four miles below Fort Des Moines, where they took up their winter quarters, and awaited the arrival of their chief and goods. So, on his way up Pasishamone called on Mr. Mikesell for assistance in moving them. For this purpose he took two wagons, one drawn by an ox and the other by a horse team, and got as far as Timber creek the first day, and camped near where Mr. Prunty now lives.

Here our informant witnessed a feat of speed and power of endurance on foot, that we think would be hard to surpass by any of the boasted pedestrians of the present day, who walk for a wager. Just at sundown, when the movers were preparing their supper, a strange Indian entered the camp and asked for food and permission to rest there for the night, saying that he was very tired and hungry. His request being granted, he sat down by the fire to await his supper, and in reply to Mr. M.'s inquiries, stated that he was on his way to the Fort to get the dragoons to help recover some stolen horses; that he had started from a place ten miles below Brighton that morning, distance about seventy-five or eighty miles. He was asked how he had managed to travel so far in one day, and only answered that in the morning he would show how it was done.

In due time the weary footman was supplied with corn and meat, of which he ate like a hungry Indian, ravenously and abundantly, till sleep gradually overcame him, and he sank back upon the ground and remained motionless as a log till morning. Then, no sooner was he awake than astir, with limbs not the least stiffened by the previous day's exercise, and ready to renew the journey. When ready to start he told Mr. M. that he might now see how it was done, and immediately set off on a run, making long, easy strides, which speed he kept up with no apparent variation till out of sight, and perhaps, till he reached the Fort. He was afterwards heard from, that he was quite successful in his mission, as he undoubtedly deserved to be.

At the close of the second day the party reached their destination, and camped on the east side of the creek, some distance from the village. Soon after dark a great noise was heard in the village. It somewhat resembled singing, interspersed with shouts and other loud voices, making a commingling of sounds strange and weird-like. And this uproar continued with very little intermission till morning.

Mr. M. was much surprised at this, and early in the evening signified to the chief his intention to go over and see what was the matter. But Pasish, who had just arrived from the scene of the mysterious noise, shook his head gravely, and added, "White man better not go—Indian drunk—hurt white man."

This explanation satisfied "white man" for the time being. He thought it quite probable that the whole village was on a grand spree, and it would not be advisable for him to get in their way. But he noticed that Pasishamone and his braves were astir all night, going and coming at all hours, without showing any signs of drunkenness, but rather demeaning themselves with more than usual sobriety.

All this lent a doubt as to the truth of Pasishamone's statement, and tended to deepen mystery. So in the morning our informant endeavored to risk an attempt to solve it at all events. Seeing the chief come over from the village, and stealthily put a couple of wooden bowls under his blanket, with which he immediately set out on his return, Mr. M. concluded to follow him unobserved. On reaching the village he saw a long wickeup, which appeared to be the place of meeting, from the number of persons about it and going in and out. Seeing no evidences of drunkenness or carousal, he ventured to the door of the hut to see what was going on within. In the centre was a row of kettles hung over a fire, and in each kettle was corn soup and a piece of meat, some of the pieces consisting of the ribs and back-bone of what proved to be a couple of fat dogs. The animals had been skinned except the heads and feet, and these had been scalded or singed to remove the hair, and then nicely roasted or baked to a beautiful brown, emitting a savory odor. They occupied a wooden bowl at each end of the row of kettles, and were reserved for the old men, who regarded them as the choice part of the feast.

The food now seemed to be ready and in waiting for those who were to partake of it; but the preparatory ceremony which seemed to be of a religious character, was not yet quite completed. Around on each side of the wickeup were seated rows of men, singing a jargon that sounded like some of the senseless fal-da-ral that serves as the chorús of a comic song, most of the time keeping their eyes turned upward with a devout expression. At length the singing ceased, and an old man rose to his feet, and in a low, solemn tone, made what appeared to be a prayer. No sooner was it concluded than every Indian was on his feet, having their bowls in readiness, and began an indiscriminate dipping into the soup and dog, and to feast like men who had been undergoing a fast.

This was evidently a thanksgiving feast, made partly as a sacrifice to the Great Spirit, in whom all unchristianized Indians entertain a crude belief, and partly as a feast of welcome to their chief, who had been some time absent from his people. The slaughtering and dressing of the dogs and other preparations were performed during the night, attended by the noise that was heard. During the ceremony no one seemed to notice the presence of the white man, but after it was all over Pasishamone approached Mr. M. with an apology for having lied to him the evening before:

"White man no like dog. Tell white man Indian drunk; he stay away."

Before closing this chapter we shall take occasion to relate an incident to show further that these people were far from being devoid of a religious sentiment; that they believed in the presence, power and mercy of God, and in the immortality of the soul, though their ideas about these matters were not according to the revealed Word.

The incident relates to the death of a child belonging to one of Keokuk's braves. The child had been severely scalded, and the party stopped at Mikesell's to nurse it; but it was evident that it was even then in a dying condition, and the Indians made preparations to hold such religious services over it as they supposed would secure its happy admission into the spirit land. For this purpose they set up a large tent at the foot of the hill, near the house, in the center of which they placed the little sufferer, on a bed. Seeing there was no hope of its recovery, and that it must soon die, Keokuk and a number of his braves seated themselves on the ground in a circle about the death bed, where they performed with appropriate solemnity a series of religious exercises till the child died. These exercises seemed to be principally singing and prayer. The singing was somewhat monotonous in tone, and a constant repetition of certain words or notes like "la, ha, ha, la, la, ha," and was accompanied byt he rattling of a gourd of beans over the head of the child by one appointed to that duty. This was said to have been intended to soothe the spirit in its exit from the body, and waft it happily away. When the singing ceased the worshipers bowed themselves forward, their heads between their knees, covering their faces with their hands, and thus remained for some minutes in silent prayer, audible only in an occasional sigh or groan; but the rattling was continued without intermission. At the proper time the chief would resume the chant, and the others would rise to a sitting posture and join in it. Thus they continued to do for several hours, with great earnestness and patience, and until the spirit of the little one had taken its departure. So intent were they in their devotions that they appeared to take no notice of visitors, several of whom came to the door of the tent to witness the strange performance.

Who will say that such sincerity, such faith, though unattended by the light of Christianity, will not be rewarded by Him who knows the heart, and who, we have reason to believe, will make due allowance for the errors of unavoidable ignorance?

After the child was dead immediate preparations were made for the funeral. It was the intention of the friends of the deceased to dispose of the body after the singular custom frequently practiced by the people in the burial of their dead, that is by tying it in the top of a tree. Observing that this was their intention, Mr. Mikesell interfered, and finally induced them to put it in the ground. He told them that the crows and buzzards would find it, and it would eventually fall down and its bones would get scattered. So they concluded to take his advice and give it a white people's burial. For this purpose Mr. David Worth, who lived in the neighborhood, furnished a coffin, and the few toys that belonged to the little fellow were put in with him, and he was buried a short distance north of the house where Mr. M.'s orchard now is.

When all that remained of his child was hid away from him the grief stricken father gave vent to the sorrow of his heart in a prayer of faith that might well become a Christian in behalf of a living child. Though uttered in the Indian language, it was well enough understood by our informant to warrant him in giving at least the substance. He asked the Great Spirit to take good care of the little one. He was very sorry to give him up, "but," said he, "you, God, know best, and I know he'll be happy with you."

It was the custom of the Indians to regard such articles of food and drink as they were particularly fond of themselves as worthy articles to sacrifice to the Great Spirit, and to offer to the spirits of their departed friends. Whisky, in spite of the baneful effects its use had upon them, was regarded as a very acceptable offering.*

On one occasion the noted chief Keokuk obtained a quart of whisky from Mr. Mikesell, expressly to make an offering of it to the Great Spirit, and a treat to the souls of some of his friends who had been very fond of the beverage during their life-time. Having received the liquor in a bottle, he sat down by the fire and mumbled a prayer, which may have been a formal dedication of it to the sacred purpose intended, and an invitation to the Great Spirit to accept the offering. Pretending to have received a favorable answer, he poured a quantity of the whisky into the fire and the blue blaze flashed up the chimney. He then asked the Great Spirit if he might treat some of his spirit friends. Permission being granted, he turned out about enough for a dram, naming the person for whom it was intended; then another, and another, till the whole quart of bad spirits was consumed in a succession of blue blazes, and a pretty large company of good spirits had each enjoyed a drink.

To some readers this story may seem highly improbable, and even blasphemous, but when we take into account the fact that these ignorant creatures, like some of their more enlightened white brothers, regarded whisky as one of God's blessings, they deemed it their duty to make burnt offerings of it, as the Israelites of old did of their cattle. Tobacco, much valued by the Indians, was frequently offered in the same way.

---

* The fondness of the Indians for strong drinks was so universal, and in some instances so intense, as to lead to the belief that it was more natural than acquired. Such was the intensity of their appetite for this stimulant that they would sacrifice almost any thing to obtain it. We give an instance:

An Indian came to Mikesell's and begged for a drink of whisky. He said if he could get one more drink he would be willing to die. Mr. M. thought he would test the sincerity of this statement, and told the suffering applicant that he would give him a drink if he would let him hang him. With the utmost coolness the poor fellow agreed to the proposition, and a rope was looped on his neck, and passed over a joist ready for the execution. He then received his liquor, drank it with great satisfaction, and closed his eyes in confident expectation of dying. Mr. M then pulled on the rope till the poor wretch was nearly choked; still he showed no opposition to the painful process, and when let down and sufficiently recovered to speak, expressed surprise that the bargain had not been fully carried out on the part of the hangman. He said he supposed it was the last drink of whisky he should need in this world.

CHAPTER XII.

Red Rock Township continued—Claiborn Hall—Elias Prunty—An Adventure—A Difficulty Overcome—A Milling Trip—Killing Wolves—Another Indian Thanksgiving.

Among the very earliest permanent settlers in this township was Claiborn Hall, still remembered as a somewhat prominent personage in political and religious circles, being an active and efficient member of the democratic party, the editor and proprietor of the first paper issued in the county in support of that party, and a minister of the Gospel in the Christian denomination.

Mr. Hall was born in Virginia in 1819; moved with his parents to Boone county, Mo., in '29; and in the autumn of the same year moved to Menard county, Ill., where his parents still reside. In the spring of '43 he came to Iowa and settled four miles north of the present site of Red Rock village. Having secured his claim, Mr. Hall cleared about thirteen acres, and got it planted about the 31st of May. After harvesting this crop he sowed the ground in wheat in the fall, having brought the seed from Illinois, and harvested from it a remarkably heavy yield in the summer following. A load of this wheat he got floured at Keosauqua, distant about a hundred miles.

In the spring of '45 he returned to Illinois and secured the co-partnership of Miss Susan T. Duncan, a former acquaintance, with whom he immediately repaired to his western home, and converted his "bachelor's hall" into a country residence; and, it may be equally important to state that during his residence here he organized and superintended the first Sabbath school in the northern part of the county.

In '46 he was elected county surveyor, held the office one year and then succeeded to that of probate judge, which he held two years. In '49 he was elected sheriff, moved to Knoxville and held that office two years. In November, '50, his wife died, whereupon he put his official business into the hands of his deputy, Isaac H. Walters, and went to Illinois, where he spent the winter at the residence of his father. In the spring he returned and resumed the duties of his office; and at the expiration of the term was elected to the triple office of recorder, collector and treasurer; held it two years, and then voluntarily retired from the field as an office seeker.

Some time during the term of his last named office he formed a co-partnership with L. D. Jackson, (now deceased), in the mercantile business, and purchased an old stock of goods from L. W. Babbitt, to begin with. This business he continued only two years, when he sold out, purchased a farm near Knoxville, to which he retired with his second wife, whom he had married shortly before.

But again, in '56, he brought himself into public notice by becoming the editor and proprietor of the first Democratic newspaper published in the county. Being a warm politician, and somewhat enthusiastic in the interests of his party, he purchased the press and type for a paper to be devoted to the support and dissemination of its principles in Marion county, and in June of the year above mentioned, the "Democratic Standard" made its appearance. But being entirely without experience in this line of business, he succeeded but poorly, and after a short time disposed of the concern to a company.

Soon after his retirement from the publishing business Mr. Hall was elected to the office of county superintendent of schools for two years, and with the close of this term he finally retired from the political arena as an office seeker, and has since divided his time and talents as a farmer and a minister of the gospel In '64 he returned to Illinois for permanent residence, where, in December of that year, his second wife died.

The next person that succeeded Mr. Hall as a settler in the same neighborhood, was Elias Prunty. He was born in Scott Co., Ky., in 1809, moved to Morgan Co., Ill., in the fall of '33, and in the fall of '43 to Red Rock township, three miles north of the village.

On reaching the residence of Thomas Tuttle, where Pella now stands, Mr. Prunty began his search for a claim, and continued it in the direction of the river till they reached Red Rock village, then consisting of one or two small cabins. Here they found Claiborn Hall, who was camped on his claim, and proceeded at once to secure a location in the immediate neighborhood, and put up a cabin.

Mr. Prunty's family consisted of his wife and four children, and his stock of domestic animals were two horses and two cows that he brought with him. But, like most of the early settlers, he was without a supply of provisions for the winter; and was obliged to repair to the Old Purchase for such articles of consumption as were indispensable to life. He obtained his supply of corn and meat from Round Grove, Jefferson county, and to this place he made four trips during that first winter, leaving his family exposed to whatever inconveniences might be incidental to their entire separation from neighbors, and to the annoying visits of the Indians, who made them a call every few days. They were, however, kindly treated by Mrs. Prunty and the children, and manifested no disposition to be uncivil in return.

On these trips Mr. P. went prepared to "camp out," for there were but few cabins on the trail he had to follow, till he reached the Old Purchase. On one occasion, having camped n Cedar creek, he awoke in the morning under a covering of snow ten inches thick. On getting up he found the weather extremely cold, the fire extinguished, and his horses apparently nearly frozen. After feeding his team he hastily kindled a fire and prepared a drink of warm coffee, then renewed his journey with what speed he could make through the deep, unbroken snow, intending to reach home that day. But when within three miles of the place, night overtook him and he found it extremely difficult, if not quite impossible, to keep in the right direction, to say nothing of following the obscure, snow-covered path that was his only dependence for a road. But being much chilled, and comparatively anxious to reach home, he drove on until he was compelled to admit the unpleasant suspicion that he was lost. At length, not knowing exactly in what direction he was traveling, he quite despaired of reaching home that night, and proceeded to split up his wagon bed for fuel. Pretty soon he heard the barking of a dog, and, immediately setting out in direction of the sound, soon found himself at home once more. The dog had heard the noise, and gave the signal that probably saved his master's life.

In the spring Mr. Prunty found it necessary to get a team suitable for breaking prairie, and traded his horses for oxen. Still he had no plow, and what was worse, had no money to buy one with. A breaking team would be of little use without that indispensable tool; and the difficulty had to be overcome in some way. The only thing of considerable value that could be spared, was a feather-bed; and this Mr. P. sold to Adam Goal, (many years since a resident of Monroe, Jasper county;) got the cash, went to Fairfield, purchased the plow, commenced breaking the sod in April, and succeeded in breaking, planting in corn, and fencing thirty acres that season.

In June, after getting the ground fenced, Mr. Prunty, in company with Joel Worth, made one of those long, laborious and adventurous, but not less indispensable milling expeditions that seemed inseparable from pioneer life at that early period. They had to go eight miles south of Brighton to get corn, paying twenty-five cents per bushel for twenty-seven bushels in the ear. This they had to shell, which delayed them several days at that place; and when they reached Cedar creek they found it bank full, and fording impossible. Here they remained a week awaiting the abatement of the flood, or for a chance to get ferried over, and at length obtained canoe transportation in the manner described in the fourth chapter of this work. For this service they paid the ferryman two bushels of meal after they could get it ground.

Being disappointed in getting any grinding done at the mill to which they first intended to go, they went down Skunk river some distance, to another called Sugar Creek Mill. Here they encountered another raging stream called Lick Run. It was narrow, but seemed almost too threatening to ford. But the attempt could not well be avoided; so in they plunged, and succeeded in getting through with no greater loss than a slight damage to one sack of corn by getting it wet.

After two days longer delay they obtained their meal and started on their return trip. To add to their discomfort, it had rained almost incessantly from the time of leaving home, was still raining, and the roads were in an almost impassable condition. Their progress was therefore slow and exceedingly toilsome; and at length their cattle finally failed, six miles below Oskaloosa, rendering it impossible to get further without help. Help could not be obtained short of home, a distance of at least thirty-five miles; but Mr. Prunty concluded to try and get there that day on foot. He traveled as rapidly as he could but night overtook him when he was yet four miles from home, exhausted with weariness and want of food, not having had anything to eat that day. Mr. P., however still thought he could reach home, and trudged on as well as the darkness and his exhausted condition would permit. But at length he lost the trail, and commenced wandering about in search of it, and became completely bewildered. Thus he continued to do till he fell over the abrupt bank of a small creek. This unpleasant interruption completely discouraged him from further efforts to find the way home that night. So he gathered up a bed of grass, upon which he stretched himself to rest, and, notwithstanding the loneliness of his exhausted situation, in a country infested with wolves and other wild animals, and his necessarily anxious state of mind, his over-exhausted physical energies gave way to repose, and he slept soundly till day-light. On rousing up and looking about, he recognized his locality, found himself only two miles from home, and was soon there, after an absence of just twenty-one days.

So soon as possible Thomas Black was sent with a yoke of cattle to the assistance of Worth, and the provisions were finally got home without any further serious difficulty, though it was found that some of the meal was materially damaged by the dampness and heat of the weather.

During the absence of Mr. Worth on this occasion his family became reduced to short rations in the way of food; and the rain and flooded state of the streams rendered communication with the neighbors difficult. The nearest neighbors to the Worths was a German family named Metz, living a short distance across a narrow stream. This stream was sometimes filled to overflowing, rendering it dangerous if not quite impossible for the ladies of either house to pass and re-pass, no matter how urgent the need; and borrowing, if it ever was excusable, was then. The pouring rain would extinguish the fire on the ground hearth during the night, and there was no such a thing as a friction match about the house to re-light it with. And what was worse than this, Mrs. Worth had neither bread nor meal, and between her and her neighbor was the impassable gulf. She, however, could communicate a knowledge of her needs; then the two women would wade in on each side of the stream so far as they dared, and Mrs. Metz would throw a loaf bread or a fire-brand into the extended apron of her neighbor.

Mr. Prunty relates an instance of wolf-killing that may serve to illustrate what we have already said of the great number and boldness of these animals. An ox belonging to James Harp died and the carcass was left within easy gun-shot of a claim pen belonging to one of the Harps. Mr. P. was then invited to participate in the sport of shooting the wolves that came in large numbers to feed upon it. A bee-tree had just been found, and the sportsmen sat up all night eating honey and firing upon the wolves, a large number of which they killed by partially random shooting by star light. The slaughter had been fearful, for morning light revealed the ground strewn with the dead and wounded, though the number of the living did not seem to have been diminished, as they continued to swarm about the bait night after night, heedless of the danger.

But we may not conclude this chapter before relating another Indian thanksgiving feast, as witnessed by Mr. Prunty. The event took place in the autumn of 1844, at a place near Red Rock village, and on the line between the United States and the Indian Territory, as designated by an inscription on a board fastened to a post. Some fifty warriors had collected at the place, under the leadership of Kish-ke-kosh, and participated in the ceremonies. A couple of long logs had been placed together and a fire was burning between them, over which was the carcass of a dog fastened to a stick by which it was rolled from one end of the fire to the other till it was well singed and roasted, and was swollen to a rotundity that made it rather an unpalatable looking object.

During the roasting process, the warriors sat in a circle around an upright pole midway up which were fastened bears' claws, birds' claws, dogs' feet, and bunches of tobacco; and on the top birds' wings and beaks; and all were slowly burning by the aid of some combustible material. They seemed to be engaged in a sort of conference meeting around this singular sacrificial altar, each brave rising, one at a time, and speaking a few words with the solemnity peculiar to a religious exercise. And their appearance was not less remarkable than their performances; each one wore a string of bear and eagle claws around their necks, and had polecat skins tied about their knees.

So soon as these exercises were finished, they partook of the dog, and then retired, probably for the purpose of holding a dance; for such gala days were usually closed with this performance, the braves alone participating in it. The dance was performed in a circle, each performer following the other in a half bent attitude, keeping step to the tap of some kind of instrument by one who occupied the centre, and singing a sort of chorus. The step was not rapid, nor intended to be musical, but they were alternate as in walking, uniform as in military marching, and each foot was brought down with a force that sounded upon the beaten earth like the stroke of a sledge. The performance was not altogether unpleasant.

In addition to being a thanksgiving occasion, it was a preparation day for a two or three months' hunt, and the sacrifices were to propitiate the favor of the Monatou, that he might give them success.

Several years later Mr. Prunty moved to near Vandalia, Jasper county, where he resides at this present writing.

CHAPTER XIII.

Red Rock Township Continued—Joel B. Worth—A Critical Situation—Sickness and Loss—A Tough Joke—David Worth—A Prairie Fire—James A. Chestnut.

Joel A. Worth and Thomas Black were the the first persons who succeeded Mr. Prunty in the settlement of the northern part of the township. Mr. W. was born in Ky., Aug. 17, 1817, emigrated to Ill. in '29, and from thence to Fairfield, Iowa, in Nov. '43, in company with Thomas Black, and their families.

Here winter overtook them, and they were compelled to secure quarters for their families till spring. Having provided corn and fuel, they set out for the "New Purchase" in search of a permanent location. At the close of a cold day in December they got as far as where Pella now is, and being unable to reach a more sheltered place, they put up a sort of cat-faced tent to windward of a scanty grove that grew near where the Central University now stands, and prepared to pass the night there. But a serious difficulty interfered with an important part of this preparation, which was to kindle a fire. Everything was damp, the wind was blowing a strong, cold blast, and our wayfarers were in imminent danger of perishing unless they could get something warm for the "inner man." They had one box of matches, but these seemed to have been either worthless at the start or had become damaged, and they were not aware of it till at this critical moment. One after another they refused to ignite, till nearly the entire box was exhausted, and all hope of obtaining the life sustaining heat was as nearly extinguished. At length only two matches remained, and upon these seemed to depend their weal or woe. Fortunately, or it may be providentially, to their great joy, these two matches happened to possess the vitality requisite for the crisis. With the utmost care a fire was started, and a warm supper restored the adventurers to comparative courage and comfort.

Next day they reached their destination and took up their quarters with Mr. Prunty till claims could be selected and houses built. The claim selected by Mr. W. proved to be in section 1, town. 77, range 20, on which, on the 14th of Feb., he put up a cabin, and on the 19th of March had the pleasure of introducing his family to their new home.

That spring, by joining teams with Black and Prunty, Mr. Worth got fifteen acres of his land broken. From this, notwithstanding the lateness of the growing season, he succeeded in raising a pretty fair crop of sod corn, and that without any fencing, there being then little or no stock in the country to trespass upon the crops.

During his early pioneer life here Mr. Worth suffered some adversities that may be worth relating. Soon after returning from the milling trip related in the preceding chapter, he fell sick of a fever, brought on by severe exposure, from which he did not fully recover for four months. Then early in the spring following ('45) one of his oxen died, leaving him without any kind of a team by the aid of which to replenish his store of provisions, that threatened soon to be exhausted. Being entirely without means he could neither purchase another ox nor the necessary supply of food. This was a trying situation, and the only way to get out of it was to sell the remaining ox for what he could get, and invest the money in provisions. This he did, getting eleven dollars for the animal, and with Allen Tice, to whom he had sold it, went to Illinois and returned with three barrels of flour and one of salt. This supplied them till the corn became fit for use; and Mr. W. was enabled to get another team in time for another season's cropping.

An anecdote may not be out of place here. It occurred at a

time when provisions were very scarce, especially meat, as most of the game had been killed or driven away by the Indians. Mr. Worth had been out hunting, and returned with what appeared to be the hind quarter of a small deer. The meat looked tempting to Mrs. W., who had a genuine fondness for venison, and she was eager to have a mess of it so soon as it could be cooked; so she took immediate charge of it, and owing to the want of grease to fry it with, put the whole into a large pot to boil, and hastened the process with a good hot fire.

After blubbering away at a lively rate for about an hour or more, the good lady thought it about time the tender young deer was done, and proceeded to test it by prodding it with a fork. But, to her surprise, the meat seemed about as tough, if not a little tougher, than when it was put there. Impatient at this, she rushed the fire, and kept the pot in a foaming temperature for some time longer. Then again she prodded the ham, and was not only surprised but puzzled to find it even tougher than ever, so tough, indeed, that it fairly resisted the sharp points of the fork. She declared she had never seen nor heard of the like before, but was determined to boil it down if such a thing could be done. But it was evident that the longer it was boiled the further it was from being done, till finally it became as black and hard as a piece of old sole-leather. It was truly a curious kind of venison, and Mrs. W. was at her wit's end as to what further disposition to make of it. At this her husband could no longer restrain his merriment. What was the matter? Why, her young venison was a piece of a big old catamount, all muscle, that contracted and became harder by contact with heat. It was a tough joke, and it may be supposed that the cook appreciated it no more than she did the venison.

During the year following, (1845), Mr. Worth moved into Jasper county, just across the line, where he still lives in the enjoyment of a comfortable competence as the reward of his early trials in pioneer experience.

During the autumn of the same year that Joel Worth settled in this township, he was followed by his brother David, who had been to the country on a prospecting tour in the month ot August previous.

On his way up the last time, Mr. W. had an opportunity to witness one of those grand, and sometimes fearful conflagrations that were so common before the prairies were sufficiently settled to interpose any obstruction to the sweeping march of the devouring element. He had camped, with his family, a short distance from a house in the vicinity of Black Oak Grove, Mahaska county. Sometime during the night they were awakened by a suffocating cloud of smoke, and an alarm of fire; and had barely time to get the wagons moved to a bare spot of ground adjoining the house, and secure the tent, before the whole prairie was swept by a long column of fire, producing a night scene at once grand and terrific. Stables and fences were with difficulty saved, and fighting fire was the order for the remainder of the night.

As they neared their destination, they were met by Thomas Black, who had been on the alert for their appearance, and had seen the wagons five or six miles distant on the prairie, where there were then no groves or improvements to obstruct the view. They were gladly welcomed. To those who were citizens of the country at that early date, having been a year, or at least a few months, separated from the society they had been all their lives accustomed to, the arrival of a new comer, especially if he happened to be a relation or acquaintance, was an event of no no small importance, and the greeting was comparatively joyful. Mr. W. located on section two, which was bounded on the west by the United Sates boundary line. He has been nearly ever since a citizen of the county, and now lives on section eight.

Among other early citizens of Red Rock, still well remembered by most of the old settlers, was James A. Chestnut whose name, it may be remembered, appears in the list of first grand jurors. He was born in Ireland, February 1, 1803; came to America with his parents at the age of two years, landing at New York. From thence he came to Indiana; from thence to Iowa in '41, and settled in Van Buren county, where he remained for a short time; then moved to Mahaska county and took a claim precisely where Oskaloosa now is. But, not foreseeing the value this land would ultimately attain to, and, like many others, thinking the lands along the river would always be worth much more than the high prairie, he sold this claim, and settled at the head of White Breast Prairie, where the old Ewing farm now is.

After a short residence here he went to Lee county, where he remained a year; then returned and settled in Red Rock village in '48. In the spring following he went to California where he remained nearly two years. On his way home he contracted the cholera at New Orleans, and died at Natchez.

Mr. Chestnut was known as a worthy citizen, and for some time a class leader in the M. E. Church. His widow remained at Red Rock till very recently, when she went to Missouri with one of her sons.

CHAPTER XIV.

Red Rock Township Continued—Stedling on Indian Credit —A Search Warrant—Mock Trial of a Horse Thief—Lynchiny Horse Thieves.

We have spoken of the thieving propensity of the Indians; but truth will not permit us to say that they were the only class of people given to this vice during the early settlement of the country. We are informed that much of it was done by the whites on Indian credit. In those days the settlers along the river permitted their hogs to run at large, much as they do now, each owner depending upon a certain ear-mark whereby to distinguish his own from his neighbor's swine. But these marks did not always prove the ownership of the animal, particularly after it had "fallen among thieves." All that was needed to destroy this evidence was to cut off the ears, or even the head, and secrete them. Not unfrequently these ears were found in possession of the Indians, un oubtedly furnished them by the real thieves in order to direct suspicion from themselves and fix it upon the "reds." Or, as the latter were in the habit of buying their meat of the whites, they would sometimes thus come into possession of a dressed hog, minus the ears; and, on being asked about it, any answer they might give was no certain proof, *pro* or *con.* Thus it was a difficult matter either to prove the property or convict the thief.

At one time two brothers named Bell, living in the nighborhood of Red Rock village, were strongly suspected of being the perpetrators of numerous thefts of live stock and other kinds of property. Yet, thus far, no proof sufficient to convict them could be found, and they were permitted to go unmolested by law.

Among such articles as disappeared so mysteriously as to lead to the belief that they had been stolen, were two or three fat hogs belonging to 'Squire Russell, that he had in a pen, near his house, intending them for his own use. Of course the 'Squire was justly enraged at being thus robbed of such valuable property, and determined to make an immediate effort to recover it. To this end he issued a search warrant, put it in the hands of the constable, and then, in company with another person, making a party of three, went to help serve it.

To the Bells they went; but no signs of the pork, alive or dead, could be found around the premises; so it was determined to search the inside of the cabin, though much against the protestations of the occupants. Still nothing of the article was visible till, at the suggestion of the anxious 'Squire, a pile of corn in a corner of the room was pulled down, disclosing the hairless, headless, and disemboweled corpses of three hogs. Of course the 'Squire was sure they were his; but in the absence of all proof marks, he could not identify them sufficiently to take lawful possession of them. It was necessary to find the heads and ears first, and, though the prospect of doing so must have been rather slender, the party proceeded to make a thorough examination of the grounds within a reasonable distance from the house. Presently their attention was attracked by a number of crows, a short distance in the grove, that appeared to be discussing some subject of peculiar interest to themselves, flying up and down and caw-caw-cawing in an excited manner. Thither the searchers went, hoping to find the heads to be the subjects of this crow demonstration, but in this they were disappointed. Instead of the heads they found the hide of an ox, the marks of which proved it to have been once worn by an animal belonging to a Mr. Flanders, and that had been mysteriously missing for some time.

After some further search all hope of finding the heads was abandoned, and the 'Squire was compelled to leave his pork where he found it. The ox hide was taken to town and hung upon a shed at the 'Squire's, till it could be claimed by the owner. But that night it disappeared again, and was never more found.

An occasional instance of horse-stealing also occurred, the country then being so thinly settled as to render the chances of escape much better than in older and more populated districts. But, once captured, the thief had a fair chance of being subjected to punishment under the rulings of Judge Lynch.

On one occasion an individual who was suspected of being engaged in this business, was captured and conveyed to 'Squire Russell's for trial. The trial was to come off at night, and it was known to all parties, except the prisoner, that it would be a sham, merely intended to frighten him and run him out of the country.

So, when the case was called, a Mr. Martin appeared for the prosecution and John Cameron for the defense. But, during the progress of the trial, Cameron assumed to have little hope of clearing his client, and privately advised him to get away if he possibly could. But the prospect of doing so seemed extremely hazardous, for several of the spectators were armed with rifles, and appeared to be watching the prisoner closely. His counsel, however, kindly interfered in his behalf, and he was permitted, on some pretense, to leave the court room for a few minutes, attended by Cameron himself and several of the guard. No sooner were they out than Cameron whispered to him to run for his life and never be seen in the country again. The poor fellow, whether guilty or innocent, took his lawyer's advice, and, without stopping to say good-bye to any one, made off toward the brush with all the speed that the darkness would admit of. And to hasten him, several shots were fired after him, accompanied by the yells of the guard apparently in hot pursuit.

Agreeable to the advice of his lawyer, he was never more

seen in the country. A day or two after, an Indian exhibited a wallet he had found in the timber, that proved to have belonged to the fugitive. It contained a letter addressed to him by some enamored damsel who was, perhaps, blissfully ignorant of his character and calling. Unfortunately for a more romantic conclusion of this story, the letter was lost, and both its contents and the name of the writer have been forgotten.

Another of these rascals did not fare quite so well. He was captured by Ray Alfrey, on the stolen horse, taken to town, tried, severely whipped and driven from the country. And another instance was that of a fellow named Sutton, who, after being tried, convicted and whipped, had the audacity to return and steal another horse. He was taken a second time and lynched; but even this failed to cure him. He stole yet another horse and was making off with it when overtaken and shot dead.

Mention has been made of the Williams family, who were early settlers in the neighborhood of Red Rock village, and were frequenters of the place, "hale friends well met" with those who were fond of liquor and the diversions common to a semi-desperado sort of life. Particularly was this the case with Mat, whose fisticuff duel with "Old Blank" is related in another place. We close this chapter with another little incident in which Mat took an active part.

A man named Henry Lott, living near town, lost a bell, which was afterwards found by the elder Williams. Whether truly or not, some of the younger Williamses were informed that Lott had accused their father of stealing the bell. This enraged the boys desperately, and they immediately resolved to have revenge. Being well fired up with bad whisky, Mat and John made a night raid upon Red Rock and the surrounding country in search of Lott, determined to give him a summary "cleaning out." One of the actors in the drama stated that they did not wait for a quiet admittance into any house, but kicked upon every door they came to.

At length they found the object of their search in bed at Colonel Alley's; and, without waiting for parley or explanation, they pulled him out of bed and out of the house, where they subjected him to some rough treatment for a short time, Lott all the time pleading not guilty, and offering to go with them to town and satisfy them as to the truth of his plea.

R. R. Watts, a justice of the peace, who happened to be Lott's bed fellow at the time, being unable to command the peace, determined to secure the arrest of the Williamses, went to Knoxville next day, where he obtained a warrant and sent the sheriff to arrest them. At the June session of the District Court, 1846, John and Mat were brought up for trial on a charge of assault. In John's case the evidence against him did not prove sufficient, and he was discharged, and Mat was remanded for trial before Landon J. Burch, justice of the peace, where he was found guilty and fined.

CHAPTER XV.

Red Rock Township Continued—The History of a Couple of Claim Battles.

Prominent among the numerous claim troubles that arose between the settlers of Red Rock, was one in which the noted Col. Alley and a person named Shoemake, were the principal actors. This difficulty assumed almost the preparations of a riot, and came very near resulting in bloodshed.

The claim that become the subject of dispute, is the land now owned by Mr. Talbot, one of the proprietors of the Otley mill, and the claim cabin stood on the knoll, about where Mr. T.'s house now stands, a short distance northeast of town. Each of the contestants claimed to have a just title to the property and both were so determined to maintain their rights that for a time nothing like a compromise could be even hoped for. And, as if to aggravate the difficulty, and bring matters to a crisis, the Colonel, on the alert for an opportunity to take advantage of his enemy, one day found Shoemake absent, took a team and wagon, moved his household goods to another place and took possession of the house. But, knowing that he could not retain it alone, he called to his aid a number of his friends, armed for an emergency and supplied with whisky. Thus equipped, they turned the cabin into a fortress and awaited an attack from Shoemake, who they knew would come well supported. For this they had not long to wait, for Shoemake, on discovering what had taken place, was greatly enraged, and lost no time in collecting a squad of his friends with the avowed intention of ousting the usurper. They readily came to his aid to the number of about fifty. In the meantime the Colonel's forces were swelled by reinforcements to about the same number, though they did not all take shelter in the fort.

A regular battle was now imminent. The opposing forces were near enough to each other to make a lively and interesting thing of it, and each was apparently determined to carry his point at all hazards. But the time was principally occupied with a combat of words, at times so hot that, apparently, any overt act would have been the signal for an appeal to arms. Yet, happily, not a gun was fired, and at length a better state of things triumphed. A compromise was offered by some of the more peacably disposed of the Shoemake party, and the Colonel sent for to consult. The result was that, rather than risk the hazardous plan of fighting it out, he gave Shoemake $175.00 for the claim, and retained possession of it. Thus ended what, to all appearances, came very near being a bloody affair.

One more instance of the kind may here be related, though we have been informed since the above was written that it occurred some time previously thereto, and should have so appeared in this history. We find it difficult, if not quite impossible, to arrange every incident in the exact order of its date, and therefore ask the reader's indulgence.

In 1845 a claim on the north bank of the river, a short distance below town, was owned by two brothers by the name of Wilson, who had put a house on it, and cleared and fenced a few acres of ground. But, as their residence was distant from the claim, (see history of Summit,) they were not constantly there, and were some times absent for several days; and this led some persons to regard the claim as justly forfeited, and subject to be "jumped." Thereupon a man named Sigler, newly arrived, and on the lookout for a place, pounced upon it. The Wilsons, not wishing to eject him in the summary manner usually done in such cases, concluded to try the civil process of law, and applied to Colonel Alley for help. But this wily limb of the law refused to undertake the case without a retaining fee of ten dollars, saying that Sigler would undoubtedly apply to him on the same business, and he would not consider himself bound to any one without a fee in advance. So the Wilson brothers paid him the ten dollars, and suit was entered.

The first business was to send the constable (John Babcock) for Sigler. Not finding him at the claim pen, the officer went over the river to a certain place where it was understood he, (Sigler,) made his home occasionally. Here he (Babcock,) met a stranger of whom he inquired the whereabouts of Sigler, and the stranger informed him that Sigler was to be found at another house in the neighborhood. But upon inquiring at the place designated, the constable discovered that he had been deceived; and on returning to the place where he had seen the stranger he further discovered that the stranger was Sigler himself, and that, surmising the officer's business, had put him on a false trail till he could get safely out of the way.

Sigler was not seen in that neighborhood again, but the Wilson brothers having been put to some trouble and expense on his account, determined that they would not pay another lawyer's fee in a like case, but would take the usual means of ejecting an intruder.

An opportunity to carry out this determination occurred soon after. One day, being informed that an old man named Cannon was in the house with the apparent purpose of holding the claim, the young men immediately repaired to the place with the intention of driving him out, should he refuse to go voluntarily. But, in consequence of the intruder's age, they thought it would be scarcely proper to lay violent hands upon him; so, after repeatedly ordering him to go, he persistently refusing, they moved his things out, and then put out the fire. The weather was quite cool, and Mr. Cannon, not having any means of renewing the fire, was compelled to seek shelter elsewhere. The Wilsons then closed the door, fastened it with a padlock, and went home.

Next morning, whilst on the way to the claim, accompanied by David Ray, who was to assist them in some work they were going to do on the premises that day, they met three men, Wm. Cannon, a son of the old man, James Chestnut and Andrew Stortz, who rather abruptly informed them that the old man was in the house again, and that they meant to keep him there. This bit of intelligence roused the ire of the boys, and they instantly replied that they would oust him, even at the risk of their lives. The other party then made some attempt to drive them back, and in so doing Stortz made some demonstrations toward Scott, (the elder of the Wilson brothers,) with a club. But Scott being armed with an ax, stood his ground so threateningly that the Cannon party deemed it unsafe to make any further attempts, and left our heroes to go their way.

But it was now found to be advisable to obtain some help. They had ample reason to believe that the Cannon party would be reenforced to some extent; so Freeman Wilson immediately returned to invite a few of their friends to help them meet the emergency. About fourteen men responded to the call, and in a body, marched to the scene of action, where they met the enemy, seven in number. Scott thereupon proceeded to again remove the household goods without being resisted. After this was done a tin pan was found to be missing, but was very soon discovered in the possession of the notorious Dick Billops, who was seated upon it, on the verge of, and with his back toward, the steep bank of the river, giving utterence to some lofty phrases inspired by the presence of a well-known spirit to which he was most slavishly addicted. At this moment J. H. Mikesell, a member of the Cannon party, observing Dick's proximity to the bank, rushed upon him, and with the words, "don't say any thing, Dick," sent him a backward somersault into the river. Dick came up in a rage, and seized a rifle from the hands of James Price, and would have fired upon Mikesell, but for the interference of others.

This circumstance now seemed to be regarded as the signal for a general action, and something of a muss followed. Clubs and pistols were drawn; one man was badly gouged and another so severely punched in the side that he did not recover from the effects thereof for some time.

It now being evident that the Wilsons could not be driven from their purpose, the Cannonites withdrew. After their departure Scott, in acknowledgment of the services of his friends, told them to go up to Russell's and get something to drink, whilst he, with his brother George and Mordecai Yearns, remained on guard at the house till there should be no longer any danger of a renewal of the attack, for that day at least. It was, however, proposed by some of the leaders of the Cannon party, that if the Wilsons would remain upon and work the claim they should not be disturbed, which they agreed to do. About a year afterwards they sold the claim.

The above are related as the most important of numerous instances of claim difficulties, the narration of which would swell the number of these pages beyond the proper limits of a local history. We may only add that disturbances in relation to the rights of property were almost an every day occurrence, giving rise to arbitrations and law-suits almost without end, and to bitterness and enmity between neighbors that only time and a more settled state of things could obliterate. It was not till some time after the land sales, when most of the settlers had secured titles to their lands, and others who had been unable to do so had sold their claims and moved away, that peace was restored, with amity and good fellowship between the settlers.

CHAPTER XVI.

Red Rock Township Continued—First Preachers—Pardo, the Missionary—His Adventure at Red Rock—Poor Success with the Indians—Anecdotes of Spurlock—First District School in the North Part of the Township.

Among the first regularly authorized ministers of the Gospel who first preached within the limits of Red Rock township, were Johnson, of the M. E. church, and M. J. Post, of the Baptist; both in '44 and '45. Mr. Johnson's regular appointment was at the house of Joel Worth.

Another preacher, named Pardo, also came to Red Rock at an early date, and claimed to have been sent by the government as a missionary to the Indians. On his arrival he asked the white people of Red Rock village if they desired preaching. Being answered in the affirmative, and that they were even anxious for the gospel, he made an appointment, and preparations were immediately made for the occasion. Seats were laid down, and a large goods box provided for a stand.

After having gone through with the ordinary preliminaries for preaching, the Rev. Mr. Pardo mounted his box and began his discourse, waxing warmer and louder as he preached. But suddenly, and to him most unexpectedly, in the midst of one of his most eloquent flights, down came the box, preacher and all, causing quite a sensation among the congregation. Thinking it merely an accident, he remounted the box and resumed his discourse; but only got fairly going again when the accident was repeated. This was too much for poor Pardo. He concluded that where such an accident could happen twice in close succession, it must have had help, and was not very anxious of his success there as a minister of the Gospel.

He thereupon concluded to leave the people of Red Rock to their own destruction, and turn his attention to the real object of his mission—the Indians. But here it appears that he was destined to meet with little more encouragement than he received from the whites. When preaching to a party of them at the Phelps trading house, on Lake Prairie, relating the story of the cross, and exhorting his hearers to repentance, one of them interrupted by asking who killed the son of God, white man or Indian. "White man," said Pardo, who could not very properly avoid answering the question. "Then let white man repent," rejoined the Indian; "If God had sent his son to the Indians they would not have killed him."

At another time he was preaching to Keokuk's band, telling them that if they would repent of their sins and believe in God, when they died they should go to a land flowing with milk and honey. Keokuk, who entertained so little confidence in the promise that he was disposed to make it a subject of ridicule, replied that for his part he didn't like milk or honey, but if he, Pardo, would take him to a place where corn and whisky were plenty, he would go.

We know not if Mr. Pardo continued his missionary labors, in opposition to these discouraging evidences of unbelief; but if he did he must have been endowed with a full share of apostolic faith.

An anecdote of the notorious Spurlock is related as having transpired at Red Rock in the winter of '44 and '45. Spurlock, it may be remembered, claimed to be a preacher of the M. E. Church, and in spite of frequent expulsions and impositions of silence continued to preach occasionally. The principal charges against him were: his reputation as a maker and vendor of bad money, a charge all but substantiated; and a weakness for whisky. With a certain class he was said to be quite popular as a preacher. When he wished to preach he would obtain a jug of whisky, and this would scarcely fail to secure for him a crowd of hearers of his particular class, who liked his preaching for the sake of his liquor. At the time referred to Spurlock was crossing the river at Red Rock, moving west, when his wagon wheels cut through the ice so that he could get no further without help; so he applied to the citizens of the place, and a few volunteered. After the vehicle had been placed upon safe ground once more, the owner proceeded to manifest his thanks for their kindness by bringing forth his jug. None were disposed to slight the offer, and he concluded the performance by a hearty drink. Then, having restored the vessel to its place in the wagon, he turned to his helpers, and with much apparent sincerity, told them if they would find him a house for the purpose he would preach to them that night. They answered that they would, and Mr. J. D. Bedell kindly opened his cabin for the occasion. The novelty of the circumstance drew quite a number together, and the Rev. Mr. Spurlock entertained them with a well-timed discourse, in the course of which he took occasion to reply to some insinuations that had been made about his counterfeiting. Without denying it he said: "It is true that I make my own money, and I am not ashamed to acknowledge it. So far from that, if some of you will come to my wagon in the morning, I will show you the tools that I do it with."

This was fair, and uttered in such a plausable manner that some two or three persons, who believed confidently in the old fellow's reputation as a bogus manufacturer, thought they might have their curiosity gratified by a sight of the moulds, and, possibly, get an explanation of the process of using them. We have no right to say exactly what motive prompted this desire for knowledge. It may have been a good one. So, early next morning they waited upon Mr. Spurlock at his camp, and reminded him of his promise. And he proceeded immediately to fulfill it. Going to the back part of his covered wagon, he took out an ax, a maul and some iron wedges.

"Here, gentlemen," said he, "are the tools I make my money with. I'm not ashamed nor afraid to let you see them."

Thereupon the curiosity seekers vanished, rather ashamed of their folly in supposing that the wily old rogue would be so indiscreet as to initiate them into the mysteries of a business scarcely safe for him to follow secretly.

Spurlock was a person of remarkably tender sensibilities in relation to some things, that made him amusingly eccentric. An instance is related of him that occurred during his residence at a place called Brim's Point, Wapello county. He was the owner of a favorite cat, an animal that, for some cause or other, he was much attached to. But it came to pass that said cat died—died a natural death notwithstanding the seven lives reputed to belong to the species—causing its bereaved master almost inconsolable grief. In token of his love for the departed, he provided her a coffin, gave her a decent burial, and marked the place with a mound. To an acquaintance who chanced to stop at his house a short time after the funeral, he told with grief-choking utterance and swimming eyes, the story of his bereavement. He then took his visitor to the grave, and there, with the agony of one bereft of an only child beloved, he wept and related the history and virtues of the departed pussy.

Rev. Jas. L. Warren, whose history has already been given, was also among the pioneer preachers in this part of the county.

The first Sunday School, we may repeat, was conducted by Claiborn Hall, and the first district school in the northern part of the township, by Margaret Brown, (now Mrs. Pendray,) in 51, and in what is now district No. 5.

CHAPTER XVII.

Red Rock Township Concluded—Saw and Flouring Mills —A False Alarm—School Houses, Etc.—Census.

Among the more important enterprises established in Red Rock village and in the neighborhood, were four saw and one flouring mills. The first was a saw mill, built by Osee Matthews, junior, in 1846, on Mikesell's creek, about three-fourths of a mile north-east of town. The next was by Daniel Hiskey, in '48 and '49, on the same stream, about two miles north of town. In '54 two more were erected near town, to run by steam. The one on the east side of town was built and owned by Wilson Stanley; that on the west side by J. D. Bedel.

Only one of these mills—that of Mr. Bedel—is still standing. A few remains of those on Mikesell's creek are still visible; but of the Stanley mill, which was of a rather temporary construction, nothing remains.

The flouring mill, built by S. B. Matthews, in '54, stood in the northwest quarter of town. It was owned and run by Mr. M. till it was bought by Talbott and Setzer, who moved it to Otley, Summit township, in the fall of '69.

An anecdote is related in connection with the erection of the mill at Red Rock. It was at about the time it was finished, and preparations were being made to start it. The morning was calm, clear and frosty, and all sounds were conveyed through the air with comparative distinctness; when the settlers for miles around were suddenly startled by a terrific and prolonged scream that seemed to fill all the space, and reverberated far away. Then it would cease in a sort of die-away wail, till it would seem to recover breath, then peal forth in another unearthly scream, or succession of short, violent yells, totally unlike anything that had ever been heard in that region.

A young man, an odd genius, named Joe Copher, who happened to be in the timber, some distance from home, hunting horses, when he heard the frightful voice ran home with all his speed and reported a panther or some other wild beast in the forest. So, as soon as the report could be circulated throughout the neighborhood, a number of men got together, mounted, armed and equipped, some carrying horns for blowing signals, and attended by a retinue of dogs to assist in the hunt.

For most of the day they scoured the timber in search of the game; but were unable to discover anything capable of giving forth such a voice; and it was not till toward evening that they returned home enlightened as to the cause, and feeling as though they had been badly "sniped."

At the same time another squad of persons imagined the mysterious voice to be of a heavenly origin. They had heard of the Millerite prediction of the end of the world, and supposed that this might be a preliminary blast from Gabriel's trumpet. Having collected together to take counsel on the all important subject, they felt that they were hardly prepared for such an emergency, and thought the only thing that could be done preparatory thereto, on such short notice, was to pray. So, strange as it may seem, they invited a rampant old sinner—one who had probably never even thought of such a thing before, to lead in the solemn exercise. There was apparently no time to be lost, so the old fellow began; but hardly had he got through with the short preface to his prayer, when the glorious tidings reached them that it was only Simp. Matthews' mill whistle. Simp. had fired up for the first time, and was trying his whistle under a strong pressure of steam. Of course the praying was indefinitely postponed, and the meeting adjourned *sine die.*

Apropos to the foregoing we are tempted to relate an anecdote that transpired in the neighborhood of Red Rock at an early date. One of the settlers who happened to be hunting on the Des Moines bottom, not far from the river, was surprised at an unusual noise. He stood still and listened for a few minutes, when the strange sound grew louder and louder every instant, as though the monster was coming rapidly through the forest, from down the river. Its breathing resembled the labored respiration of a wind broken horse, only much louder and more boisterous, and seemed to be well nigh exhausted by a long run. Our hero listened till he thought the creature, by the rapidly increasing distinctness of its breathing, and the sound of its footsteps, was coming directly toward him. His fears thus excited, he could readily imagine that it was in pursuit of him; and so he thought it would not be advisable to remain there an instant longer. With the same reasoning that taught Falstaff that "discretion was the better part of valor," he fled, making his way home as rapidly as he could get through the trackless woods. Now and then he would halt a little to listen for his pursuer, whose terrible blowing seemed to indicate that it was gaining upon him; but much to his relief, after gaining the upland timber, fatigued and excited, the breathing of the mighty beast indicated that it must have taken another direction. The sound was more distant, and rather past the point where the flight commenced.

He therefore pursued his way homeward more leisurely, and there related the adventure much to the surprise of the folks, who were as ignorant as himself of the character of the animal. However it was not long after that they were enlightened. It was about, if not quite, the first attempt at steamboat navigation of the Des Moines, and a little stern-wheeler was slowly making her way against the strong current of that stream during a freshet.

These incidents were related to us as facts, though it may be supposed that they were more or less exaggerated. But, when the fact is known that some of the early settlers had never heard a steam whistle, nor seen a steamboat, nor were even advised of the existence of such wonders in their neighborhood, their mystification, if not actual alarm, is not to be wondered at. The story is, at least, not without a foundation in fact.

The first regular school house in Red Rock village, was built in 1854 or 1855, but was burned soon after. Since then the citizens have put up a large two-story building for the purpose and the schools are well attended. The place also contains several other good buildings, among which is a substantial brick church erected by the Methodists, in 1856 or '57. Two dry goods and one or two grocery stores receive the trade of a large extent of the surrounding country, on both sides of the river. Red Rock must ever remain a permanent crossing place. During low water the fording is easy and safe, and at all other times a good ferry boat is ready to accommodate travelers.

The population of Red Rock township by the U. S. census of 1870, is as follows:

Native	1308.
Foreign	26
Total	1334.

CHAPTER XVIII.

Summit—Geography and History—Names of First Settlers —James Price—The Wilsons and Others—A Conflict with Indians—A Veteran Coffee Mill—A "Settlers Rights" Difficulty—First P. O.—First Sunday School—Day School—Otley.

This township is technically known as town. 77, range 19, and is bounded on the north by Jasper county, on the east by Lake Prairie, on the south by Polk, and on the west by Red Rock. The larger portion of it, consisting of the north and east, is prairie, being the dividing ridge between the Des Moines and Skunk, commonly known as the "Divide." The largest body of timber is in the southeast quarter of the township. There are no large streams in this township. The numerous small creeks take their rise on the "divide," and flow each way into the Des Moines and Skunk.

The coal fields of Summit are quite extensive. The principal ones now worked are along a small stream in sections 21 and 28, about a mile south of Otley. The first mine was discovered and opened by John A. Scott, in 1849; and this was the only one that was worked for several years. The next opening was made by Wm. Fisher, some time in '61 or '62, since which time numerous openings have been made in this locality by Fisher, Durose, Price, Barnes, and others. The veins of coal average from four to seven feet in thickness, and is of a good quality. Much of that mined by Mr. Durose has been shipped at Otley for Des Moines and other localities west.

Summit was originally a part of Red Rock, till April 6th, 1854, when, in response to a petition of numerous citizens, it was declared by the county judge a separate township. The name first proposed and filed in the court record was Harrison; but *Summit* being the choice of a number of settlers from Summit county, Ohio, it was so named.

The first election was held soon after the township was organized, at the house of Jacob C. Brown, and the following are the names of the officers elected: John Ribble and A. F. McConnell, justices of the peace; Geo. Reynolds, I. N. Crum, and Ira Kelsey, trustees; Abram B. Scott, clerk; Ira Kelsey, assessor; and A. Donnel and P. P. Harp, constables.

Some changes were effected in the civil geography of this township, which, though they were the result of partizan wire-working, and occurred at a comparatively recent date, we shall take the liberty of sketching briefly. In 1862, in response to a petition of a portion of its citizens, the township was enlarged by the addition of that portion of Polk (town. 76, range 19) lying north of the river. This change not being agreeable to the Republicans of the township, they petitioned the board of supervisors to have the above mentioned territory, locally known as the "White Breast Settlement," re-attached to Polk, which was accordingly done at the September session, 1864. But, owing to the neglect of the clerk, John B. Hamilton, to transmit to the board of trustees an official report of the change, much embarrassment and partizan feeling resulted at the election that fall in relation to the admission of the vote of that district. A hot dispute was carried on for some time that very nearly resulted in personal violence. But the difficulty was finally settled by the admission of the challenged votes.

Soon after this the Democrats again petitioned for the attachment of the disputed territory, which act was received by the opposite party as an acknowledgment that it was *not* a part of the township at the time of the election. The petition was granted, and White Breast was now indisputably a part of

Summit; and so it remained till 1867, when the board was again asked to return it to Polk, where it still belongs.

Prominent among those who settled in the township at the earliest date, are James Price, the Wilsons, David and Allen Tice, and Andrew Metz. Among those who came later, were, Joseph S. West, the Harps, I. N. Crum, James Dueese, S. S. Roberts, Alex. B. Donnel, and Allen Lanehead. Most of these are still residents of the township. Others who took claims at a very early date, but did not become permanent settlers, will be incidently mentioned as we proceed. Most of the first settlers located in and along the edge of the timber, and it was not till '45 that the divide began to be permanently occupied.

James Price was born in Clark county, Ohio, September 14, 1817, emigrated to Cass county, Michigan, at the age of thirteen, and from thence to Burlington, Iowa, in 18—. From there, early in the spring of '43, in company with Jonathan Donnel, he came into this county, and selected a claim where he still lives. The first cabin they built was a few rods below the coal mine owned by S. S. Roberts. Some slight remains of this pioneer building are still visible. This house he occupied with his family on the 22d of June.

That spring Mr. Price broke nine acres of prairie on his claim, planted it with corn, and realized from it a surplus of two hundred bushels, which he sold for fifty cents per bushel. On the following season he obtained some seed wheat from Fairfield, and obtained from it a fair crop. During the first summer he went to Burlington to mill, and in the winter to the nearest mill on Skunk. On the occasion of his winter trip he had to ferry his load over that river in a canoe. On his return from a trip to Fairfield, it rained much of the time, then turned so cold that his clothing was frozen stiff on his body. On another occasion, returning in company with Ray and Samuel Wilson, from a milling expedition to Skunk, a heavy snow storm obstructed the way so much that it was necessary to make frequent halts till one or another should go forward in search of the path and break the drifts.

Besides the nine acres he broke for himself, Mr. Price broke some for two or three of his neighbors, among whom were Samuel Martin, David Fritz, and Wm. Adams, who made claims in what is now section twenty, but remained in the settlement a short time. The unfortunate career of Sam Martin may still be remembered by most of the old settlers. Having stolen a horse at Council Bluffs, he returned to Red Rock, was followed there, arrested and lynched by whipping; after which he descended the river in a canoe belonging to A. B. Donnel, and is now supposed to be in Idaho.

Humphrey Blakeway also came up with Mr. Price, and made a claim of land now owned by John Ribble, in sections 27 and 34. The same was also claimed by David Ray, who had built a house on it to hold it. In consequence of this some trouble arose between the claimants, that was finally settled by Ray buying the claim of Blakeway.

Another temporary settler, named Wm. Hodge, overtook Mr. P. on the way up, and made a claim on land now owned by S. S. Roberts, section 28, and another on section 17. Hodge remained in the country but a short time. He was afraid of Indians, and a contact with them was the cause of his speedy departure from the country. Being in company with Jonathan Donnel on a bee-hunting expedition, they were visited by a party of Indians, who, seeing some barrels they (the hunters) had in the wagon to put honey in, supposed they contained whisky, and began to beg for some of it. On being refused they took hold of Mr. D. in a rough though friendly manner, intending to over-persuade him to comply with their wish. This, to Hodge, looked like fight, and he took up an ax to defend his companion; seeing which the Indians drew their knives and made a rush at him, whereupon he fled, to the great amusement of the savages, and never returned to see how his companion fared alone in their hands.

The Wilson family, consisting of four sons, two daughters, David Ray and their mother, took claims and settled in sections 33 and 34, June, 1843. They were natives of New Jersey, which state they left in 1836, and came to Indiana, and from thence to Burlington in 1840. On the third day of their journey from Indiana, October 24th, John, the father of the family, died, aged 56 years.

Since their settlement here, two of the sons, one of the daughters, and the mother have died. Samuel died September 28th, 1844, and was, so far as is known, the first white person that died in the township, and his remains were the first deposited in the burying ground on the farm of James Price. George* died June 16th, 1855, and on the 22 of January, 1870, the mother, Ruth Wilson, died, aged 82 years.

During the first two years of their settlement here, the Wilsons, in company with others, were subjected to some severe privations and inconveniences in the matter of subsistance. For some time corn was necessarily the only kind of breadstuff that could be procured. As we have before stated, the mills for grinding were so distant that they could not be applied to for a supply at any time, so that necessity, "the mother of invention," called into requisition such temporary substitutes for mills as could be manufactured at home, and as we have already described as in common use at that early period.

In this emergency, however, the Wilsons were fortunately blessed in the possession of a strong, old iron coffee mill, that they had brought from the east. This mill was firmly fastened to the wall, and, on one occasion, was kept in almost constant service for more than two weeks, doing its work slowly enough to discipline the patience of the young milleress, (now Mrs. W.

---

*George Wilson settled in Polk directly after their arrival in the country.

B. Keeler,) but producing a good article of meal, fine enough to be successfully sifted through a fine hair seive, that the family had also thoughtfully provided themselves with on leaving their eastern home.

This venerable mill now belongs to Freeman Wilson, and is still in the service, not as a corn-cracker, but legitimately as a coffee mill. We are informed by the owner that it has had the honor of pulverizing more than $400 worth of coffee, besides the corn, since it has been the property of the family. They esteem it as a worthy keepsake.

David Ray settled in the township, in the same neighborhood and at the same date with the Wilsons, to whom he was related by marriage. He now lives in Red Rock township.

Joseph S. West, who was the first person that held the office of justice of the peace, within the present limits of Summit, and whose name appears among the first grand jurors in the county, was a native of Mason county, Kentucky, where he was born in 1810, and from whence he immigrated to Iowa in 1844. On his arrival here he purchased a claim in the southern part of the township, from Gadis and Nye, the two traders mentioned in the first chapter of this history, where he has constantly resided ever since.

Charles Harp was a native of Tennessee, from whence he immigrated to Illinois, and from thence to Iowa in 1844, and settled on section 21, in this township. He was the head of a numerous family, the most of whom are still residents of the township. He died in the winter of 1847, and his widow survived him, and occupied the homestead, till in the winter of 1870, when she died.

Isaac N. Crum was a native of Illinois, from which State he moved to Iowa and settled in Summit in '45, where he opened the farm he still owns, but resides in Otley, engaged in the merchantile business.

David and Allen Tice moved from Illinois and settled where

David still lives, near the western line of the township, arriving there on the 18th of May, 1843, and lived in a tent till a house was built. They did little or no farming that season, but shipped their provisions from Illinois, except such wild game as they could take fit for meat. In the spring following they planted three acres of corn, and sold some of it in the fall for $1.50 per bushel. They were among those who made early provisions for fruit. In 1845 they shipped from Illinois about fifty apple trees, that they planted that spring, in a piece of grubby, unfenced land. The trees are all still living, except two, and are good bearers.

Andrew Metz was a native of Germany, immigrated to and settled in the west side of the township in 1844, and died in 18--.

Alexander B. Donnel was born in Pennsylvania, March 20, 1806, and immigrated to Ohio in 1818, and from thence to Iowa in 1844. In '45 he purchased land in company with S. S. Roberts, with whom he had been associated in business for several years. In '49 he, in company with many others, started for California, and died near Fort Kearney, in June. Other members of the family, some of them still living in the township, settled here in 1848, and the mother died early in the spring of '56, aged about 80 years.

Soon after the settlement of this family here, a report got abroad that they intended to enter a number of claims in the neighborhood, and this brought the club together to enforce mutual protection in case such was the design. But upon visiting the residence of the supposed intruders in a body, and with such warlike threats as were thought necessary to frighten them into compliance with the rules supposed to be indispensable to "settlers' rights," yet without avail, it was discovered that it was not the intention to interfere with the just title of any claimant. Failing to bring the enemy to any more definite terms, the club adjourned, and this was about the last demonstration of the kind made by them.

A somewhat amusing instance of claim jumping may be related here. Just previous to the event related above, Andrew Donnel had made a claim and hauled some logs to the ground preparatory to the erection of a house thereon. But, after a few days absence on some other business, he returned to the place and found, to his astonishment, and, we presume, somewhat to his grief, that the house was already built and occupied by Mr. John A. Scott, who still owns and occupies the land. Mr. D. preferring not to disturb the intruder, made another claim in the neighborhood, which proved to be far superior to the first in value.

The first postoffice in Summit township was called "Divide," and John A. Scott was commissioned P. M. in '47. But, as Mr. S. did not serve, the office was immediately discontinued, and he carried the mail to Red Rock for several years. At first, not having any regular mail bag, he took the small amount of matter directed to that place tied up in a handkerchief.

In the summer of '57 a post office was established on section 16, called Newark, Wm. H. Anderson P. M. Some years after this it was shifted into the hands of various persons, and finally got settled at Otley, where its name was changed to that of the village, Geo. M. Hammond, P. M. I. N. Crum is the present incumbent. Daily mails.

The first day school was taught by Abram B. Scott, in the southern part of the township. —— Watson, better remembered as "the one-armed Watson," afterwards taught in a small cabin on the divide. In the same cabin the first Sunday School was organized and conducted by Andrew Donnel and others, in the summer of '49, and preaching was had there on irregular occasions.

In the latter part of September, '67, Columbus Long, John F. Baldwin, and G. W. Johnson, employed J. B. Caruthers, county surveyor, to survey a town on land owned by them, on sections 15* and 22, being on the Des Moines Valley Railroad, at a station previously located by Col. Otley, engineer of this road, and called it Otley, in honor of that gentleman.

The first goods sold were by I. N. Crum, who still continues in the business there, and is also P. M. There are now five stores in the place, three good church buildings, and a proportionate number of dwellings and shops. Being situated on the railroad it is necessarily a point of considerable shipping by farmers and merchants south of the river.

Population of Summit by the U. S. census of '70:

Native	1,262
Foreign	222
Total	1,484

*In July, '48, a town was laid out on the west half of section 15, and called by the pretentious name of American City. It was surveyed by Stanford Doud in the interest of James D. Putnam, S. S. Mangrum, I. N. Crum, and George F. Hendry. Nothing but the stakes ever indicated the existence of a town there. The land is now owned by J. F. Baldwin.

CHAPTER XIX.

Polk—Geography and Early History—"White Breast"—Death of White Breast—Names of Early Settlers—First Schools—First Preaching—First Saw Mill—Richard R. Watts—John Babcock—Destitution—Rouseau and Coalport.

On the 4th of July, 1848, town. 76., range 19, was declared a township to be known as Polk, thus dating the beginning of its municipal history on the seventy-second anniversary of our national independence. The place of holding elections was appointed to be at the house of Warren D. Everett.* The formation of this township took that part of Red Rock in town. 76, range 19, lying north of the Des Moines river.

The formation of this township was in opposition to a remonstrance of Josiah Bullington, and others; so, on the 3d of October, of the same year, in response to a petition of Jeremiah Shepperd and others, the whole of the township was attached to Knoxville. But it appears that the court shortly afterwards, in defining the boundaries of the township recognized the legal existence of Polk by describing it as all of town. 76, range 19, except the two southern tiers of sections, and all of town. 76, range 20. But on the 8th of January, 1850, town. 76, range 20 was struck off, thus limiting the township to four tiers of sections, which is as it now exists.

Polk is bounded on the north by Summit, on the east by Lake Prairie and Clay, on the south by Knoxville, and on the

* At the first election—the date of which we have been unable to obtain—about 40 votes were cast; Warren D. Everett and —— Lowery were chosen justices, and Andrew Hopkins, clerk. The names of the other officers are not remembered.

west by Union. The Des Moines and White Breast rivers run through, the first from north-west to south-east, and the latter from south-west to north-east. The township being mostly within the margins of these streams, is timbered and uneven in surface; but the bottom lands are level, and are noted for their great depth and fertility of soil. White Breast prairie, north of the river, and bordering its bank, is a beautiful strip of farming land, highly adapted to the culture of corn. And here many of the first settlers took claims, by which the place was known as the "White Breast Settlement."

The Indian name for White Breast was Waupa-Cauki, and was said by them to have originated by the circumstance of a bear having been killed near the creek having a white spot upon its breast. But at what period this event transpired tradition does not state. At an early date in the history of the settlement of this part of the county, there lived here an Indian chief also named White Breast. He is remembered by some of the early settlers as a large man, coarse-featured, and badly pock-marked. He was somewhat noted as a warrior, and loved to recount his military exploits against the Sioux; and once after their removal to the west, whilst engaged in this favorite pastime, surrounded by a small but appreciating audience, his life and his glory suddenly ceased forever. Some one, probably actuated by a love of sport, or by a malicious motive, informed a white man of a sort of desperado character, who happend to be present, that White Breast was plotting mischief against him. Without stopping to question or investigate the truth of this statement, the enraged man instantly dashed upon the chief, knocked him down and leaped upon his breast with both feet, causing his instant death.

The names of those who settled within the present limits of Polk at the earliest date are the Stevison family, George, James, Andrew and their father; Edward, George and Rachael Billaps; George Wilson, Mikel S. Morris, (who served as the first justice of the peace within the present limits of the township before its organization; Richard R. Watts, Alexander Caton, Mardica Yearns, and Andrew Stortz. These all settled on the north side of the river in 1843, except Watts, who settled near where Coalport now is. John Babcock, Warren D., Frank and John Everett, Andrew, George and William Karr, and Robert Ethrington settled in the township at later dates from '45 to '47. But few of these still live in the county, Andrew Stevison being the only one of the first named still living near where he first settled. Robert Ethrington lives in Summit.

The first school was taught by an Englishman, whose name our informant could not remember, in a small log house built for that purpose, near the creek, at the head of White Breast prairie, in '48 or '49. John Everett next taught in the same house. This little log school house also served the purpose of a church occasionally, where Warren D. Everett, Baptist, and John Demoss, United Brethren, preached in it. The flood of '51, a never-to-be-forgotten event, as we have already seen, swept the house away; and not far from where it stood, but above high water mark, now stands a well-finished frame building large enough for any ordinary use in a country district.

W. D. Everett, Jas. Karr and Mike Morris erected the first saw mill in '50, being a temporary affair, driven by horse-power. It stood near the south bank of the river.

Richard R. Watts was a native of Ohio, where he was born in 1815, moved to Indiana in '20; to Illinois in '30; to Jefferson county, Iowa, in '42, and from thence to Marion county in the spring of '43, and settled near the present site of Coalport. During his early residence here he and his family suffered some of the privations common to the times. During one winter they were dependent upon the services of a coffee mill for their daily bread, and with it they ground ten bushels of buckwheat that season.

John Babcock was also a native of Ohio. When he settled

here his family consisted of a wife and seven children, mostly girls. He was a Mormon in faith, and his wife was a member of that church. At one time during a period of about six weeks, his family was reduced to the verge of starvation, subsisting almost entirely on nettles boiled for greens. On rare occasions they obtained a piece of corn bread from Mike Morris. This kind of diet produced a change in their complexions from a natural to a dark, greenish hue, suggestive of poor health.

There were two villages laid out in this township, but they were never improved to any extent. The first is Rouseau, on the south bank of the river, in section 9. It was located by Wm. Kent, and surveyed by James Rouseau, April 25, 1850, and named for him. Here a pretended effort was once made to erect a dam and lock in the great visionary enterprise of improving the navigation of the Des Moines river.

Coalport is located in section 14, at the point of a large bend in the river, on the south side. It was laid out by Wm. Welch, May 11, '57, and so named on account of the vast quantity and superior quality of coal in its vicinity. No post office was ever established in either place, and they still remain mere hamlets.

The population of Polk township by the U. S. census, was:

Native	794
Foreign	85
Total	879

CHAPTER XX.

Knoxville—Geography and Early History—Names of First Settlers—John M. Jones—Wooden Bowls—An Indian Visitation—John Conrey----Fight with Wolves--Landon J. Burch----A Rough Experience in Pioneer Life.

At a called session of the commissioners' court, in November, 1846, it was ordered that town. 75, and all of 76, lying south of the Des Moines river, both of range 19; also towns. 75 and 76, range 20, be declared a township, to be known as Knoxville township. This included, besides all of the present township, all of Polk on the south side of the river, all of Union up to the south line of 77, and all of the present township of Pleasant Grove, included in town 76, range 20. Elections to be held at the county seat.*

At the organization of Polk in '48, and of Union in '50, the township was reduced to its present size. It is a large township, embracing mostly upland timber and prairie, of about equal area. The only considerable streams running through it are White Breast, English and Cedar. The first runs through the east and north-east part of the township, the second through the south-east, and the latter rises in the north part, runs northward to the Des Moines.

Abundant evidences of coal are to be seen in the banks of these streams, and also along the smaller creeks in the immediate vicinity of Knoxville City. Several productive veins have already been opened, principally eastward of town; and according to the report of a geological survey, recently made, the city stands over an extensive coal field of from three to

*We have been unable to find any record of the first election held in and for this township.

five veins to be reached at various depths. Fire and potter's clay also exist in the township.

Among those who settled in this township at an early date, (besides those mentioned in the general history of the county,) we note the names of the Jones family, John, Sen., John, Jun. Isaac, George and William; Elias Fuller, L. C. and John Conrey, Tyler Overton, J. R. Welch, Conrad Walters, R. S. Lowry, John Essex, M. Willcut, Michael Livingston, Lossen G. Terry, Christopher Cox, Smith Hanton, Lauden J. and William Burch.

John M. Jones (now owner of the Knoxville woolen factory,) was a native of Ohio, and one among the first white men that came to the county. Being an employee of the American Fur Company, in that capacity he traveled over most of the state in the summer and fall of 1842, and first made a claim on White Breast. Here he spent the winter in a camp, during which time he made three trips with team to Meek's mill, at Keosauqua, for breadstuff, traveling a portion of the distance on the ice of the Des Moines.

Soon after settlements were permitted, the elder Jones, with the rest of the family, moved in. Mr. Jones, Sen., was a turner by trade. Having brought his tools with him, they at once put up a temporary lathe, and proceeded to manufacture bowls from slabs split from the trunks of walnut trees. This ware, John, Jun., loaded into his wagon, hauled them to the old settlement, and peddled them out for corn, at from 25 to 75 cents apiece. A load of bowls would thus secure him a load of corn, and this he would get ground at Meek's, and return with meal enough to subsist upon for some time. Mr. J. says that some of the stumps of the trees that furnished the materials for these bowls are still visible.

They were frequently visited by the Indians during the early period of their settlement here. On one occasion the savages made the visit something of a visitation. The men were all out on a hunting expedition, leaving the mother and only sister in charge of the house, when a squad of about two hundred dusky warriors came in in single file, unannounced, and totally regardless of the fears of the two defenseless women, filling the little cabin to its utmost capacity. They immediately began searching for plunder, laying hands upon whatever they thought fit to eat. Among other things prized by them as an article of food, were a couple of pigs in a pen near the house, intended for breeders. The Indians thought one of them would make an excellent mess of soup, and, regardless of the protestations of the women, and their loud calls for the men, who they hoped might be within hearing, murdered the male swine, a shoat of sufficient age and size to possess much of the peculiar odor common to his species, threw it across the back of a pony and vanished.

This was a loss not easily replaced in those days, for hogs were scarce and money ditto. The expense of bringing such stock from a distance made the loss at least $25.

John Conrey, uncle of L. C. Conrey, settled where he still resides, a few miles south of Knoxville city, March 20, 1845, having made his claim and erected his cabin the fall previous. During the first year his nearest neighbors were from three to four miles distant, and his nearest convenience for breadstuffs was Bonaparte, Van Buren county.

Mr. C. relates an adventure that occurred in the spring following, of which Elisha Wilcutt, one of his neighbors, was the principal hero. He and Mr. Conrey had started on a hunting expedition; and after having traveled together two or three miles without seeing any game, they separated, hoping thereby to meet with better success. A few minutes after Mr. Wilcutt was surprised by five large timber wolves that came rushing down a hill, nearly abreast with each other, and met him in the most threatening manner. One large, black fellow seemed to be the leader of the gang, and fell a victim to the contents of Mr. W.'s rifle. But now having nothing to rely upon for further protection but his dogs and hunting knife, he felt the extreme danger of his situation, and called loudly for help. Mr. Con. rey heard the report of the gun, and knew by the freightened cry of his comrade, that he was in trouble, and hastened to his relief. But, on reaching the scene of action he found Mr. Wilcutt, with the help of his dogs, the victor, having dispatched two more of the wolves, the remaining two having instinctively adopted the theory that discretion is the better part of valor and fled. The adventurers named the little creek near by Wolf Run, and it has been known by that name ever since.

Landan J. Burch, a prominent old settler in the northern part of this township, and still a well-known resident there, was born in Virginia in 1801. He became an orphan early in life, and was subjected to many hardships and adventures during a long career of changes of place and occupation, till he finally located here in 1844. In relation to his adventurous experience as a pioneer, we will let him speak for himself, quoting from an elaborate paper submitted by him to the "Old Settler's Association" of this county:

"I and my brother William shouldered a parcel of provisions, a coffee pot, an axe and a gun, and left Winchester some time in January. We traveled up the Des Moines valley to White Breast creek, and there took the claim where I now live for myself, and my brother took that whereon John Fry now lives. We stayed here eight or ten days, made some little improvement, lived in camp and suffered a great deal from cold. During one day of the time it snowed, after which the weather became warm enough for the bees to come out, but still cool enough for some of them to become so chilled that they could not fly far. Then we went bee-hunting. Instead of looking up into the trees we traced up the hives by the fallen bees; and by this means we found several swarms, some of them quite rich.

"Then we had plenty of honey, but our bread and coffee soon gave out, and we went to an Indian trader at Red Rock, (or where the town now stands,) and got a supply of coffee, meal, and a little whisky. But the snow was so deep, and the weather otherwise so bad, that we could not go on with our improvements; so we concluded to go home and move our families up at the earliest practicable time.

"A thaw commenced about the time we started which was about the last of January, and continued till the ice broke on the river, and we began to prepare for moving. We had now been several years in Iowa, encountering all the difficulties attending upon a newly settled country, and I had spent what money I had brought from Kentucky. Besides improving several lots in Winchester, I had built a small boat on the Des Moines river, with which I had carried lumber from Passmore's mill, on Lick creek, to Ottumwa, to build the first frame house there, and took my pay in trade.

"On the first of March we loaded our plunder on the boat, at the mouth of Lick Creek, and started up the river. A man named Miles Wilkenson took passage with us, intending to take a look at the country, and join with me in building a mill, provided he liked the situation.

Soon after we got on the way the weather became cold and stormy, and as our boat was an open one, and our children small, we had to camp on shore every night for the sake of fire. Besides, Wilkinson had the ague, and was not able to work the boat more than half the time. In this way we got along very slowly, and were twenty-one days getting to our claims. But here we were at last, with our wives and little ones, five children each. Not a neighbor's dog could we hear bark, nor a chicken crow. Wilkinson spent two days in prospecting between where Knoxville now stands and the Des Moines river, and came to the conclusion that the country would never be settled enough to justify the building of a mill, that the toll from all the custom we would get would hardly feed a few pigs. So he went back and built a mill somewhere in the southern part of Wapello county.

"As for Bill and me, we were located, and if we had no kind neighbors to hold friendly conversation with, we had frequent opportunities to listen to the howling of wolves. Yet we were not quite destitute of neighbors. The Joneses had settled in the timber west of Knoxville; Elias Fuller had made a settlement on White Breast, and Wm. McCord had located between there and Red Rock, and he was my nearest neighhor. Two bachelors living on the river, named Johnson, I also became acquainted with.

"As soon as we got into a shelter brother Bill took my boat and went to work on the river, carrying flour from Meek's Mill, (Bonaparte) to the garrison on 'Coon river, where Des Moines City now is. The river was high, and my brother worked hard to make even small wages. At the same time I worked about home, planted three or four acres of corn, fixed up my smith tools, did some little jobs in that line for my distant neighbors, and also for the Indians, repairing their guns, etc., for which they paid me punctually, with one exception. The children also traded with the Indians in little trinkets, and thereby obtained quite a friendly understanding with them. Both the children and I acquired a knowledge of their language very rapidly; but they left too soon to enable us to become perfect in it, or to make it useful to us.

"The creek was full nearly all summer, and as I had a patch of corn on each side of it, I had to cross pretty often in a little, unwieldly canoe. On one of these trips I came very near losing two of my children.

"This was the summer of '44, during the latter part of which my brother Bill moved to his own claim, and we lived about three-fourths of a mile apart. In August our families all got sick, I being the only well one. We had got our stock up from Van Buren county, during the summer, and when sickness came the care and labor that fell upon my unaided shoulders were enough to have employed three men. Our eldest daughter died after a lingering illness of about three months. She died from the want of medical aid and attention, when there was not a soul present except I and my sick family. My wife was unable to turn herself in bed; and as for me, trouble and the loss of sleep had so nearly worn me out that I scarcely knew anything. But for the fact that I was in good health, we must have all perished.

"When I saw that my daughter was dying I went out every few minutes and blew a little tin trumpet as loudly as I could, hoping to attract the attention of some one who might be within hearing. As it happened, a young man named Moyer, was crossing the prairie at day dawn, and hearing the blast, surmised it to be a note of alarm or distress, and came to the house. He and my brother laid out the corpse, and then went abroad among our scattered neighbors, who came in and assisted us to bury our child in a tolerably decent manner.

"Having failed, on account of sickness, to make a trip the fall, our provisions gave out. We had plenty of milk, but no bread. During sickness and after, I had to beat corn in a mortar and sift it for bread; and now this process had to be kept up until the ice broke out of the river in the spring following. Then I made a voyage to the old neighborhood for a cargo of bread stuff. I shall never forget the rejoicing of the children on our return. Little ones that could scarcely utter their words plainly, would cry out, "we'll have plenty o' bread now, mother."

"On reaching Eddyville, during one of these trips, we fell in with one of the agents of the contractor, named Scott, who was there after corn for the garrison at Ft. Des Moines, and who prevailed on us to ship a load to that place, offering a high price. There was no available means of transporting it by land just then, for the roads were so bad that a team could not draw much more than would feed it for the trip.

"So we agreed to turn back. The weather was good to

start with, and if it so continued we calculated to make the trip in eight or nine days. It was important to get provisions enough to last us for that length of time. But, after insisting very hard, all the meat we could get were a couple of small thin sides of bacon. We had plenty of tea, and could have supplied ourselves with plenty of molasses, but could procure only one small jug to hold it. Meal we had none to start with, but supposed that when we should reach the horse mill, (or rather ox mill,) just above where Coalport now is, we could get a supply. But here we could get only about three quarts. We could have got some of our cargo ground, but didn't, thinking we could surely get a supply at Red Rock. But we were again disappointed, for the only eatable thing we could get there was a peck of very small potatoes, and what whisky we wanted.

"Here the weather turned cold, and the wind blew so strong against us that we had to lay by. It grew so cold that the water froze on our poles, making them so slippery and heavy that we could not use them. And to add to our troubles, our small potatoes, the only substitute we had for bread, froze and became utterly worthless. We, however, made the best we could of them by trading them to the Indians for maple sugar. And they, in turn, made the best of them by thawing them and drinking the juice with much relish.

"Having at last reached the Fort and delivered our load, we started on our return voyage with nothing to eat, hoping to reach Red Rock before we should suffer much. At that time there was but one settlement between the Fort and Red Rock, on what is now called Butcher's Prairie. By the time we reached this point the wind blew so hard up stream that we could make little or no progress, though one hand went on shore with a rope to pull while the others paddled on board.

"The situation was by no means promising, and we were compelled to land and wait for fair weather. So I went to the house to see if I could get something to eat. It was occupied by a man and his wife, whose name I have forgotten. The man was a surly fellow. No dry joke that I could pass in stating my case, could make him smile, and he looked suspiciously at me and talked as though he thought the whole world was composed of robbers, and that I had come to impose upon him. In reply to my request for something to eat, he gruffly said he had nothing for himself. But the woman wore a different countenance, and from her pleased expression I was able to glean a hope. And not only her words but her works soon confirmed it. She said we were suffering and must be fed. So she went out and killed the only chicken she had, and with that and some flour, butter and milk, she provided us a full meal, cooked. I carried it to the boat, and, after our feast, when I returned the vessels, she would receive only the moderate sum of fifty cents. She was truly a sister of charity. Blessed be her memory.

"Next morning the weather was quite calm, and we finished our voyage without any further difficulty.

"Some time in the spring or summer of 1845, I commenced building a mill, and in about twenty months began to grind. It was a poor thing. I could not make more than sixteen or eighteen bushels of meal per day, but every bushel of toll was worth 50 cents, and, as many settlers had came into the neighborhood, I got all the grinding I could do. My custom extended twelve or fifteen miles around; and after this there was no scarcity of bread."

CHAPTER XXI.

Knoxville Township Continued — Conrad Walters — First Church Organization—First Preaching—Sleepy Hearer —First School Teacher — Knoxville—First Steam Saw Mill—A Scene in the Early History of Knoxville City—John Shearer—A Pioneer School—A Critical Situation—Another—Tyler Overton.

Much respected, and still well remembered among early settlers, was the late Conrad Walters, whose name is also on record in another place as a member of the first Board of Commissioners for the county. Mr. Walters was a native ot Pennsylvania, where he was born in 1794, from which State he came to Ohio in 1814, and learned the art of printing in Wilmington, Clinton county. After various removals he finally came to Mt. Pleasant, Iowa, in 1839, and from there to this county in October, 1844, and settled six miles south-east of Knoxville. Here he remained till a few years previous to his death, at which time, July 28, 1870, he resided in the city of Knoxville. His age was 77 years.

The first religious society that was organized in this township, was by Rev. Mr. Neur, of the M. E. Church, in 1844 or 1845, and the first regular house of worship was erected in Knoxville City, in 1850 or 1851, during the pastoral charge of Rev. A. W. Johnson, of the same denomination. Rev. Mr. Neur is remembered as among the first, (if not quite the first) minister that broke the bread of life in the then wilderness of Knoxville township. An anecdote is related of him in connection with one of his first discourses here. Having become acquainted with a young man named Willis, who was at work for John Conrey, and who was also a member of his church,

Mr. Neur sent an appointment by him to preach at Mr. Conrey's cabin, on a certain night. When the time came the congregation consisted of Mr. Conrey, his wife and five children and Brother Willis. During the sermon the latter, perhaps overcome by fatigue, fell asleep and soon began to manifest his condition by some loud snoring. Observing this the preacher raised his voice a key higher, but in a kindly tone, said, "wake up, Brother Willis, I'll soon be through." This roused the sleeper, and the preacher went on with his sermon as though nothing out of the way had happened.

The first day school taught in this township, was by F. Monahan, in 1846, in what is now the north-west quarter of the city of Knoxville. School averaged twenty-five scholars. Mr. Monahan was a native of Ohio, from which State he immigrated to this State in 1844, and to this county in 1846, and settled on White Breast creek.

The history of the city of Knoxville, it being the county seat, has already been related in connection with the general history of the county, and we scarcely need transcend the limits of this work by noting its progress and present wealth. Suffice it to say that it is a place of average proportions and population for an inland city; and, being situated in a healthy locality, and in the midst of a rich agricultural and mineral region, its advantages are inferior to few other inland towns, and will soon be made superior to many by the addition of one or two important railroad connections. Knoxville is now supplied with several kinds of manufacturing establishments, a lumber yard, numerous churches, two newspapers and a large city school, all of which attest the enterprise, moral status and intelligence of the people.

In contrast with the above we note one or two incidents that may be well remembered by many citizens:

In the fall of 1854, Geo. Calvin and Ira Curtis purchased a six horse power steam engine, in Washington county, brought it to Knoxville and put up the first circular saw mill in what is now the south side of town. When the mill got into operation it proved to be quite a curiosity to the people, crowds of whom came to see it work. Now all the modern improvements that have been attached to this powerful agent for the operation of almost every kind of machinery, scarcely calls forth the wonder of an individual.

In 1850, a Mr. Henry kept a hotel near the northwest corner of the square, and during a session of the district court, the small house was crowded. One night a peddler came to lodge there, and for want of room took up his lodging in the bar-room, which place was presided over by one Eph Henby. During the night two persons named Walters and Dunham, feeling funny with liquor, pulled the peddler out of his cot by the legs, and dragged him into the kitchen. In this operation the prostrate but struggling itinerant merchant kicked one of his assailants in the breast, which was the signal for fight. The uproar now became so intense that every lodger in the house was roused, and the fighting propensity of a large pugilistic individual, named Kaufman, was stirred up. He coolly got up, dressed himself and went down stairs, declaring his intention to put a stop to the fuss or whip somebody. Finding Dunham he went about his mission at once and gave that disturber a good thrashing. At this moment Henby, the bar-keeper, anxious to restore order, but afraid of getting into the muss, thrust his head down the stairway and called out a command to keep the peace. As a reward for this unlucky interference, Walters hurled a boot at Henby, that struck him in the face with such violence as to cause blood to flow pretty freely. For this breach of good manners, Kaufman, the peace-maker, deemed it his duty to thrash Walters also, by which peace was finally restored. Early next morning the parties atoned for their fun by going to a justice's office and paying a fine. Such scenes are now remembered as things of the past.

As this chapter would be a short one, if ended here, we may venture to add a few miscellaneous items that may not be wholly without interest to some who remember them.

No old settler in Knoxville township is better remembered than John Shearer. He first came to Liberty in '46, where he remained only about three months, then moved to his present locality, a little east of Knoxville city.

Mr. Shearer shook with the ague during most of the first year of his pioneer life; was unable to labor, but by teaching school and trading in claims, he was enabled to live and save enough to buy the eighty acres of land he now lives on. Mr. Shearer's school teaching was the real pioneer kind. He was employed by subscription, two dollars per scholar for three months, and "boarded round." The school house was a little cabin originally built and used as a stable, by John R. Welch. It was supplied with a bark floor, but was neither chunked nor daubed. Rabbits were numerous in the surrounding brush, and so tame that some of them would frequently come into the house during school hours, to the great amusement of the twelve young ideas Mr. S. was trying to teach how to shoot. Once scholars and teacher took a half holiday, and employed the time in ferreting out and capturing a weazle that had taken a homestead about the timbers of the old cabin. At times, when the weather was warm, and there was no excitement to keep the scholars awake, some of the younger ones would stretch themselves on the narrow benches and go to sleep. Occasionally one would fall off, which circumstance would keep the others awake for a time.

The teacher was also a good hunter and employed much of his leisure time hunting for the benefit of his subscribers. During one short expedition he secured venison enough to last them two weeks.

Just previous to the flood of 1851, Nelson Butcher built a corn mill on a small tributary of White Breast, which was resorted to from quite a distance, and the grain accumulated so rapidly that there was not enough room for it in the small mill house, and the proprietor had to stow away at least a hundred bushels of it in his cabin near by. One night the flood came so rapidly that there was no time time to save the corn, nor even any of the household property, and the family could only think of saving themselves. Escape to the uplands was impossible, and they had to climb to the loft. This was almost floorless, only two or three narrow boards being laid across the joists. On these Mr. and Mrs. Butcher, their five children, and Mr. Shearer, who happened to be there, perched themselves as best they could and passed the remainder of the night in a painful state of apprehension for their safety, as they listened to the roar of the rising flood and felt the frail building tremble. But for one providential circumstance they would have in all probability found a watery grave. A great log came down and lodged in such a position just above the cabin as to protect it from a large amount of heavy drift-wood that must otherwise have swept it from its foundation. When the welcome daylight dawned, the besieged could more fully realize their perilous situation and be thankful for the preservation of their lives and for the relief that came by friendly neighbors. As may be supposed the corn was totally ruined. In those days corn was not so plentiful but that a small amout was deemed worth raising. In this connection we may relate an anecdote of one Billy Williams, who got himself into an embarrassing situation in consequence of his efforts to prevent a bushel of the valuable grain from going to waste. A wagon load of it had passed near his house and by some means a quantity of it was dropped along the road. Billy happened along soon afterwards and thought he had better gather it up for his own use than let it quite go to loss. But not having any basket or bag to put it in, he was for a moment uncertain how he should manage it. But presently an original idea came to his aid. He could make a bag of his pants. Being in an unfrequented place, he had no expectation of being discovered in the execution of this new idea, so he took off his pants, tied the lower ends of the legs and stuffed them as full as they would button with the ears of corn. Now being ready to bear away his prize, he looked up the road and saw two women coming toward him. They were evidently coming to his house. Mortified as he was, he shouldered his load and rushed for a haystack that stood within calling distance of his dwelling. Here he took shelter, and as no time was to be lost, he called energetically for Jemima, his wife.

"What do you want?" queried the latter, a little surprised if not alarmed at the earnestness of his tone.

"Bring my other pants," came the answer.

"Your tother pants!" returned the puzzled Jemima. "What you want with 'em out there?"

"Bring 'em along, and be quick about it!" cried the impatient Billy.

Of course she flew to obey the command, fearing that Billy might somehow be in a bad fix, but was happy to find his case no worse than it was. Billy got dressed as soon as he could and went to the house, hoping he had escaped the notice of the visitors, who were now there. But somehow the joke soon got abroad without the aid of Billy or his wife either.

Tyler Overton, who still resides where he originally settled, in the southern part of the township, arrived there on the 28th of May, 1843, in company with Henry Miller, each carrying a load of provisions on their backs from the Welch settlement north of the river. After making claims they put up a bark shanty in the nearest timber where they batched it for three weeks, making rails, making occasional trips to the settlement for provisions that he had employed some of the settlers there to bring up in wagons.

In the spring following Mr. O. went to Henry county,

where he purchased sixty apple trees, brought them up, and began an orchard on his claim, which was, perhaps, the first one planted in the township. Only about a dozen of these pioneer trees are yet living.

Population of Knoxville township by the U. S. census of 1870:

Native	4609
Foreign	141
Total	4750

CHAPTER XXII.

Union Township—Geography and Early History—Township Officers—Names of First Settlers—Simeon Reynolds—A One-man Garrison—A Family Council—Andrew Startz—Hill Milling Adventure—A Dog Trial and a Big Drunk—Samuel Teters—Sickness and Privation—A Long Walk—A Successful Wolf Hunt—Saving the Corn—Borrowing—The First School Teacher.

On the 7th of October, 1850, in compliance with a petition, it was ordered by the Commissioners that all of town. 76, range 20, south of the river, and all of 77, same range, south of the river, be called Union township, from and after the first Monday of April, 1851.

This township is bounded on the north by Red Rock, with the Des Moines river as its boundary line; on the east by Polk, on the south by Knoxville, and on the west by Pleasant Grove and Swan.

There is no stream of any considerable size coursing through this township, but many small creeks, the largest of which is Camp creek. That portion lying contiguous to the river is somewhat hilly, but well timbered. The strip margining the river is mostly flat bottom land, partly prairie, the most noted of which is Butcher's prairie. In some places the uplands terminate in abrupt rocky cliffs. The southern portion of the township is mostly upland prairie, and is a good farming district.

The first election in this township was held at the house of William Ballard, April 2, 1851. After the appointment of Wm. Ballard, Geo. Teters and Simeon Reynolds, as judges of the election, and Westley Teters and Wm. M. Norris, as clerks, the following named officers were elected: Wm. M. Norris and Samuel E. Teters, *Justices of the Peace;* Andrew Startz, Wm. Ballard and Alfred Reese, *Trustees;* James Amos, *Treasurer;* John W. Broadess, and Robert Gusten, *Constables;* Andrew Startz and Samuel Ballard, *Road Supervisors;* and Simeon Reynolds, *Clerk.* No record of the number of votes cast.

The names of a majority of those who settled in the township at an early date are, Simeon and Geo. Reynolds, Wm. Richard and John Butcher, Hiram Steel, Duncan Neil, —— Vandenford, John Flanders, Robert Gusten, Andrew Startz, Samuel, Geo. and Westley Teters, and Wm. Luty.

John Flanders now lives in Red Rock township, having sold his claim to William Ballard at an early date. Wm. Luty came from Ross county, Ohio, in 1843. Died August 21st, 1871.

Simeon Reynolds was born in Duchess county, New York, March 16, 1786, moved to Ohio in 1816 or '17, and from thence to Marion county, November, 1845, elected a member of the State Legislature and served in the House in 1847. Died April 21st, 1852.

Mrs. Amanda Reynolds, his widow, still lives on the farm they first settled on, on Butcher's prairie, and his two sons, who also took claims at the same time, live in the neighborhood. Mrs. R. was the first white woman that become a citizen of this part of the country.

On their arrival, November 2d, Mr. Reynolds and family took lodging in a little cabin formerly owned by Butcher, to whom the government had granted the privilege of making settlement there as early as 1843, in consideration of services he had rendered by repairing or making roads. The claim was at this time owned and occupied by Steel and Neal, of whom Mr. R. purchased it. Soon after this Vanderbilt entered a portion of this claim, securing a title therefor, then took a fortified position on the opposite bank of the river in order to hold it. But he was at length persuaded to capitulate by giving a deed for the land, which he did, and received his entrance money.

The first summer of their residence here was extremely warm, and for a time every member of the family was prostrated by the ague, and consequently much reduced in the way of subsistence. Discouraged at the prospect, Mr. Reynolds began to entertain serious thoughts of returning to the East; but this, he also thought, would be an arbitrary act, in case it should be contrary to the wishes of at least a majority of the family. So he convened a council of all who were of a sufficient age to understand and appreciate the importance of the question, to discuss it fully, and then vote as their judgments dictated. In spite of the most persuasive argument manifest in the pale faces of every member of this model republic in favor of returning to their old home, a decided majority was against it, and all peaceably yielded to the decision.

Some time during the winter of '45–6 Mr. Reynolds and his sons erected a new house 24 by 18 feet square, of hewed logs and lumber, there not being a sawed board about it. For some time this dwelling served as a house of entertainment for immigrants going up the country, and was often so full that there was scarcely room for all to lie down.

Andrew Startz was a native of Pennsylvania, from whence he began to move westward in 1805, till he arrived at Burlington, Iowa, in 1839, and from thence to the White Breast Settlement, in 1844 or '45, and finally settled in Union. Since then he has been to California two or three ttmes. He is now a citizen of Missouri.

In 1844 Mr. Startz wont to Burlington to get some corn he had cultivated there, and took thirty-six bushels of it to get ground at Waterville. In this trip he was greatly detained by high waters, and did not reach home till about the end of six weeks. During this time Mrs. Startz and two of the children cultivated fifteen acres of corn with hoes and kept it clean.

Such was the scarcity of breadstuffs at this time that Mr. S.'s supply of meal was besieged by so many borrowers that he soon loaned out all but about three bushels. Fifteen bushels of it were never returned.

Mr. Startz made three trips to Burlington to mill. At this time there was no settlement between Fairfield and Oskaloosa, and but few houses between that and Red Rock. On one occasion it was so cold that Mr. S. was compelled to run for several miles to keep from freezing till he could reach a shelter, which he found at Blakeway's, in what is now Summit, after midnight.

Mr. Startz was the hero of a legal contest that came before a justice's court in Red Rock, in '46 or '47, under the title of "Brown vs. Startz," the object of which was to establish the ownership of a certain dog claimed by both parties. As the parties were well known, and the case rather novel, large numbers of people came to witness the trial. After it was over, and judgment was rendered in favor of Startz, the latter proposed to treat the company, which was not objected to. But, as enough whisky could not be found, several kinds of liquors were mixed, and the result was soon perceptible and highly entertaining. A small quantity of such a compound was sufficient to disturbe the mental if not the physical equilibrium of even those who had been accustomed to drinking one kind. It is supposed that there were more tipsy people in Red Rock that day than have been there at one time before or since. Even staid old fellows who prided themselves upon their sobriety, made the unfortunate mistake of taking "a drop too much" on that occasion.

Samuel Teters, who still resides on the farm he originally claimed and entered, in the southeast quarter of the township, first came from Ross county, Ohio, in the autumn of 1844, to Van Buren county, Iowa, where he remained till the spring following, when he came to this county. As it was in March when he arrived with his family, and the weather was cold and rough, they took up their quarters with a family named Hahn, living on the north side of the river, till a place could be provided on their own claim. They then took up their residence in a small claim pen that had a bark door shutter, and prepared to battle against the inconveniences of frontier life; and it was, indeed, a hard battle to fight.

Mr. Teters was a blacksmith and gunsmith, and with a view of earning something at that business he put up a temporary shop on the bank of the river, set his anvil on a stump, and employed himself at stacking plows, sharpening plow-shares and repairing guns. In the autumn of '46 he and his family fell sick, and became so helpless that at one time they had neither fire nor water in the house for three days. Game was plenty, and once Mr. T. was able to shoot a turkey from the door, but was too weak to get it. And all this time they had no kind of breadstuff except boiled corn. But so soon as he was able to get abroad with his gun, he killed two large deers one day, one of which yielded fourteen pounds of tallow. Next day he got help to bring them home, and on the day following that he took them to Red Rock and sold them for seven dollars in cash and a sack of flour.

In the autumn of '48 Mr. Teters had occasion to go to Iowa City, a distance of about one hundred miles, to enter his land. On this occasion the utmost haste was required, and Mr. T. performed the journey in forty-eight hours, going by way of Oakaloosa, and traveling night and day.

In those early days when neighbors were so far apart, and even then few of them were in possession of those etceteras that neighbors are in the habit of borrowing and lending, the cost of borrowing sometimes overrun the value of the article borrowed. Yet such small articles were deemed indispensable, and those who chanced to have them could scarcely refuse to lend to those who had not. An instance or two may apply here. At one time a man came down from the Fort to the Butcher farm for corn. But there was nothing to measure the grain in, and the purchaser paddled down to Red Rock, borrowed a half bushel measure, and retured the same day, making a trip of sixteen miles. And it was not an uncommon occurrence for persons to go eight or ten miles to grind their axes.

Many stories are related of the depredations of those intollerable pests of every new country, the wolves. The winter of 1848 and 1849 will long be remembered on account of the depth of snow that fell and the severity of the cold. And the wolves, should any that experienced that winter yet survive, may have the most sorrowful occasion to remember it on account of their numbers that were slaughtered by their natural enemies. Weakened by starvation, and impeded by the deep snow, they were easily run down by men on horseback. Mr. William Ballard relates that he and his two sons thus killed nine in one day, and his exploit is but one in many instances.

The Indians also proved troublesome by appropriating everything to their own use that could be used for food. Once during the absence of Mr. Startz, they appropriated most of his corn from the crib; and Mrs. S., in order to save some of it, had to store it in the house. Not having any sacks to carry it in, she used a bed tick for this purpose.

Among the first persons that taught school in Union was Nancy Beckwith. This was in 1848, in the western part of the township, and in a cabin owned by Jacob Haynes.

Population of Union township by the U. S. census of 1870:

Native	755
Foreign	10
Total	765

CHAPTER XXIII.

Liberty Township—Its Geography and early History—Names of first Settlers—Martin Neel—A Precious Burden—Economy—Horace Lyman—Fording Soap Creek—Stanford Doud—Starvation—Adventure with the Indians—Weak feed and hard work.

Liberty Township occupies the southeast corner of the county, and may be described technically as town. 74, range 18. It is bounded on the north by Clay, on the east by Mahaska county, on the south by Monroe county, and on the west by Indiana township.

The principal streams running through it are North and South Cedar, and their main direction is from southwest to northeast through nearly the center of the township, and unite before leaving it. Between these streams, and on both sides of them, are heavy bodies of timber ; and these, with the numerous smaller groves distributed throughout the township, make about an equal proportion of timber and prairie.

Along the Cedar, principally South Cedar, are large bodies of coal lands. Some of these mines that have been opened and worked, are apparently inexhaustable, and measure from eight to twelve feet in thickness. They are supposed to be the richest and most extensive coal mines in the State, and are thought enough of to justify the building of a railroad between Chariton and Oskaloosa, by way of these coal fields, for the shipment of the mineral.

In 1846 one of these coal veins, in section 32, was found to be on fire, and continued to burn till it was extinguished by the heavy and constant rains of the wet season of '51. How long it had been on fire before it was discovered, is not known.

This township was the first one organized, or declared a township, by the Board of County Commissioners, the date of this transaction being April 15th, 1846. During the fall of that year the first election was held at the house of Rhoderick Peck, where Thos. Anspach now lives, on the northeast quarter of section 9. But there is no preserved record of this election, and any particulars relating to it are not remembered. The earliest one on record took place on the first day of April, 1850, at the residence of Martin Neel, about a mile east of where Marysville now is. At this election 31 votes were cast, and the following named persons elected: Andrew McGender and Isaac Willsey, *constables;* Daniel Sampson, Isaac Willsey and Wm. H. Brobst, *trustees;* Joseph Brobst, *clerk;* and Horace Lyman, *treasurer.*

The names of most of those who came and settled in the township at an earlier date, are Horace Lyman, Stanford Doud, Martin Neel, David Haymaker, Silas Brown, Benj. Spilman, David Gushway, Lewis Jones, Jacob Hendricks, and Andrew McGruder, in 1843; Thurston Day, and Wm. Simms, in 1844; James Rousseau, and Isaac Willsey, in 1845; and Wm. Bridges, and H. H. Mitchell, in 1846.

Martin Neel was a native of Kentucky. At precisely what date he settled in Liberty is not known, but it is supposed by the oldest inhabitants to have been previous to the extinction of the Indian title. He made his claim and place of residence on Cedar bottom, not far from the present site of Marysville. The land is now owned and occupied by Daniel F. Leiby.

During his early residence here, Mr. Neel suffered many of the privations incident to pioneer life At one time it was found necessary for him to go to Burlington for a short time, to work for money to purchase such articles as were sorely needed, leaving his wife and two children in their isolated, wilderness home, without any known neighbors within a distance of many miles, except Indians. At the end of two weeks

Mr. N. returned with half a bushel of meal that he had carried on foot from Burlington! It was a precious burden.

Clothing was often a scarce article with the early pioneers, and it was found necessary to practice the strictest economy in the use of it. It so happened at one time that Mr. Neel had but one pair of pants, and his wife but one dress; and, as there was no apparent prospect of obtaining a change soon, they prudently decided to save what they had by using it as little as possible. It was warm weather, and they could dispense with any surplus amount of covering without suffering any serious inconvenience therefrom, besides, like Adam and Eve, they had no neighbors to behold their condition, or at least they supposed they had not. But in this they were slightly mistaken, for one day when Martin was at work on his claim, in his every-day suit of only a shirt, he happened to observe the approach of a lady at a distance. Horrified at the thought of being so discovered in his semi-nude condition, he made a hasty retreat to the house, announced the approach of the visitor, and the modest pair had barely time to dress ere the visitor arrived. She introduced herself as Mrs. Howard who had just settled in the neighborhood, and had called to make their acquaintance. After this Mr. Neel did not deem it prudent to go pantless.

The family moved to Missouri many years ago, and the last that was heard of Mr. Neel, he was an officer in the rebel army.

Horace Lyman was born in New York, from whence he was moved to Kentucky when quite young. From there he went to Ohio, and from Ohio, to Van Buren county, Iowa, in 1839. From there, in company with Stanford Doud, he came to this county, in April 1843, and camped on Cedar, near what is still known as Haymaker's Mill, where he marked out a claim, built a bark shanty for a temporary shelter, and make his claim in due order on the first day of May. In the autumn following he sowed some wheat, and then, during the winter of 1844, in partnership with Doud and Haymaker, after which Doud sold his interest to Lyman and Haymaker.

It was not until sometime in '45 that Mr. Lyman succeeded in moving his family to his new home; and, during the time previous to this he was compelled to make frequent journeys to his old place in Van Buren county, for provisions, going on horseback, and carrying such equipage as was needed for camping out. As has been heretofore stated, the roads then were little better than Indian trails, and the streams unbridged; these journeys were attended with more or less danger, particularly during high waters. On one occasion, in attempting to ford a small stream called Soap Creek, the animal he was riding sank out of sight, forcing him to abandon it in the middle of the stream and struggle for his life. Encumbered as he was, Mr. L. scarcely hoped to escape drowning; but by such exertions as are made only when life is at stake, he reached the shore opposite where he had entered the stream. When the horse rose to the surface he spied his master and followed him. Alonzo Doud, who was in company with Mr. Lyman on this occasion, hesitated to enter any large stream till it should be proved safe to do so by Mr. L. going in advance. Fording Soap Creek was not safe, but Doud had either to go back alone or make the adventure. He chose the latter as the safer and succeeded even better than his companion.

Mr. Lyman now lives near the western border of Mahaska Co., to which place he moved in '64. He is now an extensive farmer and stock dealer.

Stanford Doud came from Ohio to Van Buren Co., Iowa, in '42, and to this township and county in the spring following, in company with a person named Henry Polly. On first entering the purchase they met with some opposition by the dragoons, and were at one time hotly pursued and narrowly escaped being captured by them. But they persisted in remaining in the country till they should be permitted to make permanent settlement; and when the time came to do so, they also made choice of and secured a claim in that beautiful strip of country near Haymaker's mill.

At one time, during their sojourn in this then wilderness, they ran short ot provisions. Strange as it may seem, game was exceedingly scarce just then. The Indians had swept the country of everything of the kind. Having anticipated a lack of provisions in time, as they supposed to procure a supply from the settlements below, they had sent a man down the river in a canoe to bring it up. But for some reason or other the messenger was delayed. Having waited, looked, and hoped for his return till almost at the point of starvation, the grim prospect admonished them that they must prepare to leave the country or die there. As they must have some means of conveyance, they concluded to dig out a canoe. This was work for men already weakened by hunger; but they went about it at once, lest their strength should so fail them that they should be unable to complete it. In the mean time one of them had killed a ground hog, which they cooked the best they could and ate without salt, which, tough and unpalatable as it was, gave them some relief.

While working at the canoe they were visted by a small party of Indians, who at first manifested much friendship by hand-shaking and conversation. Mr. Doud, though little inclined, as hungry people are, to make himself agreeable to a squad of treacherous warriors, prudently deemed it advisable to humor them. But Polly was sulky and worked away at the canoe, not deigning to look up or pay the least attention to the Indian who was trying to give him some instructions about the shape of that part of the vessel he was at work on. This want of respect or appreciation on the part of Polly so enraged the Indian that the latter took up his gun with the evident intention of shooting the offender, accompanying the act with the threatening words "nippo smokeman," (kill whiteman.) Mr. Doud understood enough of the language to know what this meant, and to respond in an equally threatening manner, at the same time pointing his own rifle at the would-be-assassin, "nippo socee." This was a critical situation for the half starved men. Mr. D. knew very well that if one of them was killed the murderers would scarely deem it prudent to let the other escape as evidence against them. But the prompt interference had the desired effect. The chief of the party bade his subordinate to desist, and they all took their departure, leaving our heroes to finish their work in peace. Fearing another visitation as much as the famine that threatened them, they got the vessel afloat so soon as it would do to float at all, and reached their destination in safety, but much reduced by starvation.

After getting well recruited, Mr. Doud returned to his claim and made such improvements thereon as enabled him to move his family to it in 1844. After many years residence here, he returned to his old home in Van Buren county, where he still lives.

Andrew McGruder settled near Hamilton in 1843. During the early part of his pioneer life he and his family suffered a full share of the hardships and privations incident thereto. For a time while making rails to improve his claim he made three hundred per day and fed on nothing but milk.

We might mention others who were early settlers in this township, whose names are not on the list. These were principally temporary settlers. Among them were three young men named Peck, Pyatt, and Sadorus, who made claims in the north part of the township, on which they made some improvements, but soon sold out, returned to Illinois, and from thence went to California.

CHAPTER XXIV.

Liberty Township continued—First Grain Mills—First Post Office—First School taught—First Sub-district Organized—A Claim Difficulty—Hamilton—"Jake's Ruin"—Whisky and Water—Marysville—Marysville Miner—Dixonville—Flight of the Goods.

In 1845 Benjamin Spillman, living in the southestern part of the township, contrived and erected a temporary hand mill for grinding corn. It consisted of a couple of native rocks dressed to a suitable size and smothness, placed one upon the other in the ordinary way, and so fastened that the open one could be turned by a crank, with one hand, while with the other the operator could feed it, throwing in a few grains at each revolution. It had the capacity of grinding five or six bushels of corn per day, and was patronized by quite a number of customers, each of whom was his own miller. Sometimes several would be waiting, each for his turn, even when that consisted of only a few messes.

When Haymakers and others began to supply the demand for breadstuff, such temporary make-shifts as the one just described, were laid away as superanuated machinery, as water mills in their turn were thrown into disuse by the introduction of steam power.

The first post office established in this township was called Elm Grove, a place still known by that name, and now owned and occupied by Jesse Bussy. The precise date of its establishment we have not been able to ascertain, but it must have been some time in '45 or '46. James Rousseau was post master.

The first school was taught by David Maymaker, in the

winter of '46 and '47, in a claim pen owned by Lyman M. Haymaker, near their mill.

The first organized school district was what is now No. 7. A hewed log house was built for school purposes, and a young man named Turk first occupied it as a teacher. The house is now occupied as a dwelling by a family named Gregg.

As in all parts of the county, claim difficulties were not uncommon, one instance of which we may record. A man named Baker came into the neighborhood of where Hamilton now is, and entered some land legally claimed by Jacob Hendricks. As it happened, there was a quantity of rails on the land just entered, belonging to Hendricks. One night these rails were all moved and piled up on the opposite side of the line. At this time Baker was absent, but his return was looked for with much interest by Jacob and his friends; and when he came they paid him their respects *en masse*, and induced him to deed the land to Jacob without any needless delay.

The village of Hamilton, occupying the south-west quarter of the north-west quarter of section 35, was laid out by Stanford Doud, surveyor, assisted by Jacob Hendricks and another individual whose name is not remembered, as chain carriers, June 1st and 2d, 1849. Proprietors, Jacob Hendricks, Isaac Willsey, Andrew McGruder, John Stilwell, H. H. Mitchell, and Martin Neel. After the town was platted into six blocks the proprietors drew cuts for the choice of lots.

The first house was built during the following winter, by Nathaniel Linn. It was a double log cabin, and the foundation was laid three feet above ground on the compact snow that bore up the entire structure, till the first thaw softened the underpinning and gradually let it down to earth.

The first postoffice was kept by Isaac Willsey. Present incumbent Theodore West. Mails daily.

The first goods were sold by Linn and Smith, consisting

principally of groceries, including a good stock of drinkables.

The first hotel was kept by Henry Edwards, in a hewed log house, since burned. The present village hotel is kept by R. R. Parker, who also owns a fine farm adjoining.

The place now contains five mercantile business houses, one church (M. E.), one Odd Fellow's Lodge, established in 1855, with now $1,000 in its treasury.

Hamilton was so named from Hamilton county, Ohio, most of the settlers having came from that State. But for some time after the town came into being it was known only by the singular and romantic name of Jake's Ruin. How it came to be so named may not appear so romantic as the name itself might indicate. During the surveying of the town, the surveyors got drunk, and Jake Hendricks became so unsteady that in the performance of his duty, as chain carrier, he had to go partly on all fours, holding to the long grass to maintain his equilibrium. Being one of the proprietors of the town, and also the original owner of the land on which it was located, he became reckless in the expenditure of time and money in the indulgence of his propensity for dissipation. Mrs. Hendricks was greatly distressed at this downward career ot her husband, and one day, having visitors, she took occasion to acquaint them of her great trouble, bitterly declaring that the town would be Jake's ruin. The words seemed so suggestive that it was thereafter so called and so known at a distance. Even strangers coming from a distance were wont to inquire the way or the distance to Jake's Ruin. On one occasion a stranger approaching the place, met Mrs. H. in the neighborhood and quite innocently asked her how far it was to Jake's Ruin. It was not till after the reason had been explained to him that he could account for the shockingly uncivil answer the lady had given him.

The early history of Hamilton was not propitious of its early prosperity. Whisky was a fashionable drink, and more convenient than water. Singular as it may seem, good water could not be reached short of 75 or 80 feet of digging, whereas now a plentiful supply can be obtained at one-third that depth, and all the old wells are inexhaustible.

Marysville is situated on the south-west quarter of the south-east quarter of section 29, on the north side of South Cedar, in the beautiful vale that margins this stream. It was laid out by James Rousseau, Feb. 11, '57, on land then owned by Joseph Brobst and Josiah Brobst, the former owning the west side and the latter the east side of what is now the main street of the village. The surveying was done by James Rousseau; John B. Ely and Jacob Stambach, chain carriers. The place was so named from the number of Marys belonging to the Brobst family, not less than five of them being in possession of that honored name. The first house was built by Jonathan Wilder. It was a frame building, and still stands. The second was by Jacob Stambach, and is now known as the old tavern stand. Andrew Kerr sold the first goods. Peter Klein was first P. M., and the postoffice was then called Ely. His successor was J. B. Ely. Present incumbent, —— Gartner.

For some years Marysville remained in a partially dormant condition, but since the discovery of vast quantities of coal lands in its neighborhood, and a railroad company organized on the basis of these lands, the place has had an upward tendency in the way of enterprise, and is now rapidly building up. The most prominent building in the place is a large woolen factory, by Welch & Co., erected last spring, '72. There is also a weekly newspaper published here, called the "Marysville Miner," by David C. Ely, and to its descriptions of the country, advertisements, and stirring appeals, much of the prosperity of the town may be attributed.

The "Miner" was first issued Feb. 7, '71, by a company, with J. W. Ragsdale as editor, from a press brought from Albia, Monroe county. In his salutatory the editor said, "As to politics, we are personally Republican, but this paper shall be independent, out-spoken, and ever ready to condem that which we deem to be wrong, even though it be in high places. As to making fair promises, we will not. We can only say to our readers that we will TRY to do our duty, and that we expect them to do the same." With the next issue of the paper D. C. Ely took editorial charge of it, and has so continued since. In his bow to the public he says: "As stated in the salutatory, this paper shall be neutral in politics, and devoted to the best interests of this section, by giving information in regard to our natural advantages over our sister towns."

In '56 Mr. D. B. Dixon caused to be surveyed on land owned by him, and now owned by Abram Pack, about two miles north of Hamilton, a town that he called Dixonville. To this place he brought and erected a store house that had been used for this purpose in Monroe county, and stored it with goods. But, unfortunately for the proprietor, the goods soon after fell under execution, and a sheriff was sent to levy upon them. It was late in the evening when the officer arrived, and he concluded to postpone the execution of his official duty till next morning. But, on going to the store next morning, he found the shelves empty. The goods, apparently apprehensive of falling under the ban of legal authority, had taken their flight during the night. Soon after this Mr. Dixon abandoned his town, and it never prospered.

Population of Liberty township by the U. S. census of 1870:

Native	1499
Foreign	33
Total	1532

CHAPTER XXV.

Indiana Township—Its Geography and Early History—Names of Early Settlers—Alexander May—A Milling Expedition—Eleven Miles to borrow Meal—George Henry—Out of Provisions and Money—Working on Sunday—In a Storm—Mush and Milk—Only Potatoes—A Perilous Adventure.

This township is technically described as town. 74, range 19. It is a southern township, and its exact location may be defined as the south-west quarter of the south-east quarter of the county. It is bounded on the north by Knoxville, on the east by Liberty, on the south by Monroe county, and on the west by Washington township.

Off the streams the prairie is almost level. The prairies are not large, and timber is abundant and convenient to any part of them. Coal is plentiful along many of the small streams, and the veins are from three to six feet thick. Those worked most are on the lands of Daniel Sherwood and Alexander May.

Indiana was declared an organized township by the board of county commissioners at their regular session, January 6, 1847, and the place for holding elections was appointed at the house of Alexander May, which was about a mile east of the center of the township.

The first election held in this township, (of which there is no preserved record,) took place at Mr. May's cabin, August 1st, 1844, which, it will be observed, was a precinct election. Benj. Sherwood and John Riddle served as clerks. The first named person was elected township precinct clerk; Alexander

May and John T. Pierce, justices, and Allen Lowe and Samuel C. Nicholson, constables.

At this election, and just previously thereto, there was a strife between parties in favor of Pierce and Lowe on the one hand, and May and Nicholson on the other, as to which pair of constables should receive the largest number of votes. Knowing the beneficial effects of something good to drink in the way of winning friends, Alonzo Smith and Samuel Coolly had prepared a barrel of "mathoglin" as a treat to the supporters of Pierce and Lowe, and won the victory by three votes.

The first election of which there is any preserved record, was held at the house of Benj. F. Williams, in Barkersville (now Attica,) April 5, 1852. Fifty-three votes were cast, and the following officers elected: Harvey Manners and W. T. Smith, justices; Nathaniel Coclerece, Samuel M. Cooly and Jacob Bonebreak, trustees; Noah Bonebreak, clerk, and Allen Lowe and John Camplin, constables.

Indiana was so named in consequence of a large majority of the first settlers being from that state. The following is a list of their names and date of settlement: Alexander May, Noah Whitlatch, Wm. Carlisle, George Henry, Allen Lowe, Samuel Coolly, Wm. Shanks, Samuel Nicholson and John Riddle in 1843; Jeremiah Gullian, Benj. Sherwood, David Sweem and Jas. Cade, in 1844; Isaac Kelsey and Lewis Pierce in 1845, and John Bonebreak in 1846.

Alexander May, who still lives where he originally settled in the township, and, with several others mentioned in the above list, formed what was known as May's Settlement, was born in Henry county, Kentucky, January 5th, 1801, immigrated to Orange county, Indiana, in 1816, to Fountain county, same state, in 1827, and from thence to Montgomery county, same state, in 1831, and from thence to his present place, arriving there June 22, 1843.

In relating his first year's experience in pioneer life here, Mr. May says in a letter to us:

"In the fall, having to lay in our provisions for the winter, John Riddle and I took my ox wagon and four yoke of oxen, and drove to the old purchase. Having to work for our grain, we put in three weeks of steady labor, by which we paid for forty-five bushels of fall wheat, and thirty bushels of old corn, one barrel of salt, one side of sole leather and one of upper. We got our grinding done at Meeks' mill, Bonaparte. No roads from Agency till we got home, only as the emigrant had made them. We were thirty-five days from home.

"The first grain we raised was threshed in the old-fashioned way with horses, and fanned with a sheet. Soon as it was ready we took it to Farmington to mill, the trip occupying fifteen days. The first wheat we got ground at Haymaker's, we bolted through book muslin stretched over a hoop. The first meal we borrowed, my wife got at Joseph Tally's on the north side of the Des Moines river. In this trip she went alone, forded the river at what is now Bellfountain, with a team of horses and wagon, the water being flank deep to the team, borrowed three bushels of meal and bought seven chickens, and returned the same day, a distance of eleven miles. These were the nearest neighbors from whom we could obtain such accommodations."

George Henry, who now lives near Knoxville, was originally from Pennsylvania. First moved from that State to Ohio, from Ohio to Missouri, and from thence to Lake Prairie, in the fall of 1842. Here, in company with Jas. Carnilius and another whose name is not remembered, they took claims and erected three cabins. But not being permitted to make permanent settlement, they returned to Missouri and remained till the spring following. Finding that the cabins had been destroyed by dragoons, Mr. Henry took a claim in what is now the northeast corner of Indian township. This was near

Wm. Carlisle's, whose family cleared a small patch of land in the timber, on which they planted some corn and potatoes. But towards fall provisions ran short, and Mr. Henry started to mill in September, leaving but little for his family to subsist on during his absence, expecting to return in a week. Having no money to purchase grain or provisions with, he hoped to obtain some due him on the way to Keosauqua, where he intended to get his milling done. But being disappointed in getting the money, he tried to get some grain on credit, and after traveling three or four miles from Keosauqua for this purpose, was again disappointed. There was now no other shift but to look for work, and if he could get it to do, earn the means to buy his breadstuff. Luckily he obtained a job of making rails, and his employer kindly furnished him a house to live in and food till he should finish the job. The contract was made on Saturday evening, and will any one censure Mr. Henry for going to work next morning? With thoughts of his family at home in an almost destitute condition, and really in danger of suffering ere he should be able to return to them with food, could he have spent the day more religiously than he did? So Mr. H. went to work on Sunday morning, and by Tuesday evening made six hundred rails, for which he received seventy-five cents per hundred, in an order to the mill, and this secured a little flour and few bushels of meal at fifty cents per bushel.

Having secured these articles, Mr. Henry set out for home with all possible haste. After going six miles, he was overtaken by a violent storm of wind and rain. He was near a house when the storm came upon him; so he concluded to go no farther, but unhitched his horses, put them into an enclosure near at hand, and took shelter in his wagon. In this frail shelter he passed the dark tempestuous night alone. Next morning, on going to look for his team he found the dead timber thickly strewn over the pasture, prostrated by the storm, and his horses luckily, and we might add miraculously, uninjured.

Mr. Henry now proceeded on his way, and being too eager to reach home to carefully regard the strength of his horses, they failed within twenty miles of their journey's end. He then went to a house near by to get some feed for them and for himself, and obtained some shelled corn; but the house could afford nothing in the way of human food but milk. He, however, made an arrangement with the family by furnishing a sufficient quantity of meal for mush, and they all supped jointly and heartily on a mess of mush and milk. By next morning the horses were refreshed for a renewal of the journey, and our hero reached home in safety, to find his family reduced to nothing but potatoes for a diet.

Just before Christmas, '43, Mr. Henry and a son of Noah Whitlatch, took two loads of flour barrels to Keosauqua. The weather was cold and stormy when they started, and a deep snow had fallen the day before. When they reached the Des Moines river, a little below Talley's ford, they found it frozen over strong enough, they supposed, to bear them and their teams, and drove on. It proved to be a dangerous venture. The ice bent under the weight of their wagons so much that the water gushed up in jets. But once started it would be as dangerous to return as to go on, and the safest plan was to make all possible speed, and they succeeded in reaching the opposite shore. On their return they found the ice gone, and had to ferry their wagons over on a canoe, and swim their teams.

CHAPTER XXVI.

Indiana Township Continued—David Sweem—Straitened—Circumstances—A Night in the Wilderness—Unknown Remains—A Lost Traveler—Indiana P. O.—First School—First Preaching—First Wedding—A Romantic Incident—A Claim Difficulty—Attica—James Barker—He fights the Dragoons.

David Sweem was born in Ohio, in 1819, moved to Indiana and from thence to this county and township in the autumn of '44.

Mr. S. was first an exhorter, and during his residence here, an itinerant preacher in the M. E. Church. He also took a somewhat active part in politics, by which he became well known in the county. His residence was near Attica, where he died Jan. 15th, '68. His widow resides in the village.

Like many of his fellow immigrants he came to this country poor, and suffered many of the privations of poverty and of a new country combined. At one time he and Jeremiah Gullian went to Keosauqua to get work for money to buy breadstuffs. Just previous to this they had lost their only cow; and, as this cow had been half the support of the family, their circumstances were much straitened by the loss. Work for wages was scarcely to be had, and all that Mr. Sweem could get to do was a well to clean out. With the wages for this job, and half a dollar he already had, he bought two bushels of meal and returned home.

Instances have been related of the scarcity of tools and such other articles, the use of which could scarcely be dispensed with, and the distance sometimes traveled to obtain the loan of them. Mr. Samuel Coolly relates to us an instance of his own experience in borrowing. Good water could not be had without digging for it; and this could not be done without a spade or shovel to do it with, and there was no such tool in the country nearer than twelve miles. It belonged to Amos Strickland, who lived in what is now Monroe county. Mr. Coolly went and obtained a loan of the spade, (the handle of which was about 18 inches long,) and started on his return, intending to make the trip in one day. But, on reaching the timbers of North Cedar, the night came on and gradually grew into impenetrable darkness. Mr. C. became bewildered, but the horse he rode—a white one, and about the only object he could see—carried him to the bank of the stream. To attempt to ford it in that unknown and dark place required a stronger nerve for adventure than the wanderer possessed; so he concluded to remain there till morning. Having tied his horse, he laid down by a tree near at hand. But neither to rest nor sleep. All night he heard the prowling of wolves and other wild animals in the vicinity. The horse evidently saw or scented them, for he was desperately restless, snorting, pawing and neighing continually. Added to this trouble were great swarms of musquitoes that were bolder and more bloodthirsty than the wolves. Morning came at last, and Mr. Coolly found his way across the creek and reached home without meeting with any other serious adventure.

The above story revives the recollection of one relating to a like adventure of less fortunate termination. In '44 or '45, Allen Lowe was driving some cattle across a trackless prairie, near the western line of the township, when some of them shied off, as though frightened at some object. Going to see what had been the cause of it, Mr. Lowe found a coat and pants, and, upon further search, the bones of a human being, scattered over several rods of ground. The bones were gathered up and buried, and the clothing was taken to Alexander May's where it still remains to be identified by whoever might come in search of the lost one. It was woolen stuff, and had been somewhat crisped by prairie fire. Evidently some poor wanderer had become bewildered, perhaps overwhelmed by a snow storm, and there alone, exhausted and dispairing, had given himself up to the sleep of death and his flesh to feed the ravenous wolves.

The liability of becoming bewildered on the prairie was much greater in the winter than in the summer, owing to snow storms, the dreary sameness of the landscape, and the obliteration of all paths by the snow. One night in the winter of '44 and '45 a man and team came to Allen Lane's and begged for shelter and food. He was from Bloomfield, and had been on a tour of observation through the country, had been bewildered and without food for two days and nights. His appearance and that of his team proved the truth of his statement of his famished condition, and he was readily provided for till sufficiently recruited to go on his way.

The first post office in this township was kept at Alexander May's, but at what date we have been unable to learn. Benj. Sherwood, P. M.; mails from Knoxville weekly.

The first school was taught by Fletcher Cain, in a little cabin near where Attica now is, in '45. Number of scholars, 16. Harvey Manners taught near the same place in '47–8. John B. Hays taught two miles south of Attica the same year. Hessey May also taught a school at her own house at an early date.

The first gospel preaching was done by Rev. Jas. L. Warren, in the summer of '43, at the residence of Noah Whitlatch. On this occasion the Dr., having sent an appointment to preach there at 11 o'clock A. M. on a certain Sabbath, walked the distance between his residence, in Lake Prairie, and the place appointed, but arrived too late. The people had collected, waited a long time, and then dispersed. After they were all gone the Dr. made his appearance, weary and heated with his long journey. After having come so far he was not disposed to return without accomplishing his mission, so he announced that he would preach at night if the people could be notified of it. Thereupon runners were sent abroad to notify them, and he was enabled to hold forth to a goodly number of hearers.

The first persons married were Samuel Nicholson and Eleanor May, daughter of Alexander May, at the residence of the latter, June 1st, '44. A little romance is connected with this matrimonial transaction, that, as it was the first may as well be related here:

The wooing had been going on for some time, and had ripened into an engagement; after which Samuel, with a view to improve his worldly circumstances preparatory to assuming so responsible a relationship, went down the river to work for higher wages than could be obtained at home. He was accompanied by Samuel Coolly, and the two Samuels hired as deck hands on a steamboat bound for St. Louis. In April Coolly returned, expecting Nicholson soon. But weeks passed, and no Samuel came. The month of May—that period so congenial to the sentimental influences of the spirit of Cupid—passed day by day and week by week, bringing no intelligence from the absent lover to his waiting and more than anxious bride elect. Whether he had been drowned, murdered, died of sickness, or had intentionally deserted her, were questions that tortured her to a degree that any reliable intelligence of the worst would have afforded some relief. At length, having abandoned all hope of his return, the sorrowing Eleanor and her father took up their luggage and started for a visit to the place and friends of their nativity in the State of Indiana. But, to their surprise, and to the happy relief of the affectionate girl, ere they had gone half a days' journey, they met the truant lover on his return. The intended visit was instantly abandoned, and the trio returned, and the union of the happy pair was consummated at the date above mentioned.

The next wedding was that of a sister of Eleanor, to Tyler Overton, in December, '44, on which occasion Mr. Overton made an adventurous winter trip to Oskaloosa for the license.

After the township began to settle up more rapidly, the people clubbed together, as described in the fore part of this book, for the government and protection of their claim interests; and out of this arose a little neighborhood trouble that might be worth relating:

In '47 a man named Jaobs, who had been employed as surveyor in this part of the county, but who now resided at Fairfield, sent to Lewis Pierce for several numbers of unclaimed land. Pierce responded by sending several numbers, but, either intentionally or by mistake, included several of claimed lots, among them those of Alex. May, Benj. Sherwood and Isaac Kelsey. These, with others, Jacobs entered at the land office. So soon as this was discovered a great excitement was manifested among the aggrieved parties. A meeting was called, and a committee appointed to arrest Pierce and bring him to trial. In case he was proved guilty of intentionally violating the rules of the club in this transaction, and should refuse to make full reparation, his punishment should be refered to the decision of Judge Lynch.

The committee went and found Pierce; but he evidently had anticipated being sent for, and had prepared himself for the emergency; for, on being invited to accompany the committee, he promptly refused, and backed his refusal with the presentation of a revolver. The committee consisted of only three persons, and they were not rash. They respected his backing, returned to head quarters and reported progress. The report was necessarily accepted, but the progress was not deemed satisfactory, so a reinforcement was sent and Pierce was persuaded to honor the meeting with his presence.

Finding himself in close quarters, Pierce, though the evidence was strong against him, plead innocent of any intentional wrong, and promised to have it righted. With this promise, he was released for the time being; and it is probable that he immediately set about fulfilling this promise, for it was not long after that that Jacobs received intelligence of the state of affairs, and was also informed that the club would visit him at Fairfield. At such a distance he might scarcely be supposed to fear an attack; but such was the terror inspired by threats of the organizations—they having proved themselves capable of fulfilling them in a number of instances—that distance was not deemed safety. So Jacobs wrote to the claimants that he would deed them their land on the receipt of the entrance money, and interest on the same at the rate of six per cent. annually. The club agreed to this proposal and peace was restored.

On the 26th of July, '49, James Barker and Nathaniel Cochreece caused to be surveyed on the northwest quarter of section 11, a town that was called Barkersville, in honor of one of the proprietors. Surveyor, James Rousseau. James Barker erected the first house on the survey, a one-story brick, that is now occupied by Wm. Thomas. Barker also sold the first goods, and was, at the same time, first postmaster. Mail once a week. It was first carried from Knoxville, in a pocket handkerchief, by M. M. Marks. B. F. Williams afterwards bought Barker's store, and also took charge of the postoffice. Present post master T. S. Cathcart. Mails daily. The first hotel was kept by a German named Michael Himmelhaver. Fare, ten cents per meal. The house still stands, near the Attica House.

The first school in town was taught by Hessey May and the Rev. Mr. Neur organized the first M. E. society there.

Not long after Barkersville had been in existence, its principle proprietor, James Barker, for whom the town had been named, became so infamous in a criminal attachment for another man's wife, that the name was regarded as a disgrace to the town, and by common consent it was changed to Attica.

Attica now has three stores, one hotel, and three potteries. The clay for the manufacture of the ware is obtained from land near by, owned by Wm. Sharon.

James Barker was noted as a desperate character in this locality. After having acted upon the free love principle by deserting his own family and domesticating himself with another man's wife, with whom he lived for some time, he disappeared altogether, in such a way that his disappearance is still shrouded in mystery. It is supposed by some that he met with a secret and violent death at the hands of an enemy.

An anecdote is related of Barker that we may as well close this chapter by recording, though we are not able to give the exact time or place:

With a wagon stored with articles for trade with the Indians, including whisky, he came into the new purchase long before the time stipulated for settlement, hoping to evade the notice of the dragoons and do a good business. But one day he discovered a squad of these prowling guardians of the treaty approaching at a distance. Quickly as possible he drew his wagon into a brushy hollow, then took a jug of whisky and went out to meet the troopers. On meeting them the captain told him he must get out of the territory or he would have his wagon and team confiscated. Barker swore he wouldn't.

" What will yo do?" asked the astonished captain.

" Fight," answered Barker.

"How?"

" With my jug," said Barker; " and I'll whip you too;" saywhich he gave the weapon a swing and landed it on the pommel of the captain's saddle. Barker's tactics were invincible, and the regulars soon fled, rejoicing in their defeat as much as Barker did in his victory.

Population of Indiana by the U. S. census of 1870:

Native	1321
Foreign	11
Total	1332

CHAPTER XXVII.

Perry Township—Geography and Early History—Lead Ore—Names of Early Settlers—Asa Hughs—The Brans Family—A Wild Cat Adventure—Hezekiah Gay—Bennington—E. H. Baker—Some of his Peculiarities—Lucky Duck Shooting—A Woman's Adventure with a Deer—First Preachers and School Teachers—Census.

At a session of the county commissioner's court, January 6, 1847, it was ordered that town. 77, range 21, be called Perry. This name was in honor of Commodore Perry, of the Lake Erie victory notoriety. It was suggested by some of the citizens that it should be called Cincinnati, but this name was not adhered to after the township was organized.

As above defined it included all of the present township of Perry and all that of Swan, except two sections and four half sections belonging to town. 76, range 21, since added to Swan. The place of holding elections was at the house of Wm. Markley.

At this election about fourteen votes were cast, and Dan. Kiger and Hezekiah Gay were elected justices; James M. Brans and Joshua Linsey, constables; Asa Hughs and Joshua Linsey, trustees, and James M. Brans, clerk. The first pre cient election was held at the house of Asa Hughs, April 7th, '46, 13 votes cast.

This and the next election were held north of the river, and the two following south of it; but the flood of 1851 caused a dissatisfaction among the people, owing to the inconvenience of crossing the river, and so, at the July session of the commissioners' court, 1852, it was ordered that that portion of town. 77, range 21, north of the Des Moines river, constitute the township of Perry. Election to be held at the town of Bennington. At this election Harrison Freel was elected justice, but we have no record of any other officers.

Perry is the northwest corner township of the county, and is bounded on the north by Jasper county, on the east by Red Rock, on the south by Swan, with the Des Moines river as its boundary line, and on the west by Warren county.

The township is mostly timbered, and, with the exceptions of the bottom lands on the river, somewhat hilly. Coal is abundant along the north bank of the Des Moines river, and on the small streams. Lead ore has also been found in the bank of the river; and, at an early day, the remains of furnaces were discovered in the vicinity of the ore, supposed to have been used by the Indians in smelting it. Walnut Creek is the largest stream running through the township.

The following are the names of those who settled in the township at the earliest dates: Hezekiah Gay, Joshua Linsey, Dan. Kiger, Chas. Owen, Asa Hughs, Robert Alison, Alfred Vertrice, and Mordica Yearns, in '45; Peter Brans, and his two sons, James M. and Benjamin, Thomas Car, Wm. Hughs, Wm. Gregory, Samuel Waterman, and Joseph McWilliams, in '46. Numerous other names might be added of persons who settled at a still later date, had we space to admit them. Of the above named but three still live in the township, six went to California many years ago, one to Missouri, five are dead, and one's whereabouts is unknown.

Asa Hughs first moved from Indiana to Iowa in '36, and settled in Marion county, on Lake Prairie, in '44, from whence he moved to Perry in '45, and made a claim on Walnut creek, in what is now section 12. Here he lived, surrounded by a numerous family till the date of his death, Feb. 13, 1863.

The Brans family were natives of Pennsylvania, from whence they moved to Ohio in '25, and from thence to Mahaska county, Iowa, in '45. In the spring of the year following, James came and took up his residence on the place now occupied by Mrs. Mullins, in the north-west corner of Red Rock township, where he remained till he had put up a cabin on his own claim, where he still lives. His father, Peter Brans, died November 4th, 1860.

Perry township being a rough, timbered region, wild game was quite plentiful at an early date, and even within the past few years wild cats and lynxes have existed there. We may relate a little wild cat adventure, of which J. M. Brans was the hero. It occurred in the spring of '46, when Mr. B. was employed in making rails some distance from his house. Observing a large elm stump, about twenty feet high, with a hole in it near the ground, he incautiously put his head in it to see what discoveries he could make. And the discovery he did make caused him to withdraw his countenance as speedily as possible; for, within a very short distance of it was a great mother wild cat and her three kittens. Mr. B. had no gun, so he closed the hole securely, went for help, and soon the old cat was ousted from her den, killed by dogs, and the kittens captured. After being retained a short time they were not deemed a safe breed to adopt as a part of the domestic circle, and were dispatched.

Hezekiah Gay was a bachelor, and is well remembered for his eccentricities. For some time after his settlement in the township, he lived by himself in a rude shanty near the present site of Bennington, and was much occupied with speculative ideas of manufacturing machinery to be operated by the water power of the Des Moines river. Full of his plans of constructing an immense woollen factory, he was often seen with a miniature trough filled with water, taking the level of the river, to ascertain what height he should build his dam to have sufficient power. But there was other power needed than water, and this Hezekiah had not, either in purse or in credit; so the water power was never brought into service. He then became interested in a shingle machine; and this involved him to an extent that subjected the property to an execution. About this time Hezekiah was seen on his way to "Tool's Point," (now Monroe,) to procure a rope as he stated to a neighbor, to serve as a belt for his machine. This was the last seen of him in Perry, and to this day his whereabouts is unknown.

In August, from the 10th to the 14th, '48, Wm. Gregory and E. H. Baker caused a town to be surveyed on the north bank of the Des Moines river, on the east half of section 9, and called it Bennington. Stanford Doud, surveyor. Gregory was the owner of the claim, and Baker had it surveyed, sharing equally the profits on the sale of lots. Baker then put up a store room and dwelling together, and in the fall following moved his goods from Red Rock and began business. He also secured the appointment of P. M.

Shortly before Bennington was laid out, June 14, Hezekiah Gay caused a town to be laid out on the north half of section 9, and called it Perryville. This was done in competition with Baker's and Gregory's contemplated town. But neither of the places prospered, and, in process of time, were abandoned by their proprietors, leaving no more of them than their names. Two or three small houses occupy the town plat of Bennington, and one of the citizens keeps a ferry, which is on the main road between Pleasantville and Prairie City.

Gregory opened a farm in the country, where he died many years since, and Baker moved to Prairie City, and from thence to Colfax station, where he still lives.

Baker will always be remembered by many old settlers as one of the most eccentric characters that ever existed in Marion county. Many stories might be told to illustrate this fact, a few of which we give. He sometimes took a whim to sell no goods on certain days, and his best customers could not move him from his purpose. On another day he would be extremely accommodating to everybody. Then he would positively refuse to sell coffee on a certain day, or would accommodate only certain customers with it, refusing even those who had come quite a distance, and were prepared to pay for it, however promising to supply them liberally on the day following.

In his transactions as postmaster, he was at one time known to retain letters when called for by their owners, so as to give him apportunity to advertise them. Their appearance on the list was clear proof that they were in the office when called for.

At one time a customer called at the store and found Baker at work in his garden. And here his oddity was so conspicuously manifest that if he had thereafter been tried for murder and convicted, he could have plead insanity with some plausability. He was at full length on his abdomen, and bareheaded, his bald crown glistening in the hot sun, as it bobbed up and down to the motion of his work; and as he hoed to the length of his hoe-handle he would drive the blade deep in the ground and pull himself forward. Thus he toiled away as though his life depended upon it, and would not stop a moment to talk to or wait upon a customer.

But the most heartless instance of his whimsical behavior is the manner in which he received his aged mother, whom he had not seen for many years. She had come from Illinois to make him a visit, and had brought him a valuable present. It was late in the evening when she arrived, and a neighbor accompanied her to the house of her son and knocked for admittance. Baker asked who was there, and, on being informed that it was his mother, he informed the visitors that he was in bed, that he would not get up to admit even Jesus Christ, that she might go to John Young's that night, and he would see her in the morning. And no pleading of the old lady or her escort could move the unworthy son to open the door. Mortified and grieved beyond expression, she retired and resolved not to see him. So, early next morning, before breakfast, she sat out on her return home. Baker, on hearing of her departure, was pricked to the heart, mounted a horse and went in pursuit of her. After a hot chase of several miles, he came up with her. He apologized for his want of civility in not admitting her, stating that he was not in a condition to receive her just then, and asked her to return with him. But Mrs. B. was exasperated beyond conciliation, and no pleadings of her son seemed to have any effect upon her purpose, only to make it stronger. So she went on her way, and he returned to his bachelor home, conscious that he had made a grievious mistake.

Among those who settled in Bennington at an early date was a family named Moon. During their residence here they were victims to the ague, which reduced them so much in strength and finances that they were at one time on the point of starvation, and pro' ably would have perished but for one little circumstance that seemed a direct interposition of Providence in their behalf. Mrs. Moon went down to the river to try to do some washing, when she saw four wild ducks swimming in still water near the shore. She immediately returned and informed her husband of the discovery. He was too weak to carry the gun, but proposed to do the shooting; so his wife took the gun and he followed. Coming within easy shot of the game, Mr. Moon took rest against a big tree and fired. The shot was effectual, causing one duck to turn on its back. It was to be supposed the others would have taken flight, but not so; they merely fluttered away a few yards and then returned to their dead companion. Taking advantage of their want of discretion, the gun was soon re-loaded and another duck killed; and in like manner the others clung to the fatal spot, and likewise perished. Mrs. M. then fished them from the water with a stick, and the large family of Moons made the first full meal of them and proportionate share of grated corn bread that they had enjoyed for some time. The next day they shook easier than usual.

Mr. Moon afterwards made a claim a few miles north-east of Bennington, where he still lives. Here Mrs. M. had another adventure worth relating. One day, during her husband's absence, word came to her that the pups were playing with a deer, in a clearing a short distance north of the house. Taking one of the two guns—a heavy piece—she went out and got upon a log that was elevated upon a stump some ten feet from the ground, the better to see over the tall weeds. From this elevated position she spied the game within easy shot, confronted by the brave young dogs; and, taking deliberate aim at it, fired. But she had no time to see what effect the shot had upon the deer; for the treacherous gun shot both ways, and its reverse shooting sent Mrs. M. backwards to a horizontal position on the ground. Not being much hurt, she got up and went to look for the game; finding it down and evidently dead, she went to give it a close inspection, when it instantly roused up; and ere she had time to think of her danger, or make her escape, the enraged brute sprang upon her, knocked her down and tore off a portion of her clothing, compelling her to roll under a log near at hand, to escape further injury. From this narrow retreat she emerged in a short time, re-loaded her gun and put an end to her adventure by shooting the deer through the head.

The first preacher of the gospel that labored in this township was a Rev. Mr. Kline, of the M. E. Church. He was succeeded by the Rev. Mr. Rainer, of the same denomination.

The first person that taught school was Patience Drouylard, at her own house, in 1850. She had from fifteen to twenty scholars. The next school was taught by James M. Brans, near his present residence. He had an attendance of from twenty to thirty scholars.

The first school-house was built in sub-district number one, in 1851. It was a roughly-hewed log-house, built by William Cowman at a cost of $100.

The population of this township, by the U. S. census of '70, was as follows:

Natives	450
Foreign	15
Total	465

CHAPTER XXVIII.

Swan Township—Its Geography and Early History—First Election—Names of First Settlers—First Birth and First Marriage—C. M. Thomas—Daniel Hunt—First School—First Orchard—First Preachers—Andrew Schirner—A Severe Crisis—Wheeling—Lynching the Castners.

This township is all of town. 77, range 21, south of the Des Moines river, with the additions of 5 and 6, and the half of sections 1, 2, 3 and 4, belonging to town. 76, same range. It is bounded on the north by Perry, on the east by Union, on the south by Pleasant Grove, and on the west by Warren county. Numerous small streams run through the township, mostly from south to north. Coal abounds in various parts, and thin veins have been found in wells of considerable depth. Several veins have been opened and worked, one in the northwest part of the township, owned by John Shook; one three miles east of Wheeling, by J. F. Smith; and one near and west of Wheeling by Wm. Carte. That of Mr. Smith has been most extensively worked, and is about four feet thick. This township is rather more than half timbered, the small streams being widely margined by heavy growths, covering all the northern part, except the wide strip of bottom land along the Des Moines river, called Hoosier Prairie, so named from the number of people from Indiana who settled on and about it. Part of this tract is uncultivated, being quite sandy and subject to inundations from the river. The southern part of the township is mostly prairie, with here and there a beautiful native grove.

Swan was organized in '51, being up to that date a part of Perry, and was separated into a district township by order of the board of commissioners, in compliance with the petition of her citizens, for reasons already stated in the history of Perry. It was called Swan from the beauty and brevity of the name, by the suggestion of a former citizen of Swan township, Athens county, Ohio.

The first election was held at the house of ——— Moffett, at which Wilson Groom was elected clerk. John Shook was justice at the time the township was organized, and held over. At this time Gilson Shook was elected constable.

The first election of which there is any preserved record, took place on the 4th of April, '53, at the house of Charity Groom. Judges—John Noyes, Jacob Haynes, and Edward Murray; clerk, C. C. Wilkie; deputy clerk, J. W. Brand Number of votes cast, 37, by which the following officers were elected: J. Metcalf and Samuel P. Hamilton, justices; A. G. Young and Robert McElroy, constables; James Metcalf, Jacob Haynes, and Edward Murray, trustees; Eli M. Cole, assessor; and H. W. Groom, clerk.

The following are the names of persons who settled in this township at the earliest dates: Charles M. Thomas, Wm. H. Parmer, Jesse Johnson, James Crabb, John Firman and his two sons, John Henry and John Stroop, in '46; John Groom, Wm. Groom, Jesse Walker, Harrison Freel, the three Markly brothers, Wm. Bundren and his sister, Mary Tout, in '46; Daniel Hunt, Andrew Schirner, John Butcher, and the Childers family, in '47. Of these but seven still live in the township, to-wit: C. M. Thomas, W. H. Parmer, Jesse Johnson, John Henry, Daniel Hunt, Andrew Schirner and John Butcher. James Crabb lives in Perry, the Grooms are dead, and the others unknown.

The first white child born in the township was Emma Jane, daughter of Wm. H. Parmer, born October 8, '46. She is now the wife of James H. Easley, and still lives in the township.

The first marriage was that of Wm. Markley and Eva Groom, in February, '48.

Chas. M. Thomas was born in Pennsylvania, moved to Virginia at an early age, from thence to Van Buren county, Iowa, and from thence to his present residence in Swan, during the last week in '45. During his residence in Van Buren county, Mr. Thomas was made the victim of treachery, by which he nearly lost his life. Having a partnership interest in a claim there, he had been assisting his partner in the erection of a house, and was to receive his pay in return help. Being fond of milk he was treated to a mess of it at meal time, and took violently sick directly after, from which he did not recover for several weeks. From the sudden and violent nature of his sickness, and remarks made by his partner, it was evident that the latter had drugged the milk with a view of putting Mr. T. out of his way, and ge ting full possession of the claim.

Mr. Thomas has still in his possession a coffee mill with which the family ground several bushels of buckwheat during the early part ot their pioneer life in Swan.

Daniel Hunt was a native of New Jersey, from whence he first moved to Ohio, from thence to Iowa in '40, and to Swan in the autumn of '47, and made a claim where Asher Kise now lives. He sowed the first timothy in the township, in the spring following, one-half acre in all, and sold nine bushels of the yield in seed to James Thornburgh. Mr. Hunt is now a successful stock raiser.

John E. Groom taught the first school in the township, in a small cabin originally owned and occupied by a man named Moore, on the east side of what is now Daniel Hunt's farm, on Hoosier Prairie, at what date we have been unable to learn. At this time the grass grew tall on this prairie, and Harrison Freel plowed a pathway for his children to travel in to school, which is still dimly visible.

The first orchard was planted by Jesse Walker, on land now

owned and occupied as a farm, by Jacob Camp. Only four or five of the trees still live, the trunks of which are between twelve and eighteen inches in diameter.

The Rev. Mr. Forbes, United Brethren, was the first person remembered to have preached in this township. Revs. Johnson and Gardner were the first Methodist preachers that organized societies of this denomination here.

Andrew Schirner came from Germany in '36, and settled in Indiana. From thence he came to his present place of residence in Swan, in March, '47, and purchased a claim from Michael Keeterman. This claim was mainly in the timber, and the only improvement made upon it was a small cabin, of that temporary construction usually denominated a "claim pen," having neither floor, door nor windows. Mr. S. however, borrowed a saw of his nearest neighbor, Jesse Walker, and soon made an opening for his house, and added such other improvements as were indispensable to a dwelling. He then took possession of it with his wife and five children.

But now came a crisis such as many pioneers have had to pass through, yet all with that degree of safety that should impress upon their minds the fact that there is a Providence that rules even in the temporal affairs of this life, and grants relief just when it is most needed to save the destitute from the worst consequences of their destitution. Mr. Schirner now found his finances reduced to twenty-five cents, and his provisions to meal enough to last a day or two, besides a little coffee. Here, in a wilderness, destitute of means, what but starvation should follow the consumption of their limited supply. And, to add to the poor man's distress, the good wife, feeling, perhaps, more deeply the trying situation, as women are apt to feel it, began to weep and chide her husband for bringing them there to perish. Mr. S. thereupon concluded to try his luck at hunting, though he was not a practiced hunter, and game was not abundant. But fortunately he did not have to go far ere he found and killed a pheasant; then a couple of quails, and, on his return, a squirrel. These, with the meal and coffe, served as a temporary bait; and when they were consumed, went visiting to Jesse Walker's, where they obtained a supply of meal and meat to last till more permanent provisions could be made for their future wants. Mr. Schirner is now in independent circumstances, and refers to his early pioneer hardships in a way that gives them rather a comical than grave aspect; as events we might have wept over at the time, now assume a phase decidedly amusing to us, as we look down upon them from our elevated and independent positions.

On the 5th of July, 1851, Thomas Palson and John Rankin caused to be surveyed on land owned by them, on the north west-quarter of the north east-quarter of section five, and called it Wheeling, in honor of Wheeling, Va., as suggested by Henderson Palson. Surveyor, James Rousseau; chain-carriers, Henderson Palson and Elisha Hardin. By agreement the plat was equally divided between the proprietors, Palson being proprietor of the east and Rankin of the west side. The first house was built by James Wilson, the second by Henry Hamilton, and the third by C. C. Wilkie. That by Wilson was a frame, and the others were log houses. The first postmaster was James Wilson, and he also had the first blacksmith shop in town. Present postmaster, John Palson. Mails tri-weekly. The first goods were sold by James Walters and John Butcher. The first physician located in town was C. C. Wilkie, who is still a citizen and in practice. He came originally from New York, in 1849, resided in Knoxville several months, and finally located in Wheeling, in 1853.

Wheeling has never grown beyond the proportions of a small country village, but its location is pleasant, being on level upland prairie, surrounded by a rich farming country, with timber and coal convenient.

In concluding the history of this township we shall take occasion to relate a sensational event that took place in '49, in which a number of citizens of this and Pleasant Grove were participants.

In '47 a family named Castner came from Missouri and settled about two miles west of Wheeling, where James Thornburgh now lives. The family consisted of five brothers, Jonas, William, John, Ebenezer, and James—all grown men except the last named, who was still a boy—and their mother. Jonas was married, and afterwards took up his residence near Hartford, Warren county.

The reputation of the Castners previous to their coming here was such as to justify the opinion that they were no profitable addition to the settlement, and their movements were closely observed by those who felt interested in the fair fame of the community, and the safety of property. It was believed that the Castners had been driven from Missouri for some misdemeanor of theirs there, and it was therefore deemed not advisable to permit them to remain here undisturbed longer than they should give the people an excuse for disturbing them. Such an occasion eventually transpired. Bill went to Illinois on a marauding expedition, where he aided in a daring robbery, and was caught and lodged in jail at Quincy. From there he somehow managed to escape, and was so closely pursued to within a short distance of his home that he was compelled to swin the Des Moines river somewhere below Des Moines City, and finally escaped.

News of Bill's escape from jail reached the people here, and a number of them determined to watch for his return to headquarters. Having secreted themselves so as to observe the approach of any one, they patiently watched and listened til past midntght for whatever signs might indicate the fugitive'l arrival. They knew his family expected him that night, and that his brother John had joined him after he had crossed the river; but it was now evident that the Castners believed, or at least suspected that they were watched, and therefore acted with extreme caution.

At last the deep silence of that after-midnight was broken by the hooting of an owl not far away in the timber, and this was presently answered by one near the house. This was taken by the watchers to mean something more than what owls are supposed to mean by it; but there was not the time to look for an explanation. When daylight came the squad surrounded the house, and Eb. and Jim were taken into custody. Being told that the owl signals had been heard, and that they must give a truthful explanation of their meaning or be whipped, they both denied any knowledge of it. But this their custodians believed to be false, and resolved to force them to tell the truth; so they led them away to a convenient place to administer the pursuasive hickory. Seeing what was about to take place, poor old Mrs. Castner attempted to follow, declaring that if her boys were to suffer she would suffer with them; but she was rudely driven back by one of the men, and told that they only meant to whip them, a punishment her boys had been accustomed to.

Now being convinced that he must tell the truth or be severely whipped, Jim, the boy, stated that the hooting of the owls was by his brother Bill and John to let him and Eb. know where they were, so that they could take them something to eat. This was satisfactory, and Jim was released. But Eb. concluded that he would stand the thrashing rather than tell, and the whip was vigorously applied; after which he was a second time admonished to confess or have the process repeated. Now being convinced that a confession would be more agreeable than another application of the gad, he corroborated Jim's statement.

They then led their custodians to the place of rendezvous, and their statement was further corroborated by the trail they had made through the dewy grass. But the fugitive brothers had again fled, and it was believed that pursuit would then be in vain.

They thereupon turned their attention to the further disposal of their prisoners, by ordering them, with the whole family, to quit the country within a given time, or abide certain consequences. But, as the time of grace expired without any movement on the part of the offenders to comply with the command, the citizens again collected to enforce it. They compelled the Castners to rig up their conveyance and load their plunder, and then accompanied them beyond Bremen, Monroe county, where they left the next morning, after having seen them start on another day's journey.

Some time after this Eb. returned to his brother Jonas', in Warren county, on pretense of settling up some business connected with the family. Here a number of citizens of this and Warren county followed him, and Wesley Jordan was made captain of the company. On approaching the house Jonas and Eb. who were at a spring watering their horses, having their guns with them as though they anticipated an attack hastened in. The company now drew up in line in front of the house, and Jonas came to the door and ordered their captain not to approach beyond a certain limit, which, however, he did, and called for Eb. The latter then came to the door with his head bound up and a great butcher knife in his hand. Seeing this, the captain told him the company was not prepared to hear him when coming thus armed; that he had promised to not return to the country, and that he would now be voted a limited time to leave it again or be severely dealt with. Also, inasmuch as Jonas rested under strong suspicions of villainy, he, too, would be dealt with in like manner, A vote was then ordered in Jonas' case, all being in favor of his expulsion to step one pace front. Hearing this, Jonas raised his gun and threatened to shoot any one that stepped forward. Instantly every rifle was deliberately aimed at him, the hammers of which were set and fingers pressed upon them. Seeing his critical situation, Jonas quickly stepped within doors. The vote was taken, and the Castners evacuated the country within the time specified.

Population of Swan by U. S. census of 1870:

Native	978
Foreign	23
Total	1001

CHAPTER XXIX.

Pleasant Grove Township—Its Geography and Early History—Early Settlers—Denem Halsey—Yoest Spalti—First Prairie Broken—First Orchard Planted—John P. Glenn—First Religious Society of the Christian Denomination and Others—First Birth—G. Logan—William F. Jordan—Claim Contest—The First Mercantile Transaction—First Schools—Pleasantville.

This is a middle western township, and consists simply of township 76, range 21, except sections 5 and 6, and the north half of sections 1, 2, 3 and 4, as described in the history of Swan. It is bounded on the north by Swan, on the east by Union and Knoxville, on the south by Franklin, and on the west by Warren county.

Pleasant Grove is mostly prairie, though there is an abundance of timber margining the streams, the principal one of which is Coal creek, running through the southern and western parts of the township. Butcher creek and other small streams head in the same township.

Coal abounds on all these streams, but more abundantly on Coal creek. One vein on the Cartwright farm measures about four feet in thickness, and one more recently opened on land belonging to Y. Spalti, about three and one-half.

This township was surveyed in '46 and '47 by John Bull and Jesse Williams, and was declared a township by order of the county commissioners, in January, 1847, including township 75, range 21, now Franklin, and called Pleasant Grove by suggestion of the people living in and about the beautiful grove near Pleasantville. The place of holding elections was appointed to be at the house of Wm. Glenn.

There is no preserved record of the first three elections, and we are dependent upon the memory of old settlers for the dates and incidents connected with this part of the history. The first election ever held within the limits of this township was a precinct election, as it occurred previous to its organization, April,'46. There was, however, no voting done on this occasion, there being only enough present to fill the board. The next came off in August of the same year, under some shade trees near the house of Wm. Glenn. On which occasion John P. Glenn, Wm. Glenn, and Wm. Young presided as judges, and Jesse W. Glenn and Robert Logan as clerks. About fifty votes were cast, by which John P. Glenn was chosen a justice and Thos. Hailey constable. Other officers not remembered.

At this election a well-known office-seeker, running for sheriff in opposition to George Gillaspy, made his appearance, and was so abusive in his denunciation of his opponent, that John P. Glenn, by virtue of his prospect of being elected justice, ordered the prospective constable to arrest the offender. The latter respected the authority and retired.

The first township election came off at the house of Wm. Glenn, Aug., '47. No particulars remembered, and only one incident may be worth relating, and this may show with what care the records were kept : After the election was over, and the votes were being counted by tally, by the light of a grease lamp, James Glenn, one of the clerks, accidentally threw the lamp over on his tally sheet, ruining it completely.

The names of those who settled in this township at the earliest dates are as follows :

Denem Halsey, in '45; Lewis Reynolds, Trainor Reynolds, John P. Glenn, Wm. S. Glenn, two Samuel Glenns, Daniel Vansel, Larken Young, Pleasant Prater, Wm. Young, G. B. Greenwood, John Lewis, Marion and Jas. Clifton, Richmond Miller, David Shonkwiler, Samuel Tibbett, Gilmore Robert and Harrison Logan, and Yase Spalti, in '46 ; Wm. F. Miles and Wesley Jordan and Daniel Davidson, in '47.

The first person mentioned in the above list, came into the country previous to its vacation by the Indians, and lived alone in a small cabin near the present site of Pleasantville. He was a person of tall frame, dressed principally in buckskin, and occupied himselt mostly in hunting and keeping bees. He died many years ago from disease supposed to have been contracted by exposure.

The sad fate of Pleasant Prater is well remembered by many old settlers and others. He moved to Adams county many years ago, and there, during the late war, joined the 4th Infantry. Having returned sometime after on furlough, he got into trouble with a neighbor named Carns, about some hogs, and one day Carns waylaid and shot him as he was on his way to Fontanelle. Carns was arrested and imprisoned, after which a mob broke into the prison, took him out, hung him to a tree, and then shot him to pieces.

Yoest Spalti—well remembered by old settlers as "Dutch Joe"—was a native of Switzerland, from which country he, with two brothers, Henry and Joachim, came to Iowa in '45, and settled temporarily four miles west of Ottumwa, in August. Here they remained till spring, and wintered in a shelter of their own construction, partly dug in the earth, and, for want of means, or opportunity to earn it, subsisted upon a very limited variety and amount of fare. They were frequently asked to work, but not being able to reply in a language comprehensive to any American, except *nix verstay*, they were not employed for some time, when they were luckily accosted by a German, and got work.

Yoest came up in the spring of '46 and settled at what was known as Lynn Grove, where his brother Henry now lives. Here he lived a bachelor till he started to California in the spring of '50, and died on the way. Some mystery connected with his death seemed to indicate that he was foully dealt with.

Henry and Joachim followed him to this township some

years later, and are now among the most wealthy men in the county.

Lewis Reynolds broke the first prairie in the township, on his claim a little south of Pleasantville, on land now owned by Abram Erle, in May, '46. He, W. F. Jordan, and G. Logan planted orchards in '49. The trees then planted by Mr. Reynolds are mostly still living; those of the others having been destroyed by gophers.

John P. Glenn was born in Pendleton county, N. C., September 1, 1793; moved from thence to Jackson county, Tenn., thence to Crawford county, Ind., thence to Sangamon county, Ill., from thence to Jefferson county, Iowa, in '38, and from thence to this county in the spring of '45, and settled in Polk, near Eagle Rock, where he remained one season, and raised a crop on a claim belonging to F. M. Clifton. In the spring following he moved to and made a claim on what is now section 27, Pleasant Grove, where he remained till the day of his death, September 16, 1868, aged 75 years and 17 days. Mrs. Glenn survived him 15 months, and died December 5, 1869, aged 75 years and 25 days.

Mr. Glenn was for many years a minister of the gospel, ot the Christian denomination; and in connection with Isaac Metcalf, an elder and local preacher of the same order, organized societies in various parts of the township, in '48. He also preached and organized churches in Warren and Polk counties, at an early date. James Gill also organized churches of the same order, in the township, in '48–9. Wm. Knite, a brother-in-law to Samuel Tibbett, a preacher of the M. E. Church, preached at Mr. T.'s, and organized a church there at an early date. The first building erected for religious services, was in Pleasantville, in '52, under the pastoral charge of James Woods. The building now belongs to the Methodists.

The first birth in the township was that of Jonathan, son of

Samuel and Elizabeth Glenn, June, '46. They now live in Clark county.

Gilmore Logan is now the oldest settler still living in the township. He first moved from Indiana to Wapello county, and from thence to this place, arriving on the 20th of February, '46.

Wm. F. Jordan was born in Kentucky, in 1795, and moved to Illinois when that State was yet a territory. From there he moved to where Pleasantville now is, arriving there on the 16th of October, '47, and purchased a claim of Wm. S. Glenn, on which was only a small cabin. On this claim the town of Pleasantville was afterwards located, and the cabin above mentioned still stands in the northwest corner.

Previous to its coming into possession of the Jordans, this claim was the subject of arbitration and legal contest, in which the notorious Spurlock had a hand. At this time it was claimed by the three Gillmans, father and two sons, on the one hand, and by William S. Glenn on the other; and the opposing parties agreed to settle the matter by arbitration. Spurlock, who was a justice of the peace in Wapello county, happened to be here on some kind of business, and was employed by the Gillmans to conduct their case, they agreeing to give him a portion of the contested property, as compensation for his services, provided he should succeed in securing it to them. But, after the contest had terminated in favor of the Gillmans, Spurlock refused to accept the part of the claim offered him, being of comparatively little value, and returned to his home in Wapello. There he was followed by the Gillmans some time after, of whom he purchased the entire claim for a horse and $30. The property now being forfeited to both the Gillmans and Spurlock by their absence, Glenn "jumped" it, and held it till he sold it to W. F. Jordan, who afterwards made a portion of it the town plat of Pleasantville.

Mr. Jordan's two sons, Miles and Wesley, who are still residents of Pleasantille, opened a small mercantile establishment on the part of the claim now occupied by the town. A little anecdote relating to their first business experience, may be worth telling. They began on a capital of $150, by first investing it in a load of dry hides. These they took to Churchville, (now Alexander,) Mo., expecting a handsome profit, and intending to invest the proceeds in a stock of goods. But, on reaching the place and attempting to make the trade, they found that their want of experience in the business would prove disastrous to their expectations. In purchasing the hides they had innocently included horns and tails, and now they discovered that these appendages were not in the market, and must come off before the hides were weighed. Accordingly a man was set to work with a big knife, and in a short time the village swine were in possession of a large share of the profits of this important trade. It was, indeed, the most grievious loss of all their business experience, but one that would now be scarcely felt.

Daniel Shea taught the first school, in the spring of 1847, in a small log cabin built by G. Logan, about one mile west of where Pleasantville now is. Term, three months; 20 scholars at $2.00 per head. Miles Jordan taught the next in the winter of '47 and '48.

The town of Pleasantville was surveyed by Stanford Doud, Aug. 1, '49, on the south-west quarter of the north-west quarter of section 15, and then owned by W. F. Jordan. Wesley Jordan built the first house, a frame, that is now occupied as a dwelling. He also kept the first postoffice in connection with the store. The first hotel was kept by Wm. H. H. Alley.

The location of Pleasantville would naturally suggest the name, being a beautiful, open prairie, adjoining a large, well-timbered grove that extends up the tributaries of Coal creek. Its location is also healthy; and the prospect of a railroad gives vitality to business, and promises much for the future prosperity of the place. Two fine church buildings have just been erected in Pleasantville, by the Methodist and Christian denominations.

A town called Weston, was laid out on the north-half of section 35, township 76, range 21, Oct. 8th and 9th, '56. Proprietors, P. W. and G. F. Pitman. Surveyor, Jesse H. Kent. The place never improved.

Population of Pleasant Grove by the United States census of 1870:

Native	1415
Foreign	30
Total	1445

CHAPTER XXX.

Washington Township—Geography and Early History—Names of First Settlers—Hiram Moon—An Adventure in the Snow—Allen Pearson—Joseph Pershall—A Toilsome Milling Expedition—Land Excitement—First Church Organizations—First School—New Town, or Gosport—Columbia.

Washington is a southern township, and may be described as the south-east quarter of the south-west quarter of the county, and is technically known as town. 74, range 20. It is bounded on the north by Knoxville, on the east by Indiana, on the south by Lucas county, and on the west by Dallas township.

About two-thirds of the township is prairie, though English creek that runs nearly through the center, from a little west of south to as much east of north, is widely margined by timber of a very good quality. English has numerous tributaries, and coal abounds along these streams in paying quantities, but the best veins yet worked are in section 34, owned by Clark & Williams, and average about three and a half feet in thickness.

On the 6th of January, '47, it was ordered by the county commissioners that town. 74, range 20, and town. 74, range 21, be declared a township to be known as Washington township. This included the present townships of Washington and Dallas, and so remained till about October 3, '48, when Dallas and Franklin were defined as one township, and Washington as it now is.

The earliest election of which there is any preserved record, was held on the 5th of April, '52, at which the following officers were chosen:

Allen Pearson and Joseph Grove, justices; James Fletcher and Henry Dresser, constables; Hezekiah Willey, Andrew Reed and Joseph B. Snyder, trustees, and Allen Pearson clerk.

Provious to this Joseph Pershall and James M. Brady were justices; Joseph Scott, John Riddle and Hezekiah Willey, trustees, and Allen Pearson clerk.

The names of most of those who settled in the township at the earliest dates, are as follows:

Josiah Willey, now living in Lucas county, in '46; John Asher, Wm. Clear and Wm. Hunt, in '47; the Moon family, Hyram Larkin, Geo. W., and Simon P., and Joseph Pershall in '48; Wm. Agan in '49; John Agan in '50; and John Stotz and Andrew Reed in '52. Of these, Hiram Moon, John Asher and Wm. Clear are dead, and the remainder, except Joseph Willey, still live in the township.

Hyram Moon was born in North Carolina, August 22, 1818; moved to Indiana at an early age, and from thence to this township, arriving on the 12th of October, '48, and settled on section 31, making what was then the frontier settlement in that part of the county. He was accompnaied by his three brothers, Larkin, George W., and Simon P., and another man and his son, whose names have been forgotten, making in all a family of twenty-one persons; and these wintered together in a small cabin on Mr. M's. claim. Their nearest mill for procuring breadstuff was Haymaker's, on Cedar, at which they had the good fortune to get a supply of corn ground before the commencement of that terrible winter. They also procured some wheat, of which they made an occasional substitute for corn bread, by grinding it in their coffee mill.

The following is a verbatim copy of some manuscript left by Mr. Moon, narrating an adventure of his in one of those fearful snow storms in the winter of '48- 9:

" On the 1st day of January, I went fourteen miles for some

corn, and on the second day, on my return, accompanied by my brother Simon P., it snowed on us all day, and we got within six miles of home. Next morning the snow was so deep, and drifted so hard against the axles and fore gate of my wagon, that we got only about three miles, and the horses became so fatigued that we unhitched them and tried to make our way home so. But we soon found the horses too tired to carry us, and, being too tired to walk, I took my old horse by the tail and made him drag me home through the snow. Our wagon stood on the prairie seventeen days. By this time the snow had become so thickly crusted as to bear a team part of the time; and when they went to rescue the wagon and get it home, the animals would occasionally fall through the crust, cutting their legs so badly that their trail could be traced by the blood after their tracks had become obliterated by thaws."

Mr. Moon was a minister of the Christian denomination, and preached his first sermon here, in his own house, on the first Sunday in March, '49, and at John Asher's on the same day. He organized a church in June, '49, composed of 13 members.

It is related that, in his public services, he used a large family bible, and, in the absence of a table on which to lay the cumbersome volume, he rested it upon the back of one of his brothers, who sat in a recumbent position in front of him.

Mr. Moon was a man of affliction, being much of his time prostrated by ill health, which kept him in comparative poverty; yet he continued to preach occasionally at his own house till about the time of his death, January 25th, 1861.

Allen Pearson, whose name appears on our list as the first township clerk, moved from Missouri to this township, in July, '49, settled on section 10, and bought his claim of J. Wilcut. Mr. Pearson made the first shingle roof, laid the first brick in his own chimney and put up the first timothy hay in this township.

Joseph Pershall, who was one of the first justices in the township, moved from Missouri, and settled on section 3, in the spring of '48, on land now owned by Charles McKey.

Mr. P. and his family suffered many hardships during the first few years of their pioneer experience, particularly in the way of procuring breadstuff. One milling expedition performed by two of his sons, I take occasion to relate, quoting from his written statement:

"I do not remember the year, but it was in the month of December. There was a little snow on the ground, but it was pleasant and thawing, when I started two of my boys, Phineas and Isaac, to mill. They went to Haymaker's, on Cedar, but failed to get their grinding done there. Then they went to Eddyville, and failed there also; and from there to the Skunk river mills. Here they got in company with John Harsin and Phillip Canton, stayed all night and got their grinding by late next evening. In the mean time it turned severely cold, insomuch that it was hazardous to undertake to travel. But they were all pretty resolute fellows, and anxious to get home, for they knew we must be uneasy about them by that time. So, cold as it was, they started. After getting about two miles they discovered they had left their bed clothing at the mill, and had to stop, borrow a horse and send the youngest boy back for them.

They got to Oskaloosa that night, and stayd there. Next morning it was still cold as ever, but they set out to try it again. They would drive on till they were nearly frozen, then stop and warm and go again. One evening Phillip Canton got so cold that he began to get stupid and sleepy, and sat down by the side of the road, with his back against a tree, and said he was going to rest awhile. The others tried to persuade him to get up, but he remained on his seat. They then took hold of him and raised him to his feet, when Mr. Harsin took his whip and gave him several pretty keen lashes around the legs. This made him a little mad and he was then able to travel.

"On the fifth day they got home in safety, and we were all glad to see them."

During the year 1853, the lands in this part of the county were taken up rapidly by speculators and settlers. Mr. Brumfield Long, who settled that year, on section 23, lodged as many as twenty land prospectors per night, and fed them on corn bread. The beautiful prairies here, no less than in other parts of the county, were justly attractive to land hunters.

As has been stated Rev. Hyram Moon organized the first religious society of the Christian or Campbellite order, in 1849. Rev Johnson organized the first Methodist class, with a memship of eight or nine persons, at Henry Molesworth's, a short distance east of where Columbia now is, in 1852. Mr. T. L. Strong, who lived a short distance within the limits of Lucas county, was appointed the first leader of this class.

The first school was taught by Miss Mary Crowley, (now Mrs. Beabout, living near Gosport,) in 1853. The schoolhouse was a small cabin built by Mr. T. L. Strong, above mentioned, and stood upon the line between Marion and Lucas. It was a fair representative of most of the school-houses of that period, being small, with a puncheon floor, a clapboard roof and upper floor, and a wide fire-place. The school was mostly supported from this township; and it is a fact worthy of note that at least eight persons that attended that school, have since become teachers.

On the 8th day of July, 1853, John Stipp and John Hessenflow, employed F. M. Frush, to survey and plat a town on land then owned by them, described as the south-west quarter of section 15, and the north-west quarter of section 22, and called it New Town.

The first house in the new town was built by Daniel Sampson, who opened the first store in it, and also kept the first post-office the first year of the existence of the place. The mails were at first supplied by volunteer carriers, and the office maintained by volunteer contributions. In due time it was discovered that there was another post-office in the State, bearing the same name, and it was then changed to Gosport.

Gosport is still a small village, but its location is a pretty one, being on an upland flat, within the limits of the timber that margins English creek, and contiguous to a fine farming country on the north, east and south. It contains one store, a large frame building originally erected and used as a hotel, but now unoccupied, and a number of small dwellings and shops.

On the 23d day of March, 1857, being about three years and a little more than eight months, later than the time Gosport was surveyed, Hugh S. Smith, employed Wm. Kent to survey and plat a town on the south-west quarter of the south-west quarter of section 27, and on the north-west quarter of the north-west quarter of section 34, land then owned by Mr. Smith, he having purchased it of Benjamin Litton, and called it Columbia.

James D. Steel built the first house, a round log dwelling, now not standing, John McEldoring sold the first goods, Andrew Reed kept the first post-office, and Clark and Williams kept the first hotel, and are still proprietors of the same building together with a large flouring mill.

The name Columbia, was that of the post-office, which was previously kept by Brumfield Long, at his place, about two miles west of where the village was located.*

Quite a strife arose between the people of Gosport and Columbia, on the occasion of the location of the latter. Believing that the building of another town so near their own would

---

* Columbia post-office was established November 15, 1854, and the commission came to Mr. Long shortly after. He kept it till about the 1st of January, 1857, when it was moved to the village.

be detrimental to its prospects, the people of Gosport resolved to nip the new aspirant in the bud. To this end they attended the sales of lots, intending to buy all they could of them, and let them lay vacant. But this trick was understood by the Columbians, and the lots were bid off at too high figures to warrant safe investments by the other party, and they abandoned the scheme.

The town is located in the midst of a large prairie, and surrounded by a good farming district. It contains three stores, one hotel, a large flouring mill, one church building, and a proportionate number of shops and dwellings, some of the latter being very good. The church was erected at an early date, under the pastoral charge of Rev. P. H. Jacobs, Old School Presbyterian.

The following was the population of Washington township, by the United States census of 1870:

Native	1,273
Foreign	12
Total	1,285

CHAPTER XXXI.

Franklin Township—Geography and Early History—Early Settlers—John Clark—Milling Adventure—Nathan Nichols—His Death—Peter Rowe—First Orchards—First Church Organizations—First School House—Caloma.

Technically, Franklin is in town. 75, range 21, and is bounded on the north by Pleasant Grove, on the east by Knoxville, on the south by Dallas, and on the west by Warren county.

Much the larger portion of the township is prairie, the timber narrowly margining White Breast, that runs through the south-east quarter, and a small creek called Coon creek, that runs through the north-west quarter. Coal is abundant along White Breast, and several veins have been opened and worked measuring four feet in thickness. The prairies are less broken than in some other portions of the county; and, the soil being excellent, no better farming land can be found than exists in Franklin.

On the 3d of October, '48, by order of the county commissioners, this township was defined as a part of Dallas, and so remained till about '52, when it became a part of Pleasant Grove, and so remained till the 28th of February, '55, when, by order of the county judge, it became a distinct township, to be known as Franklin township.

On the 2d day of April, of the same year, the first election in and for said township, was held at the house of John Clark, at which John McNeil and John Miller were chosen justices; Samuel Ream and William Sweezy, constables; John Clark, assessor; J. W. Hightree, clerk; Warren McNeil, Isaac Capelin and Samuel B. Wilson, trustees. There is no record of the number of votes cast.

The following are the names of most of those persons who settled in the township at the earliest dates:

Nathan Nichols and Amanda Hewland, in '46; Peter Row, William Frazer and James Frakes, in '48; John Clark, in '49; Daniel F. Smith, in '50, and J. W. Hightree, in '52.

Of these John Clark is the oldest resident settler in the township, and D. F. Smith the next, the rest having moved away or deceased. John Clark was born in Tennessee, February 14th, 1815, came to this county in '49, arriving at Knoxville on the 26th of June. Having traded William Frazer a land warrant for a timber claim on White Breast Creek, he also made a prairie claim, built a cabin on the bottom, and moved to it on the 26th ofJuly. In raising this cabin near help was so scarce that he had to resort to friends in Knoxville, and even then it required three days to put the building up.

The first milling Mr. Clark done was at Brobst's and Haymakers, on Cedar. In '55 he went to what was known as Beach's mill, now a place called Sumerset, on one of the Three Rivers, in Warren county. At that time there was, on the route to this mill, a wide stretch of uninhabited prairie, on which there was neither a tree, trail nor mound to guide the traveler who wished to cross it, and some one had set stakes at wide intervals as the only way-marks. Mr. Clark, with a wagon and two yoke of cattle, and accompanied by a man named Nathaniel Brown, had crossed this desert to Beach's, and remained there two days waiting for their grinding. Now being in some haste to get home, they set out in time to reach Hammondsburg before night. Here they concluded to tarry no longer than was required to feed and their teams and themselves, hoping to reach home long before midnight. So, without further delay, they drove on, but when darkness came they found it impossible to keep the way them selves, and thought it advisable to trust to the instinctive sagacity of their cattle to pilot them through. Unfortunate trust! The brutes, left to themselves, had lost their reckoning, and were as much at fault as their masters—if indeed they cared particularly about what direction they traveled. At all events, after plodding along in this way for a long time, Mr. Clark began to think something was wrong, and set about making a calculation of their locality as well as it could be done by starlight, the result of which calculation proved that they were far out of their way, indeed so far as the breaks of White Breast, not far from the south-west corner of the county. And here, to add to their vexation, the wagon ran into a slough, at which Brown became alarmed and begged Clark to camp till daylight. But the latter was not disposed to lay out if such a contingency could be avoided; so they got the wagon out and proceeded, making a guiding point of certain stars, and reached home at about one o'clock.

Nathan Nichols taught the first school in '53, in a house left vacant by one of the Frakes. The house stood on the bottom near White Breast, in section 26. It was long afterwards moved to Mr. Richies, and is doing service as a stable.

The death of Nathan Nichols will long be remembered on account of the painful circumstances under which it took place. He and Mrs. Hewland, who was a widow, and a relative of his, had come from Ohio together, and were living together south of White Breast, till a grown son of Mrs. H.'s created a disturbance that caused him to take up his abode alone in a small cabin not far distant. One evening, some time after taking up his lonely abode, he went to Mrs. Hewland's for a pitcher of butter-milk. On receiving it he took a hearty drink of it, and was observed to take another ere he reached his domicile. Nothing more was known or thought of him till next day, when his non-appearance about the premises induced some one to go to his house. There they found him dead, and all the evidences to prove that he had died in extreme agony. He was lying upon his bed with his head hung over the railing, and his face black, whilst over him and upon the floor were strewed large quantities of feathers from the bed-tick that he had evidently torn open in his struggles. At one time some suspicious of foul treatment were entertained, but no conclusion was better to arrive at than that the poor man died from a violent attack of bilious colic, induced by the excessive draughts of butter-milk he had taken into his stomach. Mrs. Hewland afterwards returned to Ohio.

Peter Rane went to California in '52, and returning after an absence of two years, found that his wife had gone to Missouri, and followed her. He never returned. Frakes went to Wapello county,

Jackson McClain and John Clark planted the first orchards in '52. Of the sixty trees planted by Mr. C., but two now live. McClain's are mostly living.

Rev. A. Colborn was the first preacher in the township, and John Demors organized the first society of United Brethren in '51. The meeting was held in sub-district number one, and the class was composed of persons belonging to various denominations. Revs. Banebreak and Sleeper also preached and organized a church of United Brethren at Coloma.

The first house erected for school purposes was in district number one, in '50. Soon after its completion Chas. Smith, now living in Pleasant Grove, came and asked the privilege of dedicating it to educational purposes by delivering a lecture on slavery. The request was granted, and this was the first lecture of any kind delivered in the township. W. M. Stone made the first political speech ever made in the township in this house in '56, in favor of John C. Fremont for President.

Daniel F. Smith kept the first postoffice in '57, called Coloma, the name it still retains. Mails once a week between

Chariton and Newton. Present postmaster, F. A. Harding; mails weekly.

The population of Franklin, by the U. S. Census 1870, was:

Natives	723
Foreign	45
Total	768

CHAPTER XXXII.

Dallas Township—Its Geography and Early History—An Incident Connected with the First Election—Names of Early Settlers—Nicholas Helms—The First Mill—First Marriage and Birth—Thomas Kirton—An Adventure Through the Snow—Destruction of Wild Game—The Bauer Brothers—Peter Yrentz—Hiram Teakel—Henry Harstman—Church Organizations—First School—Newbern—Dallas Town—A Hunting Adventure—Conclusion.

Dallas is the south-west corner township of the county, and is technically described as town. 74, range 21. It is bounded on the north by Franklin, on the east by Washington, on the south by Lucas county, and on the west by Warren county.

White Breast runs through the north-west quarter, and a nameless branch of English takes its rise in the interior, and runs through the south-east quarter of the township. Timber is more abundant than in Franklin, but covers much less than half the surface. Coal abounds along these streams, and numerous veins have been opened, averaging about three feet in thickness. One owned by John F. Willis, near Dallas Town, is worked. But the richest coal fields are to be found in the west and south-west.

From the 6th of January, '47, till the 2d of October, '48, this township constituted a part of Washington, after which it was ordered that it and town. 75, range 21, (Franklin,) be called Dallas; and so remained till some time during the year '52, (at precisely what date we have been unable to ascertain,) it became a distinct township. The first election after this, was held at the house of Thomas Kirton, April 5th, '52, at which the following officers were chosen:

Joseph Bauer and William J. McClain, justices; Hiram Teakel and John Clark, constables; Peter Yrentz, Alloys Bauer and Thomas Kirton, trustees.

An election was held in November, '48, at which time nine votes were cast, by settlers in what is now Dallas and Franklin; but, as in so many cases, the record was poorly kept, carelessly handled and finally lost.

A day or two after this election, Joseph Bauer being on his way to Fairfield, was requested by Nathan Nichols, the clerk, to carry the poll-book to Knoxville. Not having been an officer of the election, Mr. Bauer objected on the ground of the illegality of such a performance, but was finally persuaded to take and deliver it to George Gillaspy, the sheriff of the county. But by missing the right way to Knoxville, Mr. B. was so much delayed that he did reach there till some time in the afternoon; and then, being in much haste to be on his journey again, he found George directly, and handed him the documents.

"Are you one of the board?" asked that dignitary.

"No," answered Bauer, and was about to add some explanations, when the great man cut him short with:

"Then I don't want your poll-book," and abruptly turned away, refusing to have anything more to say about it.

This scene took place in Babbitt's store. Gillaspy walked around the counter and appeared to be engaged in something else, whilst Bauer stood thoughfully discussing the matter with himself, but unable to decide what he should do with the precious document. To return with it to the proper authority was scarcely to be thought of, as other business urged him to be on the way to Fairfield, and he would not risk the responsibility of carrying it with him. At length his own perplexity and the provoking silence of the great George, roused his wrath, and decided him instantly. He drew the poll-book from his bosom, dashed it upon the counter and drew the attention of George to it in this emphatic manner: "Here, take your poll-book and do what you d—n please with it," then abrubtly left the presence. It was not till after his return from Fairfield that Mr. Bauers learned that it had been found necessary to send for Nichols that evening to come to Knoxville, present the poll-book and take the oath required by law in such cases.

The following are the names of persons who settled in this township at the earliest dates:

Nicholas Helms, with his four sons, and Wm. Willis, in '46; Thomas Kirton, Henry Wagoner, Joseph Bauer, Peter Yrentz, and Hiram Teakel, in '58; Alloys Bauer in '49; Henry Ghor ing, Henry Harstman, and Jacob Smith, in '50, and Jacob Fight in '52.

Of these, Thomas Kirton, Wm. Willis, Henry Ghoring, Henry Harstman, Joseph and Alloys Bauer and Hiram Teakel live in the township. Nicholas Helms is dead, and his four sons are supposed to live in Missouri. Henry Wagoner, Jacob Smith and Jacob Fight are also dead.

Nicholas Helms was from Ohio, and he, with his sons, took claims in what is now the southwest part of the township. During his residence here he was a useful citizen to the extent of his means. By the erection of a tempoary hand-mill, worked by a crank, he supplied many of the early settlers with meal when it was impossible to obtain it from the great distance people then had to go for breadstuffs. Particularly during the winter of '48 and '49 did this little corn-cracker prove to be of inestimable value; for, as has already been shown, it was impossible to get any distance from home on account of the great depth of snow. During this period, every family within reach of this mill, who had a peck of corn to convert into meal, came to it; and the faithful little make-shift was kept at work day and night, grinding a peck, or even a mess or two, for one and then another, as their turns would come, each customer taking his own turn at the crank.

In the family of Mr. Helms occurred the first marriage in the township, that of his son Jesse and Miss Sarena Wind, whose parents resided within the limits of Lucas county. The wedding took place in Dallas, December 25, 1847. And to this couple was born the first child born in the township, Henry Helms, Aug. 2, '48.

Thomas Kirton was born in Yorkshire, England, came to Canada, where he resided five years, from thence to Illinois, and from thence to Clay township, in this county, in '43, and from thence to this township in the spring of '48. He purchased a claim where he now lives in the north part of the township, of an individual named Geo. Leach, an adventurer of some notoriety in this part of the country at that time, and suspected of being a horse-thief. After selling to Mr. Kirton, Leach moved his residence to Franklin township, near where John Clark now lives, where he passed the winter of '48 and '49, making it rather his temporary home. Once during this winter, being at Pleasantville he set out for home across an uninhabited prairie, the snow being nearly three feet deep on the level, and blown into drifts of much greater depth, and unbroken trail, this adventurer came very near ending his career. After struggling through the trackless waste till within about two miles of distination, he became so exhausted that further progress seemed impossible, and it occurred to him that he must perish. In view of his impending fate he cut a small stick, flattened it, wrote his name thereon, and stuck it up in the snow, in order that his remains, if ever found, might be identified, and then laid himself down to die. But here the horrible idea of leaving his carcass to be possibly found by some fellow being, but more probably to be devoured and scattered by wolves, came upon him with such force that it roused him to a determination to make another effort for his life. This he did, and by such efforts as only the fear of death can nerve a sufferer to make, he reached his home alive.

We may as well add in this connection, that such was the severity of that winter that much of the wild game perished in this portion of the county. In one instance a number of deers, being unable to travel, huddled together and remained in one place in the timber on White Breast, where they trampled a circuit a few rods in circumference, keeping the snow down by their feet and the heat of their bodies, whilst it arose like a wall around them. Here they remained till their prison walls vanished under the warth of spring, and those that were alive escaped. A great many turkeys were also found dead in the spring.

Joseph and Alloys Bauer, who reside in the western part of the township, were natives of Hanover, Germany, from whence they came in '33 to Indiana, and from there to their present residence (section 19) in '48 and '49. Joseph made his claim and Alloys purchased his of Leander Bennett, a temporary settler, who had came from Illinois in '46.

Just previous to the commencement of the severe winter of '48 and '49, Joseph had procured the grinding of four bushels of meal at Burch's, on White Breast, and on this, with pounded hominy and what little grinding they could occasionally get done on Helm's hand mill, they subsisted all winter. Leander Bennett had also taken a sack of corn to Burch's; but being unable to get it ground soon, he returned without it, thinking he might be able to go or send for it another time. But the snow soon put an end to all hopes of the kind till spring. And then, after so long waiting, he found that the mice had made nests of the sack and taken their winter's subsistance out of its contents. A fortunate circumstance for the mice.

During their first two or three years residence here the Bauers, being destitute of any kind of earthern vessels, barrels or even boxes, or lumber to make them of, used wooden troughs to store their provisions in.

Peter Yrntz moved into this township from Eddyville, late in the autumn of '48. Owing to the lateness of the season he did not get his stock feed and provisions moved up before the first snow fell; and as all kinds of provisions were scarce in the county, he subsisted by borrowing from his neighbors for his own subsistance, and broused his cattle in the White Breast timber.

Hiram Teakel was a native of Tennessee, from which State he moved to this, and to this township in the winter of '48 and settled where John Graves now lives, near Newburn, and purchased the claim of Freeland Willis, giving him $5 for it. On this he built a cabin, broke and fenced ten acres, and after living on it two years, sold it, and purchased another claim of Adam Uchler, in section 17, where he now lives.

On moving up from Eddyville, and nearing his destination, Mr. T. found no road and scarcely an object to guide him aright across a treeless prairie; and at the same time the snow was so deep that the fore wheels of the wagons were nearly burried in it. The teams, one a horse team and the other oxen, could make but slow progress. But by constant and untiring efforts they at last succeeded in reaching their chosen place of habitation, and are now, in common with many of their cotemporaries in the privations and sufferings of pioneer life, reaping the rich reward of their perseverence through difficulties.

Jacob Smith planted the first orchard in the township, but none of the trees are now living, having perished from exposure and neglect.

Henry Harstman was born in the province of Hanover, Germany, December 17, 1818, and left that country for America, in 1847, first settled in Ohio, from whence he came to Indiana, and from thence to his present residence on section 8, in September, 1850. Here he purchased a claim of 160 acres, of Henry Wagoner, for thirty dollars. This claim had no improvements on it, and Mr. Hartsman proceeded at once to erect a cabin 18 by 20, near the creek. Here he lived for some time, during which he occasionally suffered severely with the ague, and was at one time, for nine consecutive days, without any other food than potatoes. This, however, was not for the want of grain, plenty of which Mr. H. had stored away, but for the want of ability to get it carried to a mill and ground. He is now the owner of a well-improved farm of 490 acres.

The western portion of Dallas is mostly settled by Germans, a part of whom are Lutherans in doctrinal faith, and the others Catholic. Rev. J. F. Shearer, an American Lutheran minister first organized a society of those holding to that faith, in 1854. About sixteen families were united, making a membership of 45. But, as Mr. Shearer could only speak English, his place was soon taken by Rev. Wilhelm Hounderdosse, from Germany.

The Catholic church was organized in 1854, by the union of nine persons of that faith, by whom a hewed log church was soon erected, 16 by 18 feet, with bellfry. This organization was not effected by the aid of a priest, and it was not till after the erection of a house of worship, that Father John Krekel held services in that community. A frame building is now in process of erection for a parsonage.

Wm. Demoss and —— Johnson first formed societies of United Brethren and Methodists, in 1851–2.

Asa Davis taught the first school in a round log cabin built for the purpose, in 1852. Henry R. Klingman taught next.

Newbern was surveyed by F. M. Frush, by request of Ransome Davis, on the south-east quarter, of the south-east quarter of section 31, September, 9th, 1851. One of the chairmen was Joseph S. Howard, now Professor Howard, of McGee College, Missouri. The other is not remembered. It was so named by Mr. Davis, from a town of the same name in Indiana. Nine lots were sold at auction, at from four to eight dollars per lot. Mr. Davis built the first house within the town plat, (a hewed log,) that stood in the north side of the village. Jesse Moon sold the first goods, till he disposed of the business to Fletcher Kane. The first post-office was kept by Joseph Howard, father of Joseph S., mentioned above. He received his commission in the spring of 1853, not having been previously consulted. His successor was Fletcher Kane. Present incumbent John Willes. Mails daily. Chicago post-office on the north-east quarter of the north-east quarter of section 17, was established in February, 1872, Julius Teakel, postmaster. No public mail service, but matter supplied from Newburn by private conveyance. There was no town laid out here, but the place contains two stores and several dwellings, and is situated on White Breast creek. Christopher Anderly, first opened a store there, in 1867, and jocularly gave it the name of Chicago.

The first hotel was a log house, kept by Rufus Murry. Dr. C. Taylor was the first practising physician, located in the village. He is still a resident practitioner.

There are now two stores, two hotels and rather more than a proportionate number of good buildings. A small part of the village lies in Lucas county, and the entire location is very good, being surrounded by an excellent and well-improved farming district, convenient also to coal and timber.

Dallas town is located on the southwest quarter of the the southeast quarter of section two. It was surveyed by F. M. Frush, in September, 1857, at the instigation of Richard Willis, on land purchased by him of a Mrs. Eckles. Mrs. E. was a grass-widow, whose husband was at that time alive and not divorced from her, and upon this ground the opinion was held by some that the title of the land given by her was not secure. This report materially injured the prospects of the village for a short time; but the fact that Mrs. Eckles had purchased the property with her own money, restored confidence, and a goodly number of lots were at length sold.

The embryo city was at first called Ohio town on account of the number of settlers from that State, in the neighborhood. But it was eventually found advisable to change it to Dallas, in conformity to the popular habit of calling it so when Dallas post office was about all there was of tho town, and was there before it.

Dallas post office was established in 1855, and was first kept by John Parrett, in a little log house still standing, but unoccupied. Present P. M., P. Buckalew. The first house was built by Hiram L. George, who also sold the first goods. The place now contains one store, two blacksmith shops, a commodious M. E. Church building, and a good school house. The one store enjoys the trade of a fine farming country lying south and east of it.

Mr. Parker Buckalew, the P. M and lone merchant of Dallas, relates to us a hunting expedition of his, with which we will close this history.

In December, 1853, being then on a visit to the country, he was ambitious of the distinction that might be accorded to any young man for killing a deer before returning to the east. Accordingly, he one day accompanied by Simon Thomas, an experienced hunter, on a hunting expedition. Having separated from his companion, and seated himself on a rise of ground in the timber for the pnrpose of ambushing the game that was expected to come that way on its accustomed round, he had the good luck to spy two large deers passing about 25 yards distant. Taking aim as well as he could through the timber, he fired, and had the glorious satisfaction of seeing one of them, a large, withered buck, drop. He ran to it with the utmost speed, and found the animal only wounded by a graze of the bullet across the back, and already getting upon its fore feet. Here, in the midst of his excitment, Parker threw his gun away, and bravely laid hold of the creature's horns. With this the latter made a violent surge, threw his assailant headlong down the hill and fell upon him. Still Parker held fast, and a rough and tumble struggle ensued, during which the buck hooked his sharp, hind hoofs in P.'s pants, and, with one violent jerk, sundered the lower half of the youthful Nimrod, leaving only the waist hand of his pants and a few shreds belonging to the legs thereof. The possibility of having his hide served in the same way now presented itself to the excited imagination of the desperate hunter with such force that he instinctively placed a big tree between himself and the flying heels of the buck, still maintaining his hold upon the horns. In this condition the deer's head was drawn around the tree, and Parker had an opportunity to get his knife and cut its throat, thus ending an adventure that, for having the quality of being at once exciting, critical and comical, is surpassed by few of its like on record.

The following was the population of Dallas by the United States census of 1870:

Native	936
Foreign	130
Total	1066

Total population of Marion county by the United States census of 1870:

Native	21,731
Foreign	2,705
Total	24,436